To my very dear Charlotte
Love
[signature]
November 1992

ALEXANDER DUFF OF INDIA

ALEXANDER DUFF OF INDIA

A. A. Millar

CANONGATE PRESS

First published in Great Britain in 1992 by Canongate
Press plc, 14 Frederick Street, Edinburgh EH2 2HB.

Copyright © A. A. Millar 1992

ISBN 0 86241 390 7

British Library Cataloguing-in-Publication Data
A catalogue record for this book is available on request
from the British Library.

Typeset by Falcon Typographic Art Ltd, Fife, Scotland.
Printed and bound in Great Britain by Bookcraft Ltd,
Midsomer Norton, Avon.

Contents

Preface

The author begs to be excused from his apparent intimacy in frequently referring to his subject as 'Alexander'. The reason and indeed the inspiration to write this biography is that the author bears the name of his subject. His mother was a Duff of Moulin and his second Christian name is that of his subject, Alexander.

The research in preparation for this biography was made particularly difficult in that when Dr Duff left for India for the first time in 1829, he took with him some eight hundred well-selected volumes. They embraced all his college prizes and diplomas. All were lost in the wreck of the *Lady Holland* off Dassen Island.

On reaching Calcutta, he immediately began to form a second library, and had made a valuable collection, when in 1834 he was carried on board a ship bound for Greenock, in a state of insensibility, owing to an attack of Bengal dysentery. To his extreme mortification, some time after reaching Scotland, he was informed that his valuable library had been sold off. It was a sore trial but nothing to what he suffered many years after, when his most valuable papers, manuscripts and correspondence were stolen by a native servant and sold in a bazaar as waste paper.

He did form another library in later life, but it was more a collection of books. When he left India for the last time in 1863, his kind friends, Messrs George Smith & Son, of Glasgow, carried the books home free of charge – no small boon, seeing the weight came to upwards of five tons. Biographies of Duff therefore must chiefly depend on his published sermons, addresses, and reports. Much of this material was used in the fullest, and, to my mind, best study: the official biography by George Smith, published in two volumes in 1879.[1] Its only faults are that it is too long for modern tastes, and, inevitably no doubt, it stresses the public figure at the expense of the private. In drawing on Smith's work for this study I have tried to redress the balance, especially in noting

[1] George Smith, *The Life of Alexander Duff, D.D., LL.D.* 2 vols. (London: Hodder and Stoughton, 1879).

the contribution that Anne Duff made to her husband's life
and work.

I would like to thank the many people who have helped
me while I was researching this book, including the staff of
New College Library, the National Library, and the Central
Public Library in Edinburgh; Colonel Ralph Stewart-Wilson,
Balnakeilly House, Moulin; the Rev Bill Shannon, The Manse,
Moulin.

1
Childhood and Schooldays

From the summit of Ben-Y-Vrackie, at 2,757 feet the only mountain of volcanic origin in the Scottish Grampian range, the breathtaking view includes the whole of the river Tummel valley, the Falls of Tummel and Loch Tummel. Loch Rannoch looks like a patch of burnished silver and in the distance are the mountains of Glencoe. Below Ben-Y-Vrackie nestles the beautiful Parish of Moulin, once the seat of Drost, a Pictish King of Atholle, which was the area first mentioned in Scottish history.

Moulin[1] was once protected by a double line of forts and the original parish church at Moulin, which was founded by Saint Colman, was built in what was the centre of the Pictish fort. The Black Castle, now a ruin, was built by the son of Robert the Bruce's sister who was created Earl of Atholle by his cousin King David II. In former days this area was of strategic importance, being situated at the head of the Tummel valley and linked by the North Road to the city of Perth; thence by the river Tay to the North Sea and the world beyond.

The village of Moulin is joined to what is now the town of Pitlochry, the latter becoming more developed because it was astride the new North Road built by General Wade. The entire area is of unsurpassed beauty, providing pastures, an abundance of game, and protected from the severe winter climate by the surrounding forests of pine and deciduous trees.

The date is 24 April, 1806, and within a few hours a baby boy, to be named Alexander, will be born, who will travel the world and forever carry with him the fond vision of this heaven in the Highlands of Scotland. We must take a brief look at the area and the people who live here in order to appreciate the idyllic surroundings in which this boy was reared.

The ancient village of Moulin was the centre and capital of the extensive civil parish of that name, which extends nearly to Enochdhu on the Kirkmichael Road and to the burn or

[1] See John H. Dixon, *Pitlochry Past & Present* (Pitlochry: Mackay, 1925).

stream at Aldclune on the North Road. In olden times the
village of Moulin was the most populace place in the parish.
In 1792 there were thirty-seven families in Moulin village and,
although Pitlochry had then began to grow, its families only
numbered thirty. The village school stood in a small paddock.
Saint Colman established the mill with the water-wheel that
allowed the people to grind their meal less laboriously than in
the old quern. The old mill dam was between Baledmund and
Balnakeilly.

In the churchyard there is an old ash tree, which in the past
had 'chaggs' or 'jougs' attached to which was a hinged iron
band on a chain, into which someone guilty of some petty
offence was placed for an hour or two. It had long been
abolished in 1746.

At the beginning of this, the nineteenth century, although
now a declining industry, flax was still grown in the parish.
There were some seventy-five acres of flax and in each field,
when in flower, looked as if a patch of blue sky had been
transferred from above to the bosom of mother earth; a
never-to-be forgotten splash of startling colour.

From the flax was produced linen yarn that was sold through
dealers, representing one of the main exports of the parish.
The yield of approximately sixteen tons of yarn provided the
principal source of cash which paid for the rents. In every
household the mother spent all her spare time spinning the
yarn, using the spinning-wheel, which at that time had replaced
the spindle and whorl. There were seven lint mills in the parish
where the flax was prepared for spinning and weaving. Fine
home-spun linen thread was also produced by a William
Forbes of Aldclune and this thread would be produced until
the end of the century. When the flax was cut, it was steeped
in pools for a certain time so as to soften or rot the husk which
enclosed the fibre. The lint pools were formed in the flax fields.
The local children bathed in these pools.

This enchanting parish, with the sparkling mountain streams
winding their way through the fields of lush green pasture, was
further enhanced with cowslips and the gay, pink, pea-shaped
flowers of the masterful rest harrow. The hedgerows of wild
raspberries and brambles, the white blossom of the bird cherry
and the ever-present faint aroma of burning wood provided an
atmosphere never to be forgotten.

It was late afternoon and James Duff, the gardener at
Balnakeilly House, was making his last rounds of the day.

He cast his admiring eye on the rich clover lawn in front of the house. The velvet green was speckled with the pink and white clover flower which provided the nectar for the honeybees. At this time of the year the bees provided the light golden-coloured honey which would, come August, be replaced with the darker amber-coloured honey obtained from the flower of the heather which would cover the surrounding hills. On this particular day James lingered no longer than was necessary as he had much more important thoughts on his mind. His first child was expected at any time.

He set off to the farm of Achnahyle where they lived in one of the estate cottages. Achnahyle farm was built on the crest of a gentle slope, with fir trees planted on the north side to give protection from the cold winter winds. The cottages were placed on both sides of a courtyard and as James approached he saw the usual hustle at the end of the working day. The returning farm workers with the children were helping to lead • the horses to their stable; chickens were being fed; and water was being drawn from the well in the courtyard. This happened every day except Sunday, yet the tempo and excitement was always the same. The day's hard toil had ended and the families were together again.

James's wife Jean stood at the door of their cottage with her friend Charlotte, the wife of the gamekeeper, enjoying the familiar scene while they waited for their husbands. These people worked the land. They were part of it, and while the tasks performed varied almost daily depending on the time of year, this part of the day was always very special.

The cottage had walls of grey-coloured stone speckled with diamond-like particles which sparkled in the sunlight. It was a local stone, mica schist, a fine-grained metamorphic rock with the minerals arranged in more or less parallel layers. The slated roof was grey-green in colour with a tracery of silver lichen. Over the door of the cottage was a small porch covered with sweet smelling tea-roses.

After the evening meal it was usual for the men of the farm to collect in the stable and James duly made his way over to chat to his friends. The atmosphere in the stable was always relaxed. The smell of oats, molasses and sweet hay never seemed to vary and in winter the heat from the mighty horses provided a most pleasant retreat.

This was the scene, the atmosphere, the way of life in this utopian community that a child, yet to be born, would cherish for the rest of his life. From his devout parents the boy would learn and believe that there was a God. He would believe in Heaven. He had lived there.

In the early hours of 25 April, 1806, a son was born to James and Jean Duff and he was named Alexander. The proud parents gave thanks to God for their beautiful, dark-haired little boy and Dr Stewart, the parish minister, called to give the baby his blessing. Little did any of them realize the impact which this baby would have on the world.

Gaelic was the language of the area but English was now superseding the Gaelic, mainly due to the revival of the teaching of Christianity within the parish by the bilingual Dr Stewart. James Duff and his girl-friend, the Gaelic-speaking Jean Rattray, were under seventeen years of age when the great Charles Simeon, in 1796, preached in the pulpit of Moulin church when on a visit to the Highlands.

Dr Stewart's life was changed on hearing the Prince of the Evangelicals of the Church of England and it was this event which inspired him in the revival of Christian teaching in the area. English and the Gaelic were henceforth preached in Moulin and used in everyday life.

Of James Duff and his wife Jean we know little, other than that which was told by their son Alexander in later life. He believed himself to owe everything to them. His parents were people of passionate religious faith, of the rugged Calvinist type, tinged both with the fire and with the sadness of the Celtic nature. James worked hard for the spiritual improvement of his neighbourhood by keeping or superintending Sabbath schools and holding weekly prayer meetings at his own cottage or elsewhere, for prayer or spiritual exposition.

In prayer James was indeed mighty, appearing at times as if in a rapture. He was equally fluent in the Gaelic and English languages and could easily adapt himself to the requirements of such mixed audiences as the Highlands usually furnished. As a child, Alexander would listen intently to his father speaking in both languages and to his mother, who was now bilingual, but still used the Gaelic in everyday use. When three years old he could instinctively understand and speak in either language. He had made a start on his mission.

The Duff family moved to an estate cottage at Balnakeilly in 1810. Their cottage was ideally placed in an open glade with a mountain stream on either side and a wealth of weeping birch, ash, larch and young oak trees, which in the slanting autumn sun seemed to surround the cottage with a setting of gold.

As a child, Alexander was almost drowned when lifting a pail of drinking water from the more easterly of the two streams. The stream had been swollen with the melting snow on the mountains; and only by grabbing a support on a rustic bridge was he able to find a footing and avoid disaster.

Alexander was an attractive and bright child with dark hair, brown eyes, and already gave indication that he would grow tall like his father. He played and helped with the work like the other children on the estate. When the stage-coach arrived at Pitlochry he would accompany the older children in a two-wheeled cart, returning with letters and parcels destined for Moulin and the local estates.

The children also accompanied the larger four-wheeled carts which were used to take produce from the parish, whence it was transferred to the goods wagons which operated in convoy on the Great North Road. The goods exported from the parish comprised wool and woollen garments including tartan cloth, linen yarn and linen goods, milk, honey, cheese, implements carved from the antlers of the deer, whisky from the local distillery at Edradour, eggs and other produce too numerous to mention. Moulin was indeed a self-sufficient community, but greater than all her produce were her sons and daughters who would leave the little parish in search of adventure and knowledge.

The children listened to the tales of the travellers, artists, soldiers and sailors who had been to far-off lands. In August each year the aristocracy would visit the area for the grouse shooting and the children would serve as beaters in driving the grouse towards the guns of the shooting parties. Alexander and his companions had indeed an abundance of sources of information.

The one school that served Pitlochry and Moulin was situated halfway between the two villages. The village schoolmaster was regarded as an exceptionally useless teacher. Amiable, ingenious and even learned, he divided his time between repairing violins and clocks during school hours, when the older children heard the lessons of the younger. During bible lessons he usually fished in the local stream while his wife took the class. The children were taught the basic subjects but an emphasis was placed on how to make and tie flies for angling; how to stalk game, how to set traps and snares, how to poach salmon, how to shoot and, for those children who were interested, how to repair violins and clocks. The children loved school but their parents were sorely perplexed!

In 1814, when Alexander was eight years old, his father heard of a school which had been established between Pitlochry and Dunkeld, where local farmers were engaged in helping to clear land for the Duke of Atholl. As the project lasted several years, the farmers moved to the area with their wives and children and the reports of the quality of teaching were very good. A place was found for Alexander and he was boarded at the school, returning the eight miles home at the weekends. He now had a sister and two brothers, Margaret, Finlay and John, aged seven, five and two years old respectively. Alexander made rapid progress during his three years at this school and a Mr Macdougall, the schoolmaster at the village of Kirkmichael in a neighbouring parish to Moulin, heard of the promising young boy from his friend Dr Stewart at Moulin. He offered to take Alexander in hand and allow him to board with him in the schoolhouse.

Alexander and his fellow pupils benefitted greatly from the manifold advantages of being taught by so brilliant a man. In the class of twelve pupils his particular friend was Duncan Forbes, who ultimately became Professor of Oriental Languages at King's College, London. All twelve pupils would ultimately gain entry to St Andrews University by bursary, which proved the unique ability of their teacher.

During his period at Kirkmichael, Alexander returned home every Saturday, irrespective of weather, and attended church on Sunday with his family. After the service he would be invited to the manse and report on his progress at school and also to keep the minister up to date with events in the neighbouring parish. On Sunday evening he would return to the schoolhouse at Kirkmichael. On one of his journeys an incident happened which, apart from illustrating some of the difficulties of travel, played a significant part in Alexander's life.

In the winter of 1819, he was making his journey home with his friend Duncan Forbes. The weather was particularly severe with deep snow and a howling blizzard. They took the shorter route across the low hill by Glen Beiarchan and Straloch, wading through the heather which was clad with deep snow. The sun had set and, being a starless night, all landmarks had become obliterated. At times the hidden ice on the lint pools would crack under their weight, soaking them with ice-cold water. At last, and in almost pitch darkness, they slid down a precipice hidden by deep snow and came to rest at the side of a river.

They lay there frozen, soaked, weak with exhaustion, completely lost and all but hopeless. They knew that only a miracle could save them and prayed to God for help. After a time which seemed an eternity they saw a small light flash some distance away. Surely their prayer had been answered. They struggled towards the source of the light which at times would disappear. On finally reaching the source, they discovered to their delight that it was a party of salmon poachers using the light to attract the fish.

The poachers helped the boys to reach a cottage and there they were given dry clothes, a meal and a bed for the night. In the morning, when it was light, they made their way home to Moulin.

In after years, when Alexander was in difficulty or danger, the memory of the sudden flash of light called forth new thankfulness and cheerful hope. Trust in the overruling providence of a gracious God so filled his heart that the earlier deliverance never failed to stimulate him to a fresh effort in a righteous cause when all seemed lost.

On another occasion, Alexander was nearly drowned in the river Ardle near Kirkmichael. He lost his footing on the bank and was dragged by the raging torrent until he managed to catch hold of a large boulder which projected above the surface. He was able to wrap his legs round the boulder and pull himself onto the slippery surface. From a crouching position, he summoned up all the strength he had and made a leap to the bank. He grasped the grass on the bank and dragged himself ashore. He lay exhausted and trembling and once again thanked the Lord for his deliverance. This river boulder still exists and is known as 'Duff's Stone'.

At Kirkmichael school the class worked hard under the brilliant Mr Macdougall who had a natural ability to inspire his pupils with his method of teaching. He conveyed knowledge in such a manner that it became firmly locked and linked in the pupil's mind. He discouraged the taking of notes as he considered that it was more important for the subject to be fully understood at the time of intake. The lesson would then be discussed openly in class, which was only possible if its content had been absorbed. Alexander would find this method of teaching used during his student days and he continued the system in his own teaching career in later life.

The master prepared Alexander for the next stage of his education. He was now fourteen years of age and Mr Macdougall considered that the boy would be best served by sending him to the grammar school in Perth, which had one of the highest reputations in the country. To do this, he needed to reach an academic standard which would gain him a scholarship, which he did.

The Rector of Perth Grammar School was Mr Moncur, a great scholar able to recognise the potential of his pupils, who had gained the very highest praise from the University of St Andrews. The opportunity which Alexander now had could not have been better. The Rector had long since abolished corporal punishment, believing that the generous youths entrusted to his charge should not be treated like savages.

Under Mr Moncur, Alexander's Latin and Greek had their foundation broadened and deepened. In the favourite optional exercise of committing to memory, he generally came off first and further developed this faculty to which much of his later oratorial success was due. Alexander left Perth Grammar School in 1821, aged fifteen, as dux of the school. The Rector presented him with a copy of Milton's *Paradise Lost* which, later in life, he referred to as having a great influence over his mental habits.

2
Student at St Andrews

In October 1821 Alexander left home for St Andrews, with twenty pounds in his pocket. This was a sizeable gift from his father, whose wage as a gardener on the estate was three shillings and sixpence a week.

St Andrews had been a centre of education since the founding of the first of the Scottish universities by Bishop Wardlaw in 1412. The spacious tree-shaded streets lie open to sun and wind, and to the eastward, the North Sea breaks against the jagged cliffs that hem in the narrow harbour. To the west is St Andrews Bay, wide and shallow, which curves in a long stretch of fine sand, fringing the famous golf links, where the Royal and Ancient Golf Club was founded in 1754.

Legend traces the beginnings of St Andrews back to the Abbot of Patras in Greece, named Rule or Regulus, who was commanded 'by heavenly vision to abscond with the arm of Saint Andro, with three fingers and three toes from his feet'. Journeying over the seas, St Rule was borne to this far neuk of the world. The King of the Picts welcomed him and built a Kirk to house his relics. Scotland early accepted Saint Andrew as its patron saint and the national flag of Scotland is the simple St Andrew's Cross, being a white diagonal cross on an azure ground. The tiny church of St Rule, with its striking square tower, is the oldest of the town's ecclesiastical ruins.

The cathedral nearby was founded in 1160 in the presence of King Malcolm, and building was begun, as customary, at the east end. Progress was slow, being delayed by poverty, wild weather and the desolating wars of Independence. Not until 1318 was the church completed and joyfully consecrated in the presence of King Robert the Bruce, the victor of the Battle of Bannockburn. In the fifteenth century, St Andrews was created a Metropolitan See, with an archbishop who exercised wide sway in Scotland, ranking only second to the Royal House. In 1513 Alexander Stewart, the Boy Archbishop, fell beside King James IV at Flodden. In the cathedral, James V married Mary of Guise.

The castle, founded about 1200 and rebuilt by Archbishop Hamilton about 1550, was the Bishop's Palace and saw as many secular deeds of violence as any secular fortress. Three of the last occupants of the See were murdered, including Cardinal Beaton, whose body was pickled in salt and cast into the Bottle Dungeon. Down the sea stairs of the castle, John Knox was driven to the French galley in which he served at the oar for eighteen months. East of the castle was the Witches' Pool, where suspect women were given the choice of drowning to prove their innocence or floating to prove their guilt.

St Andrews, despite its famous history, had very little to offer the boy of fifteen with twenty pounds in his pocket in November 1821, and a store of energy, enthusiasm and ability. After the religious atmosphere of his home and the breezy life at Perth, St Andrews, with the north-east biting winds sweeping its grey streets, seemed to Alexander a very enervating, spiritually desolate spot. Writing long afterwards about his early impression of St Andrews and the university, he described it as '. . . a veritable backwater of life, cut off even from the most ordinary of external influences'. All the members of the university senate were Moderates, and the students were generally bored with religious matters.

Social life at the Scottish universities was a simple affair in those days.[1] In order to make a university education available for poorer students, the rules of residence were of the loosest possible character. If necessary, a student might cut down his attendance at lectures to the bare minimum and win his way to the coveted degree by hours of study stolen from sleep, or after a day's teaching in some county parish school; or the day's ploughing in the fields.

Lodging in the town was not cheap and in Alexander's case, five shillings a week for a single room, which served as a bedroom, parlour and study, and that was for sharing the room with his friend Duncan Forbes. They thrived on a diet of hard work and of tea once, and oatmeal porridge, twice a day. As a treat, they could have fresh herrings and potatoes with an occasional burst of extravagance, adding ox livers for an extra one and half pence. One poor student brought a chest of oatmeal from home and with a little salt and butter, and the hot water supplied by his landlady, lived solely on this for a

[1] William Paton, *Alexander Duff: Pioneer of Missionary Education* (London: SCM, 1923), pp. 26–27.

whole year. He was too proud to confess his secret. He went hungry to bed each night yet fought his way through to become a doctor of medicine.

During his studies at St Andrews, which were to last until 1829, Alexander earned distinctions in different departments of learned and scientific studies. He carried off the highest honours in Greek, Latin, Logic and Moral Philosophy. He carried off the Essay Prize offered for the best translation into Latin of Plato's *Apology of Socrates*, and the Senatus spontaneously dubbed him Master of Arts after only two years of study. As a scholar, he earned a high reputation in classics, Hebrew, and theology. As a public speaker he showed the qualities of intellect and eloquence that would be so important in later life. One of Alexander's juniors, the son of Professor Ferrie, gives us this other and very human glimpse:

> He was passing the windows of my father's house in St Andrews with others going to some great students' meeting, and I remember Nairne, who was then my tutor, called out as they passed, 'There is Duff.' I looked, and he had on a cloak, and was going with a good thick stick in his hand, as though he expected that there might be a row.

Another contemporary recorded that there was a weight and a downright earnestness about him which everybody felt. He was the boast of the college, and was greatly regarded by the townsfolk of St Andrews.

A third fellow-student remembered:

> As a friend he was always singularly obliging, warm-hearted and constant; as a companion he was uniformly agreeable and cheerful, and not infrequently impressive in his appeals to the better susceptibilities of our nature; though generally in high spirits and mirthful, he never allowed his mirth to degenerate into boisterous vulgarity.

What the lad was at St Andrews, the man proved to be all through his life.

In the spring of 1823 the university and the town of St Andrews was set humming by the news that a new Professor of Moral Philosophy had been appointed; Dr Thomas Chalmers. He was one of the most prominent Evangelicals in Scotland and although not yet a national leader, which he later became, he was already well known as a magnificent exponent of the power of the Gospel and of the universal nature of its applications. He had been in charge of a church in a poorer district of Glasgow and had already made a deep impression on the life of that city.

Many of the residents at St Andrews remembered Chalmers as a boy, a student and afterwards as a lecturer in the town and in the university, and to receive him back again amongst them in the full blaze of unparalleled popularity, they felt to be like shedding of some undefinable radiance on themselves. The trades people calculated the effect on their scanty incomes at the coming of this great celebrity, who would attract more students and visitors to St Andrews. The students, tired of the level tones which flowed on so monotonously in lecture and class rooms were, with all the honest fervour of youth, enraptured at the thought of having for a professor a man of genius and the greatest orator of the age.

There had been three great men in Alexander's life to date: his father, Mr Macdougall of Kirkmichael and Mr Moncur, Rector of Perth Grammar School. All had brought him to where he was. Here would be the man who would finally mould him for the great task he was yet to choose. Dr Chalmers gave his first lecture in St Andrews on a Friday in November 1823.

The effect on the students was most stimulating because, instead of the dry-as-dust utterances that the aged lecturers read from yellowing pages, here was live creative thought, the actual contemporary labours of a great mind which riveted the co-operation of others. An indescribable impulse excited and sustained the students. There was not a latent spark of intellectual enthusiasm in any student that was not kindled into a glowing flame. It would be impossible not to follow where such a leader led the way, and with many, as with himself, the pursuit became a passion.

The influence of Chalmers's vision of truth, philosophical, scientific, and revealed as a whole, its parts fundamentally and essentially inseparable, could do no other than make a permanent impression on those who listened. In class the room was crowded out with more than double the number of students that had ever attended in the days of even his most famous predecessors. About half of the students came from the Scottish universities, or from England or Ireland. St Andrews, from being a backwater, became the centre of intellectual activity. Advanced students returned on their earlier studies in order to join the Chalmers class. Older amateur students from outside helped to diversify, and raise still higher, the intellectual tone of the class. Again, Alexander noted, there was no continuous note-taking among the students. Chalmers' own informality and enthusiasm made that impossible. Applause and laughter could never be restrained for long.

Alexander studied at St Mary's College, and in 1824 the St Andrews University Missionary Society was formed with Alexander as librarian. It was at this stage that he decided to devote his life to the Church and missionary work. St Andrews was no longer the backwater he had thought when he first arrived. He was now inspired and for the rest of his life believed that God had sent this great man, Chalmers, to show him the way.

Alexander's powers of oratory were further enhanced following the arrival of Dr Chalmers and his addresses were given large audience. Many were fascinated at his method of giving a lengthy address without reference to notes. At last, one of his close friends, James Craik, asked how it was done. They seemed from beginning to end to be sudden, impromptu, spontaneous outpourings, and yet there were parts that looked so artistically and artificially prepared that it was difficult to believe that they were impromptu. Alexander replied:

. . . in a general way when I was called upon to make a special speech on a special occasion, my method was this:

I abhorred the idea of addressing a great public audience on any subject without thoroughly mastering all the principles and details of it. I revolved these over repeatedly in my own mind until they became quite familiar to me. I then resolved, having a perfect understanding of the subject, to leave the modes of expressing my views, or embodying them in language, till the time of delivery. I felt, if I myself entirely understood my subject I ought to be able to make it reasonably intelligible to all thoughtful men. In the the course of a long and elaborate speech on a vital and important subject, there were often points of a delicate nature which required equal delicacy, or even nicety in giving them formal expression. These particular points I thought over and over again, until not only the thought became fixed and confirmed, but also the very modes of expressing it. So in the delivery of the speech; when these particular points came up, I did not leave them to any expressions which at the time might occur to me, but gave them in the language with which they had become riveted and associated in my own mind; but coming up in this way in their natural place and connection; strangers might not know but they were the spontaneous effusion of the moment, like all the rest of the speech.

This was far better than earlier days, when committing a speech to writing and then to memory had always seemed to Alexander to prove more or less a failure.

While studying at St Andrews, Alexander devoted a considerable time to the study of languages, to the extent that by 1829 he had mastered German, Russian, Persian, Arabic, Chinese and Hebrew. By 1827 he had positively decided to become a missionary and for the next two years worked towards that goal, but he was to lose the great master, Dr Chalmers, who left St Andrews in October 1828 for a professorship at Edinburgh. A year later, in 1829, Alexander Duff M.A. was licensed by the Presbytery of St Andrews to exercise his gifts as a probationer of the Holy Ministry. The young man was now ready for the work which had been long awaiting him and he had done his utmost to prepare himself.

In the spring of 1829, Dr Ferrie, Professor of Church History at St Andrews, proposed Alexander as the first missionary of the Church of Scotland to Calcutta. Dr Fernie had written to Dr Chalmers before making the proposal. On 12 March, 1829, Alexander wrote to Chalmers informing him that he was willing to go to India. A characteristically long letter, mixing flowery language with passages of genuine eloquence, it showed the seriousness, humility and respect with which he had come to his decision. Having prayed about Dr Ferrie's invitation, carefully examined his own motives and qualifications, and consulted his friends, Alexander felt he was now ready to reply to the committee in the words of Isaiah, 'Here am I, Send me' (Isa 6:8). He went on:

The work is most arduous, but is of God and must prosper; many sacrifices painful to 'flesh and blood' must be made, but not any correspondent to the glory of winning souls to Christ. With the thought of this glory I feel myself almost transported with joy; everything else appears to fall out of view as vain and insignificant. The Kings and great men of the earth have reared the sculptured monument and the lofty pyramid with the vain hope of transmitting their names with reverence to succeeding generations; and yet the sculptured monument and the lofty pyramid do crumble into decay, and must finally be burnt up in the general wreck of dissolving nature; but he that has been the means of subduing one soul to the Cross of Christ, hath reared a far more enduring monument – a monument that will outlast all time, and survive the widespread ruins of ten thousand worlds; a trophy which is destined to bloom and flourish in immortal youth in the land of immortality, and which will perpetuate the remembrance of him who raised it throughout the boundless duration of eternal ages.

Alexander returned to the parish of Moulin to spend some time with his family and friends, as it would be his only opportunity before his ordination and departure for India. The family had been increased by the addition of another child, Jean, who was born in March, 1815. His parents, brothers and sisters, and indeed the whole population of the parish and the neighbouring estates, were thrilled at having their now famous son return.

He was invited to the houses of many of the estate owners in order to be formally congratulated and to be given letters of introduction to their friends whom they thought might be of benefit to him on his travels. The minister at Moulin Church, now the Rev David Duff, came over to the cottage at Balnakeilly to inform Alexander that a farewell party had been arranged for the people of the parish at Balnakeilly House by the gracious consent of the Laird, Captain Alexander Stewart.

The farewell party was the greatest event held in the parish in living memory. The stately Balnakeilly House, having been completely rebuilt in 1821 following a fire which destroyed the original building, provided an ideal setting for the celebration. By permission of His Grace, the Duke of Atholl, the music was provided by the Pipes and Drums of the Atholl Highlanders. A feast fit for their 'prince' was provided, with an ample supply of Atholl Brose (a mixture of malt whisky, honey and cream) and locally produced beer.

Since childhood, the girls of the parish had been taught to spin the local flax and produce linen. Every girl was expected to produce enough linen for her future household and was not allowed to marry until this was done. From the wool they

produced tartan cloth and Alexander was duly presented with
a fine selection of linen and tartan cloth.

On this particular occasion the girls of the parish excelled
themselves and adorned their persons in a most competitive
way to attract the attention of this handsome and eligible
bachelor. Alexander gave no hint of wishing to acquire a wife
at this stage.

From several pulpits and platforms before his departure for
India he delivered rousing missionary discourses and appeals.
In the fine old Kirk of Leuchars, preaching from Romans 1:14,
he exclaimed:

> I am debtor both to the Greeks and to the Barbarians.
> There was a time when I had no care or concern for the
> heathen: that was a time when I had no care or concern
> for my own soul. When by the grace of God I was led to
> care for my own soul, then it was I began to care for the
> heathen abroad. In my closet, on my bended knees, I then
> said to God, 'O Lord, Thow knowest that silver and gold
> to give to this cause I have none; what I have I give unto
> Thee, – I offer Thee myself, wilt Thou accept the gift?'

The tears trickled down his cheeks as he uttered these words.

Next to his own people, none took so keen an interest in
the career of Alexander as a patriarchal couple in Blairgowrie.
Patrick Lawson and his wife became young again in the
company of students and Alexander in particular. They had
extended many invitations in the past to the young students.

Alexander had a problem at this stage in his life, following
his interview at the General Assembly in May. He told his host,
Patrick, that he had been asked abruptly whether he intended
to marry and had replied that he had never even given thought
to the matter and in any case had not met a suitable girl.

Patrick responded, in terms that Alexander accepted:

> I do not approve of young men fresh from college taking
> wives to themselves when newly married to their church,
> before they can possibly know the requirements of their
> work. But your case is wholly different. You go to a
> distant region of heathenism, where you will find little
> sympathy among your countrymen, and will need the
> companionship of one like-minded to whom you may
> unbosom yourself. My advice to you is, be quietly on
> the look-out; and if, in God's providence, you make the

acquaintance of one of the daughters of Zion, traversing, like yourself, the wilderness of this world, her face set thitherward, get into friendly converse with her. If you find that in mind, in heart, in temper and disposition you congenialize, and if God puts it into her heart to be willing to forsake father and mother and cast in her lot with you, regard it as a token from the God of providence that you should use the proper means to secure her Christian society.

No reference seems to have survived to Alexander's meeting with the girl of his choice, their courtship, which must have been short duration, or of her Christian background. Whatever the circumstances; as later events will unfold, their union could only have been by divine influence. This fifth person of inspiring influence in Alexander's life became, by far, the most important. The first four, his father, Mr Macdougall, Mr Moncur and Dr Chalmers, had all helped prepare him for his task. His wife would carry out the task with him and even when she knew her life was drawing to a close, she kept it from him and prepared a home for him to continue with his work.

Just before Dr Chalmers ordained the missionary, Dr Inglis married him to Anne Scott Drysdale of Edinburgh, on 9 July 1829. As Alexander said more than once after her death, it was a happy marriage and no missionary had ever had a more devoted wife.

Alexander's ordination followed on 12 August, 1829, at St George's in Edinburgh. Dr Chalmers conducted the service. At this time it was confirmed that they would be leaving for India in September. His father had watched with grateful pride the consecration of his son to a higher than an ecclesiastical bishopric of souls. A few days later Alexander wrote to his father at length, and this was followed by a further letter dated 25 August. This was on the theme of God's present and future blessings. Alexander was blessed in being called to missionary service, his father would be blessed in giving him to it. The letter ended:

will you be a loser by so giving me up to the Lord, and so praising Him for His goodness in having called me to so mighty a work? No, God will bless you with the blessing of Abraham, will enrich you with His faith and reward, and will reward you a thousandfold for your willing resignation and cheerful readiness in obeying

God's command. The Lord bless you, and my dear mother, and all the people of God at Moulin. Adieu! Your dear and affectionate son,

Alexander Duff.

Despite the fact that he had been married for only a few weeks, no reference was made to his wife.

3

Leaving for India

On 19th September, 1829, the Duffs boarded a ship for London at Leith and duly arrived at London, where they became guests of Alderman and Mrs Pirie, whose task it was to look after them and to arrange a cabin for them in the *Lady Holland*, an East Indiaman bound for Calcutta. The cabin was specially fitted out for them as they had a considerable amount of luggage, including his now large library of books and manuscripts.

Dr Inglis of the General Assembly had applied to the Directors of the East India Company for Alexander and his wife to sail to India with the classification of 'Interlopers'. This was a passport rating distinct from the conventional civil, military and naval service of the East India Company. Alexander had been supplied with letters of introduction to the Governor-General, Lord Bentinck, the Earl of Dalhousie and many other men of influence. The *Lady Holland*, having filled up in the Thames with a cargo valued forty-eight thousand pounds, entered the English Channel. Her first stop was Portsmouth, where she shipped passengers. She became windbound for a week at Spithead and finally set sail from Ryde on 14 October. Plunging heavily into a storm outside the Isle of Wight, the ship made for Falmouth. When the gale had abated, she again set sail for Madeira. The bay of Biscay proved unusually friendly, but contrary winds did not allow the ship to reach the Roads of Funchal until 7 November.

The *Lady Holland* was a stately vessel, carrying cargo, provisions, livestock to provide fresh food on the voyage, and thirty-two passengers. As an East Indiaman, modelled on the frigates of the Royal Navy,[1] she was built of massive oak frames, knees and planking, the timber of which had lain in the dockyard, seasoning in salt water for many years. It was as hard and almost as heavy as iron. The timbers were fastened with weighty through-and-through copper bolts; so

[1] See Arthur H. Clark, *The Clipper Ship Era* (Riverside, Conn.: 7c's Press, 1910, 2nd revision 1970).

that the ship itself became a rigid, dead structure; sluggish in moderate winds, and in a gale and seaway, a wallowing brute. She was heavy aloft and spread canvas sail by which, when close hauled, the wind held the vessel. The obsolete Tonnage Laws encouraged and almost compelled an undesirable type of vessel such as this, being too narrow, deep, flat sided, full bottomed and in a seaway, slow and often requiring a considerable quantity of ballast, even when loaded, to keep them from falling over.

A ship of the East India Company, although engaged in commercial pursuits, was under the direct patronage of the British Government and could not be regarded as forming part of the Merchant Marine of Great Britain. Like her sister ships, the *Lady Holland* served the most gigantic commercial monopoly the world had ever known. They were allowed by Royal Charter to fly the long 'coach-whip' pennant of the Royal Navy. She was indeed, built, rigged, equipped, armed and manned like the frigates of the Royal Navy. She was beautifully and luxuriously fitted for passengers, many of whom were personages of high social and official rank. She carried four hundred-and-twenty tons of general cargo and required eighty tons of ballast to keep her on her 'sea legs'.

Captains were appointed to their ships before launching and checked the ship in the final stages of building, superintending all the equipment deemed necessary for a captain which could earn him at least four thousand pounds on an eighteen-months' journey. It was known for captains to earn as much as thirty-thousand pounds on a twenty-two-month journey; London, India, China and return.

The captain and his crew were paid on a 'results basis' only. Unless the ship and its cargo arrived at its destination intact, there was no payment whatsoever and the risks were very high indeed. The stakes were high and it was therefore obvious that the policy of the master and his crew was safety first and to fight like demons if threatened. From the Company's point of view, the profits were exceptionally high and one complete voyage to India and return could pay for the building of the ship and yield at least two hundred per cent on the investment of the cargo transported.

On the *Lady Holland*'s arrival at Madeira, the captain, as usual, had intended to remain for a week and to take on a cargo of wine which would mellow on its way to Calcutta. There were three British frigates in the roads and the famous novelist Captain Marryat was in command of one of them. The week had nearly passed and the 'Agent' gave the usual ball to the captain and passengers on the night before departure. All were present at the ball except the Duffs and Lieutenant Henry Marion Durand, a young lieutenant of Engineers who would later become Sir Henry Durand and second only to Sir Henry Lawrence on the brilliant roll of the Company's soldier-statesmen. He was one of the ten passengers who attended the daily worship on board the *Lady Holland*.

About midnight, westerly gales set in with violence and drove the ships in the bay out to sea. Three of them were driven ashore and dashed to pieces. Not a life was saved. The *Lady Holland* and the Royal Navy frigates were riding the storm, but all their captains were ashore with no possible way of returning to their ships. We may imagine the position of those passengers who had gone ashore in their ball-dress with no change of clothes. Despairing of the vessel, some of the passengers began to negotiate with a Portuguese ship about to proceed to Lisbon.

During their enforced extra three weeks on the island the passengers in the different parties visited its most interesting sights, amongst others the Curral, in the centre, which was the gigantic crater of a volcano rising to a height of six thousand feet. Approached by a difficult zigzag path along many precipices which look down upon a tremendous chasm, the Curral was not seen till they actually reached it.

It was lucky that the crews of the *Lady Holland* and the naval frigates had been on board while the storm raged, as they undoubtedly saved the vessels. Eventually the captains and passengers were able to return to their ships and on the 3 December, the *Lady Holland* set sail in company with one of the frigates which had been ordered to equatorial waters to look for pirates. The ship next called at the Cape Verde Islands but was detained for another week because of pirates operating in the area.

At the time of their voyage, Don Miguel had usurped the throne of Portugal and had seized the Portuguese fleet which he sent to expel the Constitutionalists from Madeira and to proclaim sovereignty over it. Some time before the arrival of the Duffs in Madeira the eldest son of the great George Canning had been there in command of an English frigate. Animated by the liberal principles of his father, he made it understood that if any of the persecuted Constitutionalists chose to take refuge on board his ship, he would receive them.

It became known to the Portuguese authorities that he had more than three hundred of them on board. The governor of the island and the admiral of the Portuguese fleet sent him a message, that if he did not hand over the traitorous refugees they would blow his frigate to pieces. This they could easily have done, but the young Canning informed them that should they blow up his ship, it would precipitate their doom, as it would send forth the British Navy 'to put an end to you utterly'. They did not meddle with him further. However, the Constitutionalists lost their champion when Canning was drowned in a swimming accident. Thus perished one whose younger brother became the first Viceroy of India; Charles John Earl Canning, KG.

The *Lady Holland* proceeded to her next port of call, Cape Town, but because of the severity of the south-east Trade Winds, she was now nearer Buenos Aires. One morning, within two hundred yards of her, a well-known pirate ship, with at least fifty men on deck, scudded before the wind with their escorting frigate in hot pursuit. It was early February before they were approaching the coast of South Africa.

Three times the ship was driven considerably to the south of Table Bay by contrary winds, but the captain brought her back with a view of going into it. From the Cape coast there shoots out into the sea for forty to fifty miles a sandbank on which soundings can be taken. By soundings taken on the evening of Saturday, 13 February, the captain knew that he had entered this bank. His intention therefore was to avoid risk by turning his vessel back to sea, but a further sounding made at 8 p.m. made him continue inwards for another two hours.

At four bells (ten o'clock) he gave the order to turn back, but the ship bumped with alarming violence upon rocks. The concussion was tremendous and from the first moment her case seemed hopeless. The ship was on the rocks and the back of the vessel being broken, the fore part sank down between the reefs.

As in all East Indiamen, lights were put out at 10 p.m. and all passengers had retired to their berths. They now all rushed on deck and Alexander, half dressed, heard the captain exclaim in agony, 'She's gone, she's gone'. The command was given to cut down the masts in order to relieve the pressure of the wind on the ship, and to caulk the seams of the longboat in case there would be a chance of escape. The longboat housed forty sheep which were used for food on the voyage.

One of the passengers, a pleasant colonel, slept through it all because of his nightly copious draught of brandy. He was somewhat drunk and therefore not unduly concerned. Alexander suggested that it was quite possible they would all soon meet their Creator and held a short service which had a profound effect on everyone, with the exception of the colonel who was rather indifferent to the entire situation.

At the outset, the captain had ordered one of the gig boats, which hung over the side of the vessel, to be launched. It contained three seamen who were ordered to ascertain whether there was any landing place available. At the time, the captain did not know if he had struck a reef, an island or the mainland. The sea was running mountains high and it seemed that a small boat would not survive in it. After three hours' searching, the men returned to confirm that there was a sandy bay which could be reached by the longboat. The waves were breaking over the vessel but the seamen managed to float the longboat; but the rope parted and it was carried away with the other debris.

The passengers and crew were now totally exhausted and only wished for a speedy end, when the longboat was rowed back by a seaman who had been hidden in it throughout the ordeal. However, it was discovered that the longboat could only take a third of those on board the *Lady Holland* and the prospect of returning for the remainder was not great. By what seemed like a miracle, the longboat did make shore and was able to return twice. All the passengers and crew were safely landed. By the time the officers and captain had reached shore, daylight began to appear.

It was found that they had reached an island and they heard what seemed to be the braying of asses. These were in fact myriads of penguins. There were also two Dutchmen on the island collecting the eggs. The passengers and crew formed parties to collect eggs and withered grass. With a fire provided by the withered grass, they cooked eggs for all in the Dutchmen's cooking pot, this being their only food. It took the colonel some little time to get used to the situation in which he now found himself.

One of the seamen found a chamois bag containing a quarto copy of Bagster's Bible and a Scottish psalm book; somewhat shattered and soaked, but with Alexander's name written distinctly on both. All were deeply affected by what had happened and their deliverance by this almost unbelievable escape, and believed their good fortune as a gift from God. Alexander read the 107th Psalm.

Alexander had taken with him a library of some eight hundred volumes, representing every department of knowledge. All but forty had been swallowed up in the wreckage and those remaining were reduced to pulp. With the books had gone all journals, notes, memoranda and essays as dear to him as his own flesh.

The land on which they found themselves proved to be Dassen Island in the Atlantic, forty miles north-north-west of Cape Town and ten miles from the mainland at Opica. In the distance they saw the white mist which form the 'tablecloth' of Table Mountain. The Irish surgeon on board the ship set out in the Dutchmen's small skiff in order to notify the authorities and to arrange for a ship to collect the survivors. In four days they were rescued by a brig of war, sent by the Governor, Sir Lowrie Cole.

The weather-beaten party landed in the midst of the British and Dutch inhabitants who crowded round to express their sympathy and learn of the ordeal. Mr and Mrs Duff were received by the Rev Dr Adamson, son of the minister at Cupar in Fife, who had been colleague of Dr Campbell, father of the Lord Chancellor. For weeks the passengers were detained. The next East Indiaman was so full that three of the passengers paid a hundred guineas each to be allowed to swing their cots in the steerage. Mr and Mrs Duff could get a passage in the last ship of the season, the *Moira*, and that only on payment of 3,000 rupees! This sum was equal to £262-10s. in gold. From Cape Town, on 5 March, he thus addressed Dr Chalmers:

My Dear Doctor, – I know your time is precious and I shall not detain you, as my tale may be briefly told: On Saturday night, February 13th, the *Lady Holland* was wrecked off Dassen Island, forty miles north of Cape Town, but not a life was lost, not even a personal injury sustained by any one of the passengers or crew. . . . The object of writing to *you* separately, is, – that a circumstance so calamitous in its aspect may not be permitted to cool zeal or damp exertion, but may be improved, to kindle a new flame throughout the Church and cause it to burn inextinguishably. As remarked in the communication referred to 'though part of the first-fruits of the Church of Scotland in the great cause of Christian philanthropy has perished in the total wreck of the *Lady Holland*, the cause of Christ has not perished. . . . And shall the Church of Scotland dishonour such a cause, by exhibiting any symptoms of coldness or despondency in consequence of the recent catastrophe! God forbid. Let her rather arouse herself into new energy; let her shake off every earthly alliance with the cause of Christ, as a retarding, polluting alliance; let her confide less in her own resources and more in the arm of Him who saith, 'Not by power, nor by might, but by My Spirit'. From her faithful appeals let the flame of devotedness circulate through every parish, and prayers ascend to 'the Lord of the harvest', from every family; and then may we expect her fountains to overflow, for the watering and fertilizing of many a dry and parched heathen land.

This is the improvement suggested; and of all men living, you, my dear Doctor, are, with God's blessing, the individual most capable of making it. Let the committee be awakened, and, from the awakening appeals of the committee, let the Church be aroused. Who, that has heard it, can ever forget your own vivid description and eloquent improvement of the magnificent preparation and total failure of the first great missionary enterprise? From it, ours stands at an immeasurable distance; but the principle is the same. I fear that much of calculating worldliness is apt to enter into the schemes and preparations of the Assembly. And now Heaven frowns in mercy, and buries a portion of its fruits in the depths of ocean, to excite, if possible, to the cherishing of a holier spirit, and a more prayerful waiting on the Lord for the outpouring of His grace.

'Sunday sail, never fail' was the chant to which the sailors weighed anchor at Cape Town as the *Moira* set sail for Calcutta. But contrary winds drove the vessel to fifty degrees of south latitude, and then for weeks she was beaten out of her course by westerly gales, culminating off Mauritius in a hurricane which threatened the foundering of the ship. Not till near the end of May did the *Moira* sight the hardy little pilot brig which, far out in the Bay of Bengal but still in the muddy waters of the united Ganges and Brahmaputra rivers, was the advanced post of British India proper.

The hot sun was blazing with intense power as the belated East Indiaman was carefully navigated into the estuary of the Hooghly, the most westerly of the so-called mouths of the Ganges. Hardly had she moored in the rapid stream off the long, low, muddy flat of Saugar Island, when the south-west monsoon was upon her in splendid fury. The clouds hid the sun and gave birth to a storm which soon changed into the dreaded cyclone. In spite of three anchors, the *Moira* was tossed and dragged. The ship became wedged in the mud and was listing badly. The cyclone tried to pull the vessel from the mud, which would have been her end. The captain secured the ship's papers to his person and yet once again, everyone prepared for the end.

The river was of unusually vast volume, the low delta land was flooded. Poised on the very edge of Saugar bank, with some ten feet of water on the shore and sixty or seventy on the fast-flowing river-side, and wedged in this position by the force of the hurricane, the *Moira* worked for herself a bed in the clay. Nothing could be done, for the great wind of heaven was still loose and darkness which might be felt was broken only by the flash of forked lightning.

Dawn revealed the vessel leaning over at a sharp angle, but still kept from disappearing by the wedge-like compression of the of the silt of the bank. The wind, in mighty swirling eddies, raised up columns of water which came down like so many cataracts. From the extremely dangerous position of the ship it was necessary that all be put on shore, but that meant deep water. One large tree, however, was espied, and to that, the pilot and the natives succeeded in making a hawser fast, by swimming to its branches. Along this a boat was moored to the tree, and there, on somewhat higher ground, the passengers were 'landed' up to the waist in water, at the time rolling in billows. The wind drove all, passengers and crew, inland to a village where caste forbade the natives to give them shelter. Denied access to the huts that were not already flooded, the shipwrecked party took possession of the village temple. It was thus that the first missionary of the Church of Scotland was, with his wife and fellows, literally thrown on the mud of India.

The Duffs were safe and Alexander's letters of introduction were secured to his person. The date was 27 May, 1830, having left Leith in Scotland on 19 September, 1829, more than eight months before. When the tidings reached the capital, a hundred miles up the Hooghly river, numerous small boats of the covered 'dinghy' class began to appear. In one of these, Mr and Mrs Duff arrived at the City of Palaces, Calcutta; drenched with mud, exhausted after their ordeal followed by twenty-four hours in the temple. Young Durand, too, found his way to the city, to the bishop's palace, where the tall lieutenant for some days excited amusement by appearing in the dress of his kind host.

The Duffs were hospitably entertained by Dr Brown, the junior Scottish chaplain. In due time the *Moira* was dragged off the Saugar shore, badly shattered, but the cargo and all baggage was saved.

The first to visit the Duffs on the evening on which they landed were his old St Andrews companion, the Rev J. Adam, and his afterwards life-long friend and greatly beloved brother, the Rev A. F. Lacroix, both of the London Missionary Society. Next day came the venerable Archdeacon Corrie, fruit of Simeon's work; also Dr Bryce, the senior chaplain; General Beatson, and other Christian strangers who desired to welcome Alexander and his wife to Bengal.

The couple lost no time in calling at Government House where Lady Bentinck received them not merely with courtesy but with genial Christian sympathy. The Governor-General himself did not need the letter of introduction to give the young missionary a warm reception. After a private dinner, His Excellency spoke encouragingly to Alexander and learned of the missionary's plans.

Alexander was little more than twenty-four years of age when, a tall handsome man, with flashing eyes, quivering voice, and restless gesticulation, he first told the ruler of India what he had given his life to do for its people. Heir of Knox and Chalmers, he had to begin in the heart of Hinduism what they had carried out in the mediaevalism of Rome and the moderatism of the Kirk of the eighteenth century. He had also to make it a missionary Kirk. His work would be twofold – in East and West.

Need we wonder that, when the Calcutta newspapers told the story of the repeated shipwrecks, the Indians themselves remarked: 'Surely this man is a favourite of the gods, who must have some notable work for him to do in India?'

At this stage in the biography it may be of advantage to

briefly examine the history of the British interest in India, up to the time of Alexander's arrival in 1830. The young missionary had already studied the history at length and it was with this knowledge that he had prepared his plan.

4

India and the East India Company

The founding of the great East India Company, which was to become the most powerful company the world had ever known, was a typical expression of its time.[1] Various forces had brought it into being. By decree from the Church of Rome, the world outside Europe had been divided between Spain and Portugal; but Europe was in a ferment of rising capitalism. Companies of merchants had been formed to develop trade. The Dutch had already rounded the Cape, making contact with the archipelago of South-East Asia. The whole area around the Indian Ocean had been considered the preserve of Portugal and this country was now a satellite of Spain. Perhaps most important of all, Philip II, King of both Spain and Portugal, the most powerful ruler in the world, had died in 1598, ten years after the Armada. Europeans were now free to go east in search of pepper and spices as well as the fabulous wealth and riches believed to be there. This possibility tempted the merchants of Lisbon, Amsterdam, Antwerp and London. At this period, the Dutch were allies of the English in a war against Spain.

Thus the East India Company was founded with Sir Thomas Smyth, the ex-ambassador to Russia as the first Governor. In signing the Charter, Queen Elizabeth assigned a monopoly to the Honourable East India Company that was valid for fifteen years. The merchants who comprised the East India Company, this being the very first 'Joint Stock Company', numbered approximately two hundred. They started with five new vessels, the largest of which was the six-hundred ton *Red Dragon*.

The activity in Europe which was to dominate India's fate was unknown in that vast country. At this time, the Emperor of India was Akbar, third in line of the so-called 'Mughals'. He was a foreigner, a Turk who spoke Persian (which he made the language of the court and administration) and was a Muslim,

[1] See Brian Gardner, *The East India Company* (London: Rupert Hart-Davis, 1971).

whereas Hinduism was mostly the religion of the ordinary people. He ruled over all Northern and Central India, from Afghanistan to Bombay and Bengal. The court of Akbar was one of wealth and grandeur, hiding a society of rich and poor, with the Emperor at the top and the untouchables at the bottom. The stakes for the English however, which were very high indeed, included gold, silver, ivory, opium, cotton, indigo, saltpetre and countless other items.

We rejoin events in 1742, when Robert Clive, one of eight clerks was chosen to join the Company's headquarters in Madras. He was born into an impoverished family of squires in Shropshire. Clive joined when he was eighteen years of age, as a writer in the service, but found the life very dull and joined the military branch of the Company. Clive distinguished himself as brilliant leader of men and a born General, as William Pitt was later to describe him. With his victories at Arcot and Plessey against the French, Clive had conquered an empire.

The Indian prince who was then restored to his throne could do no other than reward his patrons. The 'Company' received three million pounds and Clive claimed two hundred thousand pounds. When criticized about his 'self-seeking'; he replied that he was astonished at his own moderation. He became Governor of Bengal, living in luxury with many gifts bestowed on him. A Parliamentary Commission investigated his conduct and concluded that while while he had accepted many presents, he had rendered great and meritorious services to his country. He was cleared of the charges but, depressed by anxiety, he took his own life in 1774.

Clive had suggested to William Pitt that the British Government should take over the task of ruling Bengal and the first step towards this came with Lord North's Regulating Act of 1773. By this Act, the government assumed control over the 'Company' polices in matters of administration and defence.

Warren Hastings was now Governor-General. He was a brilliant administrator who established a tradition of justice and efficiency. He returned to England in 1785, but like Clive, he had offended important people and had made many jealous enemies. His political career was finished. The Prime Minister, Pitt the Younger, agreed to the impeachment of Hastings in 1788. He was acquitted in 1795, but his fortune was gone and his career ended.

From 1786 to 1793 the Governor-General was Lord Cornwallis, a man of conspicuous honesty and courage who did much to develop further just and efficient government.

There followed the fourth Mysore war in 1799, the battle of Poona in 1802, war with Holka in 1804, mutiny at Vellore in 1806, war with Nepal in 1814; and in 1819 the pacification of Central India. The year 1820 marked the accession of George IV to the throne of Great Britain. In 1828 Lord William Bentinck was appointed Governor-General of Bengal; with authority over the Governors of Madras and Bombay. Two years later the Duffs set foot on the soil of Bengal for the first time.

Bentinck was the son of a Whig prime minister and had previously been Governor of Madras, in which he had succeeded Clive's son. He had been recalled in disgrace after the mutiny at Vellore in 1806, but was rehabilitated a couple of years later. His new mission was to cut expenditure. There was peace during the eight years of his governorship, but he was aware of the potential dangers and wrote:

'One hundred millions of people in India are under the control of a government which has no hold whatever on their affections. British India may be assailed from the north by the Gurkhas; from the east by the Burmese; from the north by the Sikhs and Afghans and the hordes of Central Asia in co-operation or otherwise with Persia and Russia; from the sea on all sides of the territory. In the native army, which lacks physical strength and moral vigour, rests our internal danger, and this danger may involve our complete submission.

Bentinck believed that India should be governed for the Indians and he endeavoured to improve their lot. Having gained favour with the authorities at home by drastically cutting expenditure (including army pay) and turning the Indian deficit into a surplus, he turned to humanitarian reforms.

The education policy of the Company had been shelved for years, but Bentinck believed that general education was the panacea for the regeneration of India and that the English language was the key to all improvements. The Company began to set up schools and colleges to teach English, and there was much encouragement to westernise Indian society. In the first place, English had to replace Persian as the official language and become the medium of the administration and the law courts, and having now heard of Alexander Duff's plans, he knew he had such a man to direct his policies.

Attempts were now made to reduce slavery, sacrifices, child marriage and female infanticide. The widespread practice of suttee, or the burning of Hindu widows on the funeral pyres of their dead husbands, was made a crime of homicide. The secret society of Thugs was abolished. Between 1831 and 1837 some three thousand Thugs were convicted of murder and executed and eventually it was wiped out. Lord Bentinck's reforms were supported in London and, in 1833, the renewal of the Company's Charter strengthened this policy.

Such was the situation into which Duff stepped on arriving in Calcutta; the centre of the most densely packed and fastest-breeding rural population in the world, with a network of rivers and canals far greater than that of Holland. Here was the focus of the whole British political system in Asia. Bengal, with its swarming sixty million inhabitants, yielding twelve million pounds sterling to the mother country, four to six million coming from Calcutta alone. The noise, the heat and dust, the continual movements of thousands of people and the singularly unpleasant aroma, due to the absence of adequate drainage because of the low-lying countryside, immediately took one by surprise.

5

Beginning the Great Task

Since their arrival in Calcutta, the Duffs had lodged with Dr and Mrs Brown. Although happy in their temporary home, Alexander knew they would quickly have to find a home of their own. He was determined that they should live beside the people with whom he was going to work, but knew full well that this would present many problems. No European had ever resided within the Hindu community, nor would any Hindu be prepared to let a house to one who would pollute it by the consumption of beef and cast a spell over the neighbourhood. While Alexander made plans to tackle this first problem, Mrs Brown became acquainted with his wife, Anne, and informed her of the local customs and what was regarded as the correct behaviour of the Europeans to the Indian people.

She told Anne of the working of the caste system. She explained the social habits of the Europeans, particularly the British. She offered to introduce Anne to Taylor's Emporium, a large European-style store which had opened in 1826 and was now the established meeting place for the ladies of the town. Mrs Brown, like Anne, had arrived in India as a young wife and knew the difficulties which this young woman would face in an environment so completely different to that which she was used. What great love had given her the courage to undertake such an adventure?

Anne explained that, like her husband, besides being a devout Christian, she was equally interested in the missionary work of the Church and that, even before meeting Alexander, she had attended meetings of the missionary societies and searched for a way in which to give her life to this great cause. As if by some divine gift of providence, she met, and fell in love with Alexander. As she made her wedding vows she knew that it was her destiny. She knew she was destined to serve her God by sharing the life of his disciple. Mrs Brown was her constant companion while Alexander prepared his plan.

Alexander had received very little instruction from the Church of Scotland except that he should open a mission

near to, but not inside Calcutta, to spread the teaching of
Christ. No reason was given to him for this instruction, but
as this was absolutely opposed to his master plan, he resolved,
there and then, that he would ignore it. It was to prove the
resolve of genius.

Caste and idolatry were rife in India. It would be his plan,
he was to recall later, that, with the blessing of God, he would
devote his time and strength to the preparing of a mine, and
the setting of a train which should, one day, explode and tear
up the whole from its lowest depths. He had resolved that
whatever scheme of instruction he might adopt must involve
the necessity of reading some portion of the Bible daily by
every class that could read it, and of expounding it to such
as could not, with a view to enlightening the understanding,
spiritually impressing the heart and quickening the conscience,
while the teacher prayed, at the same time, that the truth might
be brought home, and some at least would be turned from their
idols to serve the living God.

While religion was thus to be in the forefront, his resolution
was, from the first, to teach every variety of useful knowledge,
first in elementary forms, and, as the pupils advanced, in the
higher branches, which might ultimately embrace the most
advanced and improved studies in history, civil and sacred,
sound literature, logic, mental and moral philosophy after the
Baconian method, mathematics in all departments, with natural
history, natural philosophy and other sciences.

In short, he planned to lay the foundation of a system of
education which might ultimately embrace all the branches
ordinarily taught in the higher schools and colleges of Christian
Europe, but in inseparable combination with the Christian
faith and its doctrines, precepts and evidences, with a view
to the practical regulation of life and conduct. Religion was
thus intended to be, not merely the foundation upon which
the superstructure of all useful knowledge was to be reared,
but the animating spirit which was to pervade and hallow all,
and thus conduce to the highest welfare of man in time and
for eternity, as well as to the glory of God. All truth, directed
by the two-edged sword of the very word of God, was that
which was to pierce to the vitals of Brahmanism, save the
Hindu people, and make them instruments of truth to the
rest of Asia, even more widely than their Buddhist fathers
had sought to be.

This was the missionary's plan and he had no illusions

about the difficulties which lay ahead. Until the arrival of Duff, the greatest vernacular preacher Bengal had seen was his friend Dr Lacroix, who later confessed that during his fifty years in Bengal he did not know if he had been the means of making one convert from Hinduism. Until the arrival of Alexander Duff, the official view seemed to be that, whatever of European literature and science might be conveyed to the native mind should be conveyed chiefly through native media, that is to say, the learned languages of India – for the Muslims, Arabic and Persian; and for the Hindus, Sanskrit. This was the predominant spirit and intent of the British Government and Alexander was absolutely convinced that such a policy was wrong.

With the exhaustless energy which marked his whole life, Duff spent the hottest and wettest period of the Bengal year, the six weeks from the end of May to the middle of July, in preliminary inquiries. From early morning till late in the evening he visited every missionary and missionary station around Calcutta, from the southern villages on the skirts of the malarious Sunderban forests to the older settlements of the Dutch at Chinsurah and the Danes at Serampore. There was not a school which he did not inspect; not one of these thatched bamboo and wicker-work chapels, in which men like Lacroix preached night and morning in Bengali to the passers-by in the crowded streets of the capital, in which he spent hours noting the people and the preaching alike. He began the study of the vernacular without which half his knowledge of and sympathy with the natives would be lost. He was especially careful to visit in detail representative rural villages, that he might satisfy himself and the committee at home. From such minute investigations, and more frequent conferences with the more experienced men already in the field, he arrived at two conclusions. These were, that Calcutta itself must be the scene of his earliest and principal efforts, from which he could best operate in the interior; and that the method of his operations must be different from that of all his predecessors in India.

With one exception the other missionaries discouraged these two conclusions. He had left to the last the aged William Carey, then within three years of the close of the brightest missionary careers up to that time, in order that he might lay his whole case before the man whose apostolic successor he was to be. Landing from the river at the college one sweltering July day, the Highlander strode up the flight of steps that led to what was at the time the finest modern building in Asia. Turning to the left, he sought Carey's study. There he saw what seemed to be a little yellow old man in a white jacket, who tottered up to the visitor of whom he had already heard, and with outstretched hands solemnly blessed him.

The result of the conversation was a double blessing, for Carey could speak with the influence both of a scholar who had created the best college at that time in the country, and of a vernacularist who had preached to the people for over half a century in their own language. The young Scotsman left his presence with the approval of the one authority whose opinion was best worth having. The meeting was the beginning of an era in the history of the Church in India which the poet and the painter might well symbolize.

Duff used his personal friendship with the Governor-General to further his cause and Lord Bentinck had suggested that he should meet the one Hindu who could give him the greatest help. He gave Alexander a letter of introduction to General Beatson, the Governor of Bengal. The general welcomed him and, as directed in the letter, agreed to drive him to visit the great Hindu scholar, the Raja Rammohan Roy.

In a pleasant garden house in the leafy suburbs of Calcutta, the Raja Rammohan Roy, then fifty-six years of age, was spending his declining days in earnest meditation on divine truth, broken only by works of practical benevolence among his countrymen, and soon by preparations for the visit to England, where he died in 1834. The missionary was immediately impressed by the Raja and instantly aware that this man would play a most significant role in his plan. He listened while the Raja gave some background of his life to date.

At the close of the administration of Warren Hastings, when the bleached bones of the victims of the great famine were beginning to disappear, in 1774, a Brahman landholder and his most orthodox wife had a son born to them on the ancestral estate in the county of Burdwan, some fifty miles from the English capital of Calcutta. Rammohan Roy's father had retired in disgust from the service of the tyrant, Sooraj-ood-Dowla; his predecessors had been holy ascetics or sacerdotal lords.

Their spirit, withdrawing from worldly wealth and distinction, came out in the young Rammohan, who, though trained in all the asceticism of his mother's breviary, the *Ahnika Tattina*, renounced idolatry at the age of sixteen, when he wrote but did not publish an attack on 'the idolatrous system of the Hindus'.

That is, he gave up his father's love, his mother's care and his rights of inheritance, and he braved the loss of caste and the persecution of his friends. To this he had been led by detailed knowledge of the Bengali and Sanskrit literature in his own home, followed by a course of Arabic and Persian at Patna, and by the study of Islam. From Patna, the young and truth-loving theist went to Benares, where he learned that the Brahmanism of his day was a corruption of what seemed to him the monotheism which underlay the nature-worship of the Vedas.

Captivated for a time by philosophic Buddhism, he visited Tibet, where its practical Lamaic form disgusted him. Recalled by his father, he tried to influence him before he died in 1803. In this he failed, but he was so able to convince his mother of the folly of her lifelong austerities that she confessed her disbelief in Hinduism before her death. He had, of course, no Divine Saviour to reveal to her. The widow, however, died in the service of the idol Jugganath at Puri, having declared before she set out on the hideous pilgrimage, 'Rammohan, you are right, but I am a weak woman, and am grown too old to give up rites which are a comfort to me.'

In a brief autobiography he wrote in England, Rammohan stated that he was about twenty when he began to associate with Europeans:

Finding them generally more intelligent, more steadfast and moderate in their conduct, I gave up my prejudice against them and became inclined in their favour, feeling persuaded that their rule, though a foreign yoke, would lead more speedily and surely to the amelioration of the native inhabitants.

He won the friendship and respect of the British. At fifty he retired to philosophic ease and spiritual meditation, and became the centre of the Calcutta reformers. But he was far ahead of his timid contemporaries who, while approving the better, followed the worst. The English language had introduced him to the English Bible, and the necessity of mastering that led him to the original Hebrew and Greek. His contemporaries denounced him as an atheist and his views roused such a feeling against him that he was deserted by every person except two or three Scottish friends, 'to whom and that nation to which they belong', he later wrote, he would 'always feel grateful'. Rammohan Roy believed that fate had prepared him to help this young Scotsman.

Having listened to Alexander's statement of his objects and plans, Rammohan expressed general approval and agreed with the young reformer that all true education ought to be religious, since the object was not merely to give information, but to develop and regulate all the powers of the mind and emotions.

Rammohan Roy, though not a Christian by profession, had read and studied the Bible, and declared that, as a book of religious and moral instruction it was unequalled. As a believer in God, he also felt that everything should begin by imploring His blessing. He therefore approved of the opening of the proposed school with prayer to God. He added that, having studied the Vedas, the Koran, and the Tripitakas of the Buddhists, he nowhere found any prayer so brief and all-comprehensive as that which the Christians call the Lord's Prayer. Till, therefore, Alexander had sufficiently mastered Bengali and his pupils English, he recommended him to study and daily use the Lord's Prayer in Bengali or English, according to circumstances.

Subsequently Alexander and Rammohan Roy had many earnest and solemn discussions on the subject. The later testimony of John Foster showed that this remarkable Hindu died believing in the divinity of the mission of Jesus Christ, including his miracles, but had not come to an assurance of the deity of his person.

Encouraged by the emphatic agreement of Rammohan Roy, Alexander said that the real difficulty now was, where, or how, to obtain premises within the native city in order to commence operations; for the natives, owing to caste prejudices, were absolutely averse to letting any of their houses to a European for European purposes. Then, if a suitable place could be obtained, how could youths of the respectable classes be induced to attend, since he was resolved to teach the Bible in every class, and he was told that this would constitute an insuperable objection. At that time, Hindus regarded the Bible with something like loathing and hatred; they also felt that to take the Bible into their hands, and read any portion of it, would operate on them like a magical spell, forcing them to become Christians.

Rammohan Roy at once offered a hall in the Chitpore Road, for which he had been paying to the five Brahman owners a monthly rental of five pounds. It was used by the Brumho Sobha and the few worshippers were about to move into a new building provided by Rammohan Roy. As to the pupils, his personal friends were sufficiently free from prejudice to send their sons at his request. Driving at once to the native city, the Hindu reformer secured the hall for the Scottish Christian missionary at four pounds a month. Until now, the Duffs had been staying with Dr and Mrs Brown and were looking for a suitable place of their own to live. Within the hall were rooms which they could use as a house and Alexander thereby achieved the first essential part of his plan; to live and work in the native part of Calcutta. While Alexander was carrying out his reconnaissance, his friend and host, Dr Brown, was thrown from his horse and died. They did not wish to impose on his widow any longer than necessary.

Alexander made it perfectly clear to Hindu Calcutta exactly the kind of education which he intended to give. It would be a general but Christian education and he stressed that he wished no misunderstanding about the matter. After a few days, five bright-eyed youths of the higher class, mostly Brahmanical, called upon Duff. They had a note of introduction from Rammohan Roy stating that these five, with the full consent of their friends, were ready to attend him whenever he might open the school. One of these, a Koolin named Khettur Mohun Chatterjee, turned out a first-rate scholar, entered the government service, and attained to one of the highest offices which an Indian could then hold.

Having met in the hall with the five on a day appointed, by the aid of an interpreter Alexander explained to them, in a general way, his intentions and plans. They seemed highly delighted, and went away resolved to explain the matter to their friends. In a day or two several new youths appeared along with them, requesting admission. On every successive morning there was a fresh succession of applicants, till classification and weeding-out became necessary. When that had been done, a day was fixed for the public opening of the school, at ten a.m. Rammohan Roy was present to explain difficulties, and especially to remove the prejudice against reading the Bible. The eventful day was 13 July, 1830.

Having been, meanwhile, busy with Bengali, having obtained from the Bible Society's depository copies of the four Gospels in Bengali and English, and having borrowed some English primers from a Eurasian teacher, he was ready. Standing up with Rammohan Roy, while all the lads showed the same respect as their Raja, the Christian missionary prayed the Lord's Prayer slowly in Bengali. It was an unforgettable sight. Then came the more critical act. Putting a copy of the Gospels into their hands, the missionary requested some of the older pupils to read. There was a murmuring among the Brahmans among them. Their leader protested: 'This is the Christian Shaster. We are not Christians; how can we read it? It may make us Christians, and our friends will drive us out of caste.' This was the cue for the Raja, who explained to his young countrymen that they were mistaken:

> Christians, like Dr Horace Hayman Wilson, have studied the Hindoo Shasters, and you know that he has not become a Hindoo. I myself have read all the Koran again and again, and has that made me a Mussulman? Nay, I have studied the whole Bible, and you know that I am not a Christian. Why, then, do you fear to read it? Read and judge for yourself. Not compulsion, but enlightened persuasion which you may resist if you choose, constitutes you yourselves judges of the contents of the book.

Most of the objectors seemed satisfied.

The Hindu reformer visited the school at ten for the Bible lesson daily for the next month and frequently thereafter till he left for England, when his eldest son continued to encourage the boys by his presence and their teacher by his kindly counsel. During this period the other Christian missionaries in the area kept aloof when they realised what Duff was doing. The weapon of the English language seemed to them as unbiblical as his alliance with the author of *The Precepts of Jesus* was unholy. They were not convinced by his arguments or explanation that while the English language would thus be used as the channel of conveying all higher and improved knowledge, he was determined that the vernacular should be thoroughly taught to the pupils at the same time, as a channel of distribution for the masses.

The other missionaries constantly harped on the fact that many of the low caste natives in Calcutta sought a smattering of English only to carry on dealings with the sailors, whom they lured to low taverns, there to revel in all manner of wickedness, contriving at the same time to rob them of what money they possessed, and often stripping them of their clothes, and throwing them into the street. English also seemed to lead the children of the better class natives into the wildest infidelity.

With regard to the natives who wished to learn English for such purposes, Duff's reply was that, even on the low ground of the principles of political economy, he would soon by the multiplication of these overstock the market, and make it necessary for those who wished to obtain better positions to remain longer at school, so as to gain a higher degree of knowledge, which might not only enlarge the intellect but regulate morals and manners. With regard to the children of the higher classes, his trust was that the thorough inculcation of God's word, with prayer, would have the effect of preventing them from becoming utter unbelievers or atheists, and in all respects make them better men and members of society, even if they did not outwardly and formally embrace the Christian faith.

The school thus fairly started, let us look at its founder at work. The student who had passed out of St Andrews University its top scholar, its most brilliant essayist, its most eloquent debater; the preacher whose fervent utterances had thrilled the coldest assemblies by addresses which promised a rival to Chalmers himself, and were afterwards hardly excelled by Edward Irving's; the man who had been the stay and counsellor of all on board the two wrecked vessels, is doing – what? With no assistants, apart from an untrained Eurasian lad, and despised by his brother missionaries, he is spending six hours a day in teaching some three hundred Bengali youths the English alphabet, and many an hour at night, with the assistance of his wife, in preparing a series of graduated schoolbooks, named 'Instructors', which were to hold their place in every Christian English school in Bengal for a third of a century. Those who thought such work degrading for a minister later admired and imitated him.

Duff's schoolbooks were constructed on a system. The first contained lessons on interesting common subjects, in which the pupils might be drilled not only in reading but in grammatical and other exercises. The second consisted of religious lessons, taken from the most part from the Bible itself; especially the historical portions, and put into forms suitable for young people. These were carefully read, expounded and enforced on the understanding, heart and conscience, as purely religious exercises.

As to the English alphabet, which most of the pupils had to begin for the first time, he devised a plan for teaching a large number simultaneously. He obtained a board supported by an upright frame, and along the board, a series of parallel grooves. He then got the letters of the English alphabet painted on separate slips of wood. Around this upright teaching frame a large class was arranged in a semi-circle. The first letter with which he uniformly began was the letter 'O' because of the simplicity of its form and sound, and because the sound and the name are the same, as in the case in Sanskrit and Sanskrit-derived vernaculars.

When this letter was thoroughly mastered, which was soon done, the next letter which he usually put into one of the grooves was 'X'. He would then put the two letters together, and pronouncing them would say, 'O, X, Ox'. He would then tell the pupils that this was the name in English for an animal with which they were all acquainted, and would give them the corresponding word in Bengali. This always delighted them, as they said they not only knew two letters of the English alphabet, but had already got hold of an English word. After school they would gleefully shout it.

Alexander was not merely satisfied with giving the Bengali or the English word. He began to question the boys as to the properties and the uses of the objects, or different parts of the objects, which the word represented. This exercise always delighted them, for it was fitted to draw out what information they already possessed, and to stimulate the powers of observation. In this way the intellect was awakened, and the boys delighted in thinking that they had acquired something of a new power or faculty. In a word, they had become thinking beings. The same process of detailed questioning was carried out in all the classes. The boys, in their exuberance of delight, would be constantly speaking of it to their friends at home, to the pupils of other schools, and to acquaintances whom they might meet in the street. In this way, as well as for other reasons, the school soon acquired an extensive popularity among the native community, and the pressure for admission increased far beyond what the little hall could accommodate. The new method of teaching was much preferred to the old mechanical and monotonous system, and was soon imitated in many schools in Calcutta and Bengal.

Increased accommodation was secured, and the next step was taken. The decree went forth that none would be allowed to begin English who could not read with ease their own vernacular. A purely Bengali department was then created, in a bamboo shed with tiled roof, erected in the back court. Under pundits carefully supervised by the missionaries, that formed an essential and permanent part of the organization. But, for the first time in Bengal, the English-learning classes also were required to attend it for an hour daily. This contemporaneous study was judged to have had two results of vast national importance: it tended to the enriching of the vernacular language with words, and the then barren literature with pure and often spiritual ideas.

This system developed into the study of Sanskrit which, in time, the university was enabled to insist on in even its undergraduate examinations, with the happiest effects on both the language and the literature. Thus, too, Alexander carried on his own Bengali studies, the rivalry between teacher and taught, and the marvellous aptitude of the taught, adding to his one over-mastering motive an intellectual stimulus. That could not be drudgery which was thus conducted, and was in reality the laying of the foundations of the Church of India broad and deep in the very mind and conscience of each new generation.

Thus the first twelve months passed. The school became famous in the native city; the missionary had come to be loved with that mixture of affection and awe which his lofty enthusiasm and scorn of inefficiency ever excited in the Oriental; and the opposition of his own still ignorant colleagues continued. Duff now resolved that he must have a house of his own so that he could live and work in the native city. Until now they had been guests of Dr and Mrs Brown followed by living in the rooms of the college. His wife, Anne, had had no home of her own since her marriage and had stressed the importance of such a step to her husband. It was not considered wise that Anne should do so, but Alexander wished to be in contact with the natives in the street and in his own house. Many weeks passed in fruitless endeavours to find a suitable house, when a two-storeyed tenement, uninhabited for twelve years because of the belief that it was haunted, was, with much entreaty, obtained in College Square. The locality, fronting the Hindu and Sanskrit Colleges, was so central, that it was long afterwards secured for the Cathedral Mission College, and the Medical College and the university were built on the third side of the square.

Up to this time Alexander had lived to the south, on the same line of road, in Wellesley Square, fronting the Muhammadan

College and close to the site of the future Free Church building. He thus fairly planted himself in the citadel of the enemy, and he was driven from it to another quarter only by the unhealthiness of the house. He subsequently built his first college and his own house – succeeded, after 1843, by another close by – in Cornwallis Square, to the north.

Despairing of inducing the European community to follow him, in order to test the results of his first year's labour he announced the examination of his pupils in the Freemasons' Hall. To remove any prejudice that his work was low and fanatical, he secured Archdeacon Corrie as president on this occasion. It was an experiment, but he felt confident that the pupils would so acquit themselves as to recommend the school and its system. In this he was not disappointed.

The reading of the boys, their acquaintance with the elements of English grammar, geography and arithmetic; the manner in which they explained their words and sentences, and illustrated their meaning by opposite examples; the promptness and accuracy with which they answered the questions put to them – all took the auditors by surprise and filled them with admiration, knowing that the school had only been one year in operation. What astonished them most of all in those early days was the ease and freedom with which the Hindus read portions of the Bible.

They answered all questions with readiness and accuracy, not merely on historical parts but on the doctrines and principles of Christian faith and morals, to which their attention had been directed in the daily lessons. Altogether the effect produced by that examination was very striking. By those present it was pronounced marvellous. The three daily English newspapers of Calcutta had their reporters present, who gave such accounts of the examination and the new methods of instruction pursued in the school, that European Calcutta talked of nothing else.

The opinions of the English residents, official and independent, reacted on the leaders of the native community, till in the second year hundreds had to be refused admittance to the school from lack of accommodation, and the number of European visitors interfered so seriously with the regular discipline of the classes that Saturday was set apart for such inspection. The elder pupils now agreed to act as monitors and native assistants pressed their services upon the missionary.

The elementary teaching now fell to the elder pupils and

the native assistants, carefully selected by Alexander, while he spent part of his time with the English classes as they passed on to studies in sacred and secular truth. There was another immediate result. Dr Inglis and the Edinburgh Missionary Committee asked Duff to open a similar school at the purely Bengali town of Takee, forty miles off.

Takee was the ancestral seat of Kaleenath Roy Chowdery, one of the principal followers of Rammohan Roy. He and his brothers offered all the buildings and equipment for an English, Bengali and Persian school, to be supervised by Mr Duff, and taught by men of his own selection and on his own Christian system, whom in the Bengali and Persian departments, the brothers would pay. The success of the school and the example of the Chowdery family led not a few of their wealthy co-religionists in Calcutta to open new schools or to improve the old establishments.

Dr Inglis and the Church of Scotland, sorely tried by the disasters which befell their first missionary, and even before they could learn of his safe arrival at Calcutta, determined to pursue their original plan of sending out two colleagues to assist the person they had appointed, 'the headmaster of a seminary of education with branch schools'. One was most happily found in a tall, slightly stooped and pale youth from Thurso, who had first studied at Aberdeen University.

He completed his course at St Andrews a year after Alexander, but in time to know well the man whom he ever afterwards worked along with in loving harmony. The Rev W. S. Mackay, who joined the infant mission in the autumn of 1831, was so accomplished and elegant a scholar that it is difficult to say whether he became more remarkable as a learned theologian, as a master of English literature and style, or as an astronomer. A lofty and intense spirituality marked all his work, and only a robust physique was lacking in him. But even his assistance was not enough, as the school developed into a college, and branch schools like Takee demanded organisation and supervision, while other duties than that of daily teaching denied the missionary a moment's leisure. Competent lay teaching of secular subjects was required, and for this the acute but imitative Bengali intellect had not yet been sufficiently trained.

Alexander found his first English assistant in the following way. Among the passengers of the *Moira* was a Mr Clift, the son of an English squire. He was going out to one of the great mercantile houses in Calcutta. Being of a combative disposition he was placed next to the missionary by the captain. Duff discovered that he was highly educated and well read, especially in the then little studied science of political economy. On the failure of the company in which the youth became an assistant, he sought Alexander's advice. Duff at once offered him the position of assistant master at a salary of sixty pounds a year; the highest salary he was empowered to give, but invited him to his house as a guest.

Mr Clift did his work in the higher classes well. In the house his conduct was upright and at least respectful in reference to religion, on which, however, he maintained a studied silence. He was sent to the Takee branch school as its first master. After a time he returned, stricken with jungle fever, to be cared for by Mrs Duff. In the delirium of the disease he was heard repeating Cowper's hymn, 'There is a fountain filled with blood'. As he recovered he confessed that he had been trained by pious parents.

He had led a careless life. He became a changed man when he returned to Takee, from which the government took him subsequently to make him principal of an English college. The incident powerfully confirmed Duff in his conviction of what was then little recognised in educational systems, the importance of saturating the young mind with divine truth. The effect of his teaching on his students we shall now see.

6
Progress

The effect of the first year's teaching, biblical, scientific and literary, through English and through Bengali, on even the young Hindus was to lead them into licence before they could reach true self-regulating liberty; for the Bengali boy just before or at the age of puberty is the most earnest, acute and lovable of all students. The older lads, impetuous with youthful ardour and fearless of consequencies, carried the new light which had arisen on their own minds to the bosom of their families, proclaimed its excellencies on the house-tops, and extolled its praises in the street-assemblies. With their zeal they did not always observe circumspection in their demeanour and style of address, or manifest due consideration for the feelings of those who still sat in darkness. Even for the infallible Gurus and other holy Brahmans, before whom they were accustomed to bow in prostrate submission, their reverence was greatly diminished. They would not conceal their gradual change of opinion on many vital points. At length, their undaunted bearing and freedom of speech began to create a general ferment among the staunch adherents of the old faith. The cry of 'Hinduism in danger' was fairly raised.

The result was seen one morning, when only half a dozen of the three hundred youths appeared in the classroom. To the puzzled missionary the only reply was a copy of that morning's *Chundrika*. This Bengali paper had been established to fight for the sacred right of burning living widows with their dead husbands. Now, as the organ of the orthodox Dharma Sobha, of which its editor was secretary, it had become the champion of the whole Brahmanical system against evangelical Christianity of a very different type from the secularism of the Hindu College with which it had of late been allied.

The decree went forth that all who attended the General Assembly's Institution were to be excluded from caste. It was urged that a yellow flag or other symbol should be planted in front of the building to warn the unwary against the moral and religious pestilence. The Hindu society of the capital had, however, become too rationalistic in its mode of viewing the national faith, and too selfish in its desire to obtain the best education which would lead to official and mercantile appointments. The panic did not last a week. The Holy Assembly had no greater power than public opinion chose to give it.

The college thus securely established in native society, triumphing over the ignorance of his own countryman and already famous throughout India, Alexander proceeded to use at the same time the two other more immediately powerful weapons of lectures and the press. Having by his first year's work of teaching and personal influence reached a position far in excess of the Assembly's dreams, he now took three men of similar outlook into his counsels. Dr Dealtry, who succeeded Corrie first as Archdeacon of Calcutta and then as Bishop of Madras, was at that time chaplain of the Old Church, and was worthy of such predecessors as Martyn and Claudius Buchanan. John Adam had been his fellow-student at St Andrews, and was then of the London Missionary Society. Mr James Hill, also a Congregationalist, was the popular and able pastor of Union Chapel. All were eager observers of native progress, and agreed to co-operate in delivering the first course of lectures to educated Bengalis. The subject was Natural and Revealed Religion. Alexander fitted up a lecture room in his own house, which, being still in College Square, was most central for the invited class.

It was a sultry night in the first week of August when twenty of the foremost students of his own and of the Hindu College took their places in expectation. Next morning the news flew like wildfire over Calcutta. Students of the Hindu College had actually attended, in the house of the missionary, a lecture on Christianity. Soon the whole city was in uproar. The college that day was almost deserted. Continuing to rage for days, the orthodox leaders accused the government itself of breach of faith. Had the government not promised to abstain from interference with their religion, and now, insidiously, it had brought out a wild missionary, and planted him just opposite the college, like a battery, to break down the bulwarks of the Hindu faith and put Christianity in its place! In all haste, a Dr Wilson, Mr Hare, Captain Price and some native managers put up a notice threatening with expulsion students who should attend 'political and religious' discussions. That was their degree of their love of truth. The students themselves remonstrated. Alexander, therefore, thought it right to seek a private interview with the Governor-General.

Lord William Bentinck listened with the utmost attention and patience. At the close of the statement he said in substance that assuming the accuracy of the facts which he could not possibly doubt, he felt that Mr Duff had done nothing to contravene the law, nothing that ought to disturb the public peace. At the same time, he added, from his knowledge of the Hindu character, that it would be well to allow the present tumult quietly to subside. After a time it might be in Mr Duff's power more successfully to renew the attempt. So far as he himself was concerned, he could not, as Governor-General, in any way mix himself up with missionary affairs, or even officially express sympathy or approval. This was because as the charter to the East India Company specifically ordered that the British should not interfere with the religion of the natives, a principle reaffirmed by Queen Victoria when she became Empress of India.

He declared that privately, as an individual Christian man, he felt deep sympathy with the avowed object of the missionaries. He approved of the operations of all who carried them on in the genuine spirit of the Gospel. He who had been Governor of Madras during the Vellore mutiny, repeated the advice patiently to wait for a seasonable opportunity to recommence what, if Mr Duff went about it calmly yet firmly, he himself would advance by his private sympathy and support. This for the moment answered the purpose; fear and alarm were abated.

Being thus for a time freed from the task of preparing lectures in addition to his heavy school work, Alexander energetically set about mastering the Bengali language with the help of a learned Brahman pundit. By the end of one year he was able to speak it with fluency. He wrote out for the sake of accuracy and committed to memory his first sermon in Bengali. Denied lectures during the cooling-off period, the young men met in debating societies of their own. These, often nightly and in various quarters of the city, Alexander asked permission to attend, and soon an address by him was welcomed as an attractive part of the proceedings.

It was there that he first formulated his far-seeing policy on the subject of female education, which the government continued to ignore, though aiding the tentative efforts of the missionaries. At that time Miss Cooke, who became the wife of the church missionary, Mr Wilson, had been teaching the first female school in Bengal for eight years. She had been led to form it by a visit paid to one of the boys' schools of the Calcutta School Society, in order to observe their pronunciation of the vernacular, which she was learning. Seeing the pundit drive away a wistful-eyed little girl from the door, she was told that the child had troubled him for the past three months with entreaties to be allowed to read with the boys. Next day, on 28 January, 1822, she opened her first school. She started with seven girls, and in a year, with the help of the Countess of Hastings, the Governor-General's wife, she had two hundred girls in two schools.

At that early period and long after, the few hundred girls under the only partial and brief instruction allowed them before very early marriage, formed only isolated units, and were of a social class similar to that reached by street and village preachers. Many were bribed with money to attend. The middle and higher classes, whose sons Alexander had attracted to his own school, were shocked at the idea of educating their wives and daughters; and even if they had consented, as many eventually did, would not let them out of the home-prison of the zanana.

But the youths of the debating societies thought differently, and Alexander encouraged them. One evening he found the subject of debate by some fifty Hindu College students to be, 'whether females ought to be educated'. On the theory of the thing they ended in being unanimous; one married youth exclaiming, 'Is it alleged that female education is prohibited, if not by the letter, at least by the spirit of some of our Shasters? If any of the Shasters be found to advance what is so contrary to reason, I, for one, will trample them under my feet.' The brave words won rapturous applause for the speaker and led Alexander to conclude that later on, as these youths became fathers and grandfathers, female education would spread of itself, if the Christian Church supplied the necessary vernacular and English lady teachers.

Alexander now felt that his Christian educational revolution was well under way and that the fuse he had lit could not be extinguished. An education that had started, long after continued to fill the memories of the students with the best – sometimes the worst – passages of the British poets which had made quotation the mark of culture and elegance in the young debater. Sir Walter Scott, Byron and

Robert Burns were their favourites. As Alexander wrote of that tune:

More than once were my ears greeted with the sound of Scottish rhymes from the poems of Robert Burns. It would not be possible to portray the effect produced on the mind of a Scotsman, when, on the banks of the Ganges, one of the sons of Brahma – in reviewing the unnatural institution of caste in alienating man from man, and in looking forward to the period in which knowledge, by its transforming power, would make the lowest type of man feel itself to be of the same species as the highest – suddenly gave utterance, in an apparent ecstasy of delight, to these characteristic lines:–

'For a' that, and a' that,
Its comin' yet, for a' that,
That man to man, the world o'er,
Shall brothers be, for a' that.'

How was the prayerful aspiration raised, that such a consummation might be realized in a higher or nobler sense than the poet or his Hindoo admirer was privileged to conceive!

The liberals established their own English journal, well naming it the *Enquirer*. Long before, Raja Rammohan Roy had set the English *Reformer* on foot; but it had committed itself to reproducing antichristian attacks after its founder had left for England, and it was assisted in this by Englishmen who called themselves Christians. The English of the *Enquirer* and the Bengali of the *Gyananeshun*, week after week attacked Hinduism and its leaders. The campaign was carried out with courage and skill that called down on the editors the execrations of their countrymen. But all besides was negative. The Reform Bill was eagerly turned to in July, 1831, for a positive something to rejoice in as the germ of a new reformation which would sweep away tyrants and priests.

After another series of lectures and discussions on Tuesday evenings in the cold season of 1831–1832, Mohesh Chunder Ghose, a student of the Hindu College, sent his own brother to Mr Duff, with this note:

If you can make a Christian of *him* you will have a valuable one; and you may rest assured that you have my hearty consent to it. Convince him, and make him a Christian, and I will give no secret opposition. Scepticism has made me too miserable to wish my dear brother the same. A doubtfulness of the existence of another world, and of the benevolence of God, made me too unhappy and spread a gloom all over my mind; but I thank God that I have no doubts at present. I am travelling from step to step; and Christianity, I think, will be the last place where I shall rest; for every time I think, its evidence becomes too overpowering.

On 28 August, 1832, the *Enquirer* announced the baptism into Christ of Mohesh himself, in an article which concluded:

'Well may Mr Duff be happy, upon the reflection that his labours have, through the grace of the Almighty, been instrumental in convincing some of the truth of Christianity, and others of an inquiry into it. We hope ere long to be able to witness more and more such happy results in this country.

This was Alexander's first convert.

The man who proved a more than worthy successor of Rammohan Roy and sounded those trumpet notes in the *Enquirer*, became in due course a scholar and minister of the Church of England, the Rev. Krishna Mohun Banerjea, LL.D. Then he was a Brahman of the highest or Koolin class, certaint to become in Hinduism, a Pharisee of the Pharisees.

This young man was to be the second of Alexander's converts. Krishna Mohun desired that the lecture room in the missionary's house, which had been the scene of all his previous opposition to the true religion, should also be the scene of his public confession to it. He sought that there his Hindu friends, who had been strengthened in their unbelief by his arguments, might witness his public recantation of all error and public embracing of the truth, the whole truth, as revealed in the Bible. The Rev Mr Mackay conducted the service which took place on 17 October, 1832.

In the same lectureroom, on 14 December, Alexander had his third convert. Gopeenath Nundi had sought a morning interview with Mr Duff in his study, and there burst into tears with the cry, 'Can I be saved?' He told how the last of the lectures had finally driven him to take counsel with Krishna Mohun Banerjea who prayed with him and sent him next morning to the missionary. At first imprisoned by his family, they cast him off for ever by advertisement in the newspaper.

This did not shake his faith. Still, before the irrevocable step was taken, his brothers and caste-fellows implored him to desist, then foully abused him, and then offered him all the wealth and pleasure could give, including even the retaining of a belief in Christianity if only he would not publicly profess it. The last appeal was in the name of his venerable mother, whose piercing shriek none who have seen a Bengali woman in sorrow could forget. Nature could not remain unmoved. Gopeenath wept, but throwing up his arms and turning hastily away he decided, 'No I cannot stay.' He was to demonstrate his courage again, amid the captivity and the bloodshed of the Mutiny of 1857. He proved faithful unto death.

Alexander's fourth convert was Anundo Chund Mozoomdar, the youth who in the school had been drawn by the divine power of the Sermon on the Mount. Anundo was baptised in St Andrew's kirk by the junior chaplain Dr Charles, on Sunday, 21 April, 1833, before the Scottish congregation and many awe-stricken spectators.

The work went on, while the school was every year developing into the famous college which it became with the aid of a colleague so able as Mr Mackay and of the two Eurasian assistants, the faithful and earnest Messrs Sunder and Pereira. The administrative and statesmanlike genius of Alexander, had, after its first examination seized the advantage of making it a still more catholic, central and efficient institute, by uniting in its support and management all the Christian denomenations then represented in Calcutta. In his official biographer's opinion, rarely if ever in the history of any portion of the Church at any time since apostolic work ceased with John the Divine, had one man been enabled to effect such a revolution in opinion and to sow the seeds of such a reformation in faith and life, as was effected by the first missionary of the Scottish Church in Bengal in the three years ending in July, 1833.

The missionary had, so far, done his work. It was now the turn of the Governor-General in Council to fulfil his role. For what the Greek tongue and Roman order had been to the spread of early Christianity, English language, legislation, administration, commerce and civilization were to be for the spread of the gospel in India.

7

The Indian Renaissance

The second son of the third Duke of Portland, Lord William Cavendish Bentinck, was thrust out into positions where he developed for the good of humanity all those virtues and that ability which had made Hans William, the founder of the house, second only to his friend William III as a benefactor of Great Britain. It was one of the many merits of George Canning that, during his too brief term as Prime Minister, he sent Lord William Bentinck to govern all India.

It was well that to the work of Alexander Duff and the legislative and administrative measures of Lord Bentinck, applying the principles and results of that work to all India and for all time, there were added the indispensable co-operation and the supreme sanction of the British people through Parliament. For the first fruit of the Reform Act of 1832 was the East India Company's charter of 1833. That charter withdrew the last obstructions to the work of Alexander Duff and of every settler in India, missionary or journalist, merchant or planter, teacher or captain of labour in any form. It converted the Company into a purely governing body, under a despotic but most benevolent constitution so well fitted for the freedom and the elevation of long-oppressed races that the most democratic of English thinkers, John Stuart Mill, declared the system to be the best ever devised.

The new charter added a law member to the Governor-General's council or cabinet, then of five, and created a commission to prepare codes of law and procedure. To mention no others, these four men, Lord Macaulay, Sir Barnes Peacock, Sir Henry S. Maine and Sir James F. Stephen, were said to have done together more for the varied races and the corrupting civilizations of the peoples of India than the jurists of Theodosius and Justinian effected for Europe, or the Code Napoleon for France. It was the eloquence of the young Macaulay in carrying the Reform Act which resulted in his appointment as one of the commissioners. The Law Member of Council took up his abode in the best of the Chowringhee palaces, the Bengal Club, under a salute of fifteen guns. Lord Macaulay's greatest work, greater than even his penal code and his Warren Hastings and Clive essays, was to be the legislative completion of the young Scottish missionary's policy.

Yet another brilliant man was appointed to the government in India; Charles Trevelyan. On arrival in Calcutta he was twenty-eight years of age. He was educated at Charterhouse, and then went to Haileybury. He was said by Macaulay to have distinguished himself beyond any man of his standing, by his great talent for business; by his liberal and enlarged views of policy; and by his literary merit, which, for his opportunities, was considerable.

Charles Trevelyan threw himself into the different movements begun by Alexander. The two young men found themselves absorbed in one question above all others, the advantage, the positive necessity of using the English language as the medium of all Christianising and civilising, all educational and administrative efforts by its rulers to reach the natural aristocracy and leaders of the people, and through them to feed the vernaculars and raise the masses. Alexander's plans, his experience, his success, were not only accomplished facts but had resulted in imitation by every thoughtful and benevolent Englishmen in the Far East. Trevelyan became the principal link between the missionary's far-seeing practical principles on the one hand and the coming action of government in the same direction. Alexander was thus able to concentrate more on his own specific plans of education, having the political aspects being greatly helped by the Council with their new powers.

In his decree of 7 March, 1835, Lord William Bentinck declared:

> 1st. His Lordship in Council is of opinion that the great object of the British Government ought to be the promotion of European literature and science among the natives of India, and that all the funds appropriated for the purposes of education would be best employed on English education alone.
>
> 2nd. But it is not the intention of his Lordship in Council to abolish any college or school of native learning, while the native population shall appear to be inclined to avail themselves of the advantages which it affords; and his Lordship in Council directs that all the existing professors

and students at all the institutions under the superin-
tendence of the committee shall continue to receive their
stipends. But his Lordship in Council decidedly objects
to the practice which has hitherto prevailed of supporting
the students during the period of their education. He con-
ceives that the only effects of such a system can be to give
artificial encouragement to branches of learning which,
in the natural course of things, would be superseded by
more useful studies; and he directs that no stipend shall
be given to any student that may hereafter enter at any
of these institutions, and that when any professor of
oriental learning shall vacate his situation the committee
shall report to the Government the number and the state
of the class, in order that the Government may be able to
decide upon the expediency of appointing a successor.

3rd. It has come to the knowledge of the Governor-
General in Council, that a large sum has been expended
by the committee on the printing of oriental works; his
Lordship in Council directs that no portion of the funds
shall hereafter be so employed.

4th. His Lordship in Council directs that all the funds
which these reforms will leave at the disposal of the
committee be henceforth employed in imparting to the
native population a knowledge of English literature and
science through the medium of the English language;
and his Lordship in Council requests the committee to
submit to Government, with all expedition, a plan for the
accomplishment of this purpose.

Alexander's own attitude to and criticism of the last act of
Lord William Bentinck will be found in the most important of
his many pamphlets, his 'New Era of the English Language
and English Literature in India'. With the culture that had
marked his whole school and university studies, he recognised the attractions of a genuine oriental scholarship, and
reproached his countrymen for their indifference to it, for
'persevering in a truly barbarous ignorance of one of the
most remarkable nations and countries on the face of the
globe'.

He went on to distinguish the Calcutta orientalists' abuse
of public money from the pursuit of enlightened scholarship.
He then compared the government's policy to the benefits that
flowed from the Romans' use of Latin, the Arabs' of arabic, and

Emperor Akbar's of Persian. Bentinck was to be honoured for being the person:

> . . . who first resolved to supersede the Persian, in the political department of the public service, by the substitution of the English, and laid the foundation for the same in every department, financial and judicial, as well as political. And having thus by one act created a necessity, and consequently an increased and yearly increasing demand for English, he next consummated the great design by super-adding the enactment under review, which provides the requisite means for supplying the demand that had been previously created. And this united act now bids fair to out-rival in importance the edicts of the Roman, the Arabic and Mogul emperors, inasmuch as the English language is infinitely more fraught with the seeds of truth in every province of literature, science and religion than the languages of Italy, Arabia or Persia ever were. Hence it is that I venture to hazard the opinion, that Lord W. Bentinck's double act for the encouragement and diffusion of the English language and English literature in the East will, long after contemporaneous party interests and individual jealousies and ephemeral rivalries have sunk into oblivion, be hailed by a grateful and benefited posterity as the greatest master-stroke of sound policy that has yet characterized the administration of the British Goverment in India.

At the time of the 1835 decree, in that year alone, the number of Government English Schools in Bengal and Northern India had doubled, rising to twenty-seven.

It is difficult to say whether Alexander Duff showed genius in instinctively seizing the position in 1830, in working out the parallel down to 1835, or in influencing the Indian Government and the British public by his heaven-born enthusiasm and fiery eloquence. It was probably both.

Alexander now turned his attention to the teaching of medicine along the lines of those well established in Europe. We must take a brief look at the position in India at that time.

Moved by the purely utilitarian consideration of providing Indian doctors or dressers for the army hospitals, government established the native Medical Institution in Calcutta in 1822, under an English doctor and native assistants. Hindustani, the *lingua franca* of all India, was the language of instruction, and the scientific nomenclature of the West was rendered into Arabic. Four years after, medical classes were opened at the Sanskrit College to read Charaka and Susruta, and at the Madrissa to study Avicenna and the other Arabic writers. Thus, it was judged by their opponents, the orientalists dreamed they could give the people of India the blessing of the healing art as developed in the West, just as they persisted in spending that people's money on the printing of books which their scholars scorned, and in the payment of youths to learn what was despised because of its methods and what was harmful because of its falsity. Dr Tytler, the head of the new institution, was one of the most fanatic of the orientalists. His translations, afterwards condemned by his own medical brethren, proved to be among the most costly of the wasteful publications. The only anatomical instruction which he dared or desired to give, was from sundry artificial preparations or models, from the lower animals, and occasional post-mortem examinations of persons dying in the hospital.

For a Hindu of caste to touch a dead body, even that of his father, was pollution to be atoned for by days of purification and much alms-giving. To break through that iron prejudice Dr Tytler and the orientalists declared to be impossible, and they did not try, even though ayurvedic literature allowed for a primitive form of dissection.

Duff was roused, by his own principles and his daily experience in the school, to protest against Dr Tytler's folly. He declared:

> Only use English as the medium, and you will break the backbone of caste, you will open up the way for teaching anatomy and all other branches fearlessly, for the enlightened native mind will take its own course in spite of all the threats of the Brahmanical traditionists.

Alexander made his views well known on the subject and the controversy finally brought matters to a head.

In 1833 Lord William Bentinck, not less attracted by the controversy than compelled by the deplorable state of medical education, appointed a committee to report on the whole subject. They took evidence and deliberated for a year. Duff's contribution to their findings is clear from the report:

> We beg now to call your Lordship's attention to the

opinions of the Rev Dr Duff. To the question whether, in order to teach the principles of any science to native boys, he considered it necessary that they should know Sanscrit, Arabic, and Persian, the reverend gentleman replies that, 'In reference to the acquisition of European science, the study of the languages mentioned would be a sheer waste of labour and time; since, viewed as a media for receiving and treasuring the stores of modern science, there is no possible connection between them.' . . . He further records his opinion, that the study of the English language might be rendered very popular among the natives. 'The sole reason,' he justly observes, 'why the English is not even more a general and anxious object of acquisition among the natives, is the degree of uncertainty under which they (the natives) still labour as to the ultimate intentions of Government, and whether it will ever lead them into paths of usefulness, profit or honour; only let the intentions of Government be officially announced, and there will be a general move-ment among all the more respectable classes.' But the teaching of English acquires much importance when we consider it, with Mr Duff, as the grand remedy for obviating the prejudices of the natives against practi-cal anatomy. 'The English language,' he urges, 'opens up a whole world of new ideas, and examples of suc-cess in every department of science; and the ideas so true, and the examples so striking, work mightily on the susceptible minds of native youth; so that by the time they have acquired a mastery over the English language, under judicious and enlightened instructors, their minds are almost metamorphosed into the tex-ture and cast of European youth, and they cannot help expressing their utter contempt for Hindoo superstition and prejudices.'

There is an argument of fact put in by Mr Duff, which is admirably to the point. We allude to the introduction of the English language and of English sciences among the Scottish Highlanders, whose native language, to this day, is the Gaelic. The parallel is a very fair one; for no people were more superstitious, more wedded to their customs than the Highlanders . . .; but since the introduction of the English language among them, the state of things is much changed.

The same observation applied to Ireland and Wales. The result was that acquisition of the English enabled them

> . . . to pass through life with credit and not unfrequently with distinction. What is there in the condition, physical or moral, of the natives of this country that should render them incapable of acquiring English as easily as the Irish, the Highlanders, and Welsh?

It was later reported that the expectations with which this change was made were completely realized. The most intractable of national prejudices gave way before the exigencies of the dissecting room. Indian Medical Science had taken root.

Of the social life of Mr and Mrs Duff at this period we have one significant glimpse. The accession of William IV to the throne was marked by an official ball at Government House, to which they were duly invited by Lord and Lady William Bentinck. Perplexed, the Scottish missionary took counsel of a chaplain, who assured him that, viewing the invitation as a command, he was in the habit of going to Government House on such occasions, of making his bow to the Governor-General and his wife and at once retiring. This compromise did not commend itself to Alexander. Alexander frankly stated, in a letter to the private secretary, the reasons why he could not conscientiously obey the most kind and courteous command of the ruler of India. After long delay, he received the Governor-General's cordial approval of his spirit and action.

Soon after, His Excellency begged the missionary and his wife to meet him at dinner in one of those frequent gatherings where the two men discussed, in a like spirit, the highest good of the people and the government of India.

While there is obviously no record of the discussions between Lord Bentinck and Alexander, we are left in no doubt about the high regard in which the Governor-General held the young Highlander. Lord William Bentinck left the land for which he had done so much in March, 1835, and when bidding the missionaries goodbye, he made this reference, after answering those who would use the force of the conqueror and the influence of the state-paid bishop to induce the profession of Christianity:

> Being as anxious as any of these excellent persons for the diffusion of Christianity through all countries, but

knowing better than they do, the ground we stand upon, my humble advice to them is, rely exclusively upon the humble, pious and learned missionary. His labours, divested of all human power, create no distrust. Encourage education with all your means. The offer of religious truth in the school of the missionary is without objection. It is or is not accepted. If it is not, the other seeds of instruction may take root and yield a rich and abundant harvest of improvement and future benefit. I would give them as an example in support of this advice, the school founded exactly on those principles, lately superintended by the estimable Mr Duff, that has been attended with such unparalleled success. I would say to them finally, that they could not send to India too many labourers in the vineyard like those whom I have now the gratification of addressing. Farewell. May God Almighty give you health and strength to prosecute your endeavours, and may He bless them with success.

Alexander was now a central figure in Calcutta with an active interest in all events. He had a unique personality and once seen was never to be forgotten. This is illustrated by the Rev Lal Behari Day, who later wrote of his first day as a pupil at Dr Duff's school, in 1834:

I cannot say he walked into the class-room – he *rushed* into it, his movements in those days being exceedingly rapid. He was dressed all in black, and wore a beard. He scarcely stood still for a single second, but kept his feet and hands moving incessantly, like a horse of high mettle. He seemed to have more life in him than most men. He had his white pocket-handkerchief in his hand, which he was every now and then tying round his arm and twisting into a thousand shapes. He seemed to be a living personation of perpetual motion. But what attracted my notice most was the constant shrugging of his shoulders, a habit which he afterwards left off but which he had at that time in full perfection.

But what of Alexander himself now, who for four years did not cease to burn lavishly and incessantly the physical energy he had brought from the Scottish Highlands; the exhaustless enthusiasm he ever fed at its heavenly source? Alexander received his first warning in the great cyclone of May, 1833, but took no notice. The rain came prematurely that year, marshalled by the rotary hurricane which, revolving within itself, as if the destroying counterpart of the harmony of the spheres, moved rapidly over the land. From the Bay of Bengal, the mighty waters of which dragged in its devastating train, over island and mainland, forest and field, village and town, the wild fury of the cyclone rolled itself north and west. Here the storm wave and the wind bore inland for miles to some rising ground a freighted Indiaman of 1,500 tons, among the hamlets of the peasantry, where for months after it lay a marvel to all. It swept into sometimes instant but more frequently lingering death, hundreds of thousands of human beings and their cattle, whose vain struggles to cling to roofs and trees and the floating wreck of their desolated homes suggested thoughts of a greater flood and prayers for mercy. Most graphic of all was this incident, which Duff himself told.

Alexander was visiting an Argyllshire fellow-countryman who, on that dreadful day, was superintending the clearing of the jungle on Saugar Island. For several weeks before, his party had been annoyed by the nightly attacks of a tiger of unusual size and ferocity. It carried away some of their animals employed in agricultural operations, as well as two or three human beings. When the cyclone prevailed and the water continued to rise over the island, as many natives as could swim went to the Scotsman's bungalow for shelter, until it was greatly overcrowded. At last, while watching the flood rapidly rising to a level with the floor, at a distance, driven before the tempest along the mighty torrent of waters, he noticed the famous tiger evidently aiming at reaching the house. Happily he had a shotgun loaded and ready. The tiger reached the bungalow and leapt into it, causing further panic among the natives, but it worked its way through the dense mass of human beings, and did not stop till it got nose and head into the remotest corner, where it continued to lie still quivering like an aspen leaf. The Scotsman concluded that though, under the influence of terror produced by the violence of the tempest, he was then quite tame, if the bungalow escaped and the storm abated the genuine nature of the savage animal would return, and all the more speedily from the exhaustion it must have undergone swimming and struggling to reach the bungalow. So he very coolly took the gun and pointed the barrel to the heart, resting it on the skin, shot the animal instantly.

The effect on the survivors of the storm was for a time

quite as deadly. Many who escaped the flood fell by the disease which it brought when the waters subsided and the cold season of 1833–34 came round. Malarious fever, bred by the rotting carcases and vegetation, spread like a blight over the fairest portions of the rice land. Alexander could do nothing for the poor people at this stage but at least the new hospitals would give more hope in the future. Inexperienced in tropical sanitation, and bound to discharge the duty of inspecting the prosperous branch school at Takee, Alexander and his now pregnant wife Anne set off by native boat for the place, which was seventy miles due east of Calcutta. It was November and the country was only beginning to dry up. Scarcely had they left the city when they came upon a mass of putrid bodies, human and animal, through which they had to find their way.

All was beautiful to look at in the green jungle forests of the Sunderbahns, but the abundant fruit from which the Bengalis take their proverbial word for 'hypocrite' symbolised the reality. Dr and Mrs Temple received them with their usual hospitality. On the return journey to Calcutta, the young missionary was laid low by his first illness, jungle fever in its deadliest form. His fine constitution showed that robust elasticity which often afterwards resulted in rapid recovery, and after tossing amid the sea breezes of the Sandheads for two or three weeks, he was once more in the midst of the work he loved.

But with the heat of April, 1834, a remittent fever came on him which his vigour of will resisted so far as to take him, again and in that weather, to Takee. Dr Temple, alarmed at his appearance, at once sent him back, warning him against the scourge which was then far more serious than cholera: dysentery. His wife tended him carefully despite her own discomfiture in her now more advanced condition of pregnancy.

On his return at the height of the hot season he found as his guest the good Anthony Groves, surgeon-dentist of Exeter, who gave up all he had for a mission to Baghdad, and was the first and best of the Plymouth Brethren. The romantic and very sad story of that mission to Muslims under a government which punished apostasy with death, the experience of Francis W. Newman and Mr Parnell and the young Kitto, Groves told in the sympathising and sometimes amused ear of Alexander in 4, Wellington Square, Calcutta. When the two widowers and the young bachelor Newman left Baghdad, they could not leave

behind them their one convert, the lovely Armenian widow of
Shiraz, nor could she travel with them save as the wife of one
of them. So they cast lots, and the lot fell on John Vesey Parnell,
graduate of Edinburgh University; and when he succeeded his
father, the first Baron, in 1842 she became Lady Congleton.

Having come round by Bombay and Tinnevelly, where he
renewed an old friendship with a Mr Rhenius, and was
charmed by the primitive simplicity of the Indian church there,
Mr Groves found himself in a new world when among the
young Brahmans who were searching the scriptures diligently.
After a general survey of the whole school and college he was
closeted with the highest class, and left to examine them on
the Bible, on theology, and in detail on the evidences of
Christianity. Himself an excellent scholar, Mr Groves was
astonished at the intelligence and promptitude of the replies.
But the whole force of his loving nature was drawn out when
he came to examine these Hindus on the purpose and effect
of the sacrifice of the Son of God on the cross of Calvary.

His questioning burst forth into an appeal which pressed
home on their conscience the knowledge they had shown,
while he wept in his fervour, and the eyes of the young men
glowed with reflected inspiration. He exclaimed to Duff:

> This is what I have been in quest of ever since I left
> England. At Baghdad I almost daily exhorted the adult
> natives, but in the case of even the most attentive I always
> painfully felt there was a crust between their mind and
> mine. Here I feel that every word is finding its way within.
> I could empty the whole of my own soul into theirs. How
> is this?

Alexander's answer was to open the door into the large hall
and point to the busy scene, to the children in the infant
gallery lisping the English alphabet. 'There,' he said, 'is the
explanation.'

That was Alexander's last day, for a long time, in his
loved Institution. He was already suffering from dysentery,
a generation before treatment became available. Four doctors
could not help the visibly dying missionary. The last of them
called in, Ranald Martin, pronounced the case desperate, but
asked permission to try an experimental remedy which had
saved one or two of his patients. The result was that, after a long
and profound trance as it seemed to the sufferer, he woke up to
consciousness, to revival, to such a point of convalescence that

he could be carried on board the first Cape ship for home. The devoted Groves had slept beside him day and night, nursing him with a brother's tenderness; but Alexander was not the only invalid.

On the day that the stricken family were laid in their berths in the East Indiaman the *John M'Lellan*, bound for Greenock, with Groves as their fellow passenger, a son was born to Alexander and Anne Duff, to whom the name of Groves, as well as his father's name, was given. From Anne's letter about the departure to Dr Chalmers we learn that, even when thus rescued from the very gates of death, the ardent missionary implored the doctors to send him on a brief voyage, not as far as Great Britain. 'I devoted myself to the Lord,' he pleaded, 'to spend and be spent in his service in this land of India.' Ranald Martin's stern reply was, 'In the last nine months you have suffered more from tropical disease than many who have passed their lives in India. Let not a day be lost.'

As the Greenock-bound Indiaman dropped down the Hooghly his baby boy was taken to comfort him. He would have been still more cheered had he known that at that very time, in July, 1834, his old friend, David Ewart, was being ordained as the third missionary of the Church of Scotland and would soon arrive to help Mr W. S. Mackay.

Thus closed the first five years since Alexander and his wife had been sent forth with the charge of Dr Chalmers ringing in their ears. This ended the first period of his Indian service since he opened his famous Institution in the great Bengali thoroughfare of Chitpore Road, Calcutta. As the missionary was borne to the life-giving breezes of the ocean from the sweltering pestilence of a Bengal July, the precious seed he had been sent to sow had germinated and was growing up night and day.

Alexander was now summoned, though he did not know it, to do the equally necessary work of creating a living missionary spirit in the Church at home. The apparently dying apostle was really being sent on the parallel or alternating service which divided his whole career into two indispensable and co-operating sets of activities in East and West. Having set the battle in array in front, and fought for years at the head of his scanty forces, he had then to leave the post of danger in the charge of his colleagues in order to send forth more ammunition.

As consciousness returned and strength began to come back, it was natural that the young missionary should long to be left at his post, should even somewhat murmuringly marvel why he had been taken away in the hour of victory. The very elements seemed to conspire to keep him in Bengal, for the *John M'Lellan* could not breast the fury of the south-west monsoon in a Bengal July, her decks were swept again and again of the livestock laid in for the long voyage, and after six weeks' tossing she had to put into Madras for stores. By the time she sighted South Africa, Alexander had become so far reconciled to the change as to be able to write to Dr Bryce:

> The very thought of returning home at the commencement of my labours and infancy of the Assembly's mission would have, I verily believe, broken my heart, were it not that God, by successive afflictions, which thrice had me to the verge of the grave, disciplined me into the belief and conviction that a change so decided was absolutely indispensable, and that to resist the proposal to leave Calcutta would be tantamount to a resistance of the will of Providence. . . . God has, I trust, overruled all for my spiritual improvement; and I trust, moreover, that by my return for a season to Scotland the great cause may be effectually furthered.

It was during this otherwise tedious time of slow convalescence that he seems to have read the Bible straight through three times. Beginning with the enthusiastic conviction of his own success, that the Church in the world would gradually glide into a millennium of godliness, this comparative and repeated study brought him to the conclusion that missionary work is merely preparatory to the great outpouring of the Holy Spirit. In history, as in the prophets, he always found righteousness and peace preceded by judgments.

The invalid was just able to land at Cape Town, and with the assistance of a friendly arm, walk to the church, where Dr Adamson, his host five years before, baptised their child born on the day they had left Calcutta. The sea breezes had done their best for five months, and the apparently restored missionary rejoiced in the strong frost which greeted him as if from Scotland.

8

Missionary Work at Home

When the ship entered the Firth of Clyde it was Christmas Day. When Alexander landed at Greenock he found the whole country in the exuberant excitement of the General Election under the first Reform Act, which had extended the franchise from two thousand electors who returned all the Scottish Members of Parliament to something like a fairer proportion. The time of freedom in church as well as state had begun – the conflicts which ended in the disruption of the Kirk and the abolition of the Corn Laws ten or twelve years after.

The sight of election hustings was as new to Scotland as it was to Alexander and his wife. Everywhere they heard only abuse of the Duke of Wellington. In Edinburgh, Lord Campbell talked of impeaching 'the multifarious minister' who at the time held eight Cabinet offices, till it was said, 'the Cabinet Council sits in his head and the ministers are all of one mind'. It was seen in time that the Duke was only doing his duty till Sir Robert Peel should return from Italy and form the new ministry which put Mr Gladsone in office. In such circumstances who, in Kirk or public meeting, would listen to the tale of triumph so remote and so obscure as that which Mr Duff had modestly to tell. Yet the tale was really one of spiritual revolution affecting millions, compared with which the Reform Act, the policy of Sir Robert Peel, and the training of Mr Gladstone were but single events in a constitutional series!

After a few days spent in Greenock with the Rev Mr Menzies, formerly librarian of St Andrews University, and in Glasgow with his old fellow-student, Dr Lorimer, for both of whom he preached, Alexander turned his face towards the General Assembly's committee in Edinburgh. He reached the capital by what was then the easiest and quickest means, the canal track-boat on the Union Canal which linked Glasgow to Edinburgh. The Duffs joined other passengers on the narrow passenger barge.

The barge was peacefully pulled along by the little steam-boat *Charlotte Dundas* which was first introduced in 1801. How different was this journey to the sea voyages. The small boat glided smoothly along the canal through the beautiful Scottish Lowland countryside, with the land but one step away on either side and the only reason for stopping was at lock-gates. Anne's mother had died while they were in India, but they obtained a house in Pitt Street, Portobello, two miles from Edinburgh, leased to them by the trustees of her father's estate. Arriving at Portobello at this time of the year was in complete contrast to the weather to which they had been subjected for the last five years. The house stood some one hundred yards from the edge of the Firth of Forth and in winter the icy blasts blew from the north-east.

So much had happened in Great Britain and indeed the world since Alexander and Anne left London for India. Alexander would require a plan of campaign for his missionary work which would have a hearing in this exciting new age. William IV was still on the throne and the country had five prime ministers during the period. Sir Robert Peel was now in office. Andrew Jackson was in office as the seventh President of the United States of America, The first passenger train had been introduced between Liverpool and Manchester in 1830. Faraday discovered electricity in 1831. The first Parliamentary Reform Act had been passed in 1832. Slavery was abolished in the British Empire and the first state grant for education was followed by the Poor Law Amendment Act. The United States of America was now in the front of world trade with her clipper ships, sweeping the seas under a flood of cotton sails with the foam curling along their slender bows. Packet ships were sailing from New York to Liverpool in sixteen to eighteen days. This and much more had captured the imagination of the public at large. Other than the directors of the East India Company, few were interested in India or its people, far less a missionary looking for ammunition to further his cause.

The first member of committee and personal friend on whom Alexander called was Dr Chalmers, then redeeming the fame of the University of Edinburgh in its theological faculty. Most courteous and even enthusiastic was the greeting of the greatest Scotsman of his day, who added to all his other gifts, that large-hearted friendliness which is the rule of his countrymen scattered abroad. The hour sped rapidly in a fire of question and answer about the progress of the mission and the state of things in India. On accompanying his visitor to the door Dr Chalmers demanded of him, 'Where is your cloak?' 'I have not had time to get any,' was the reply. 'That will never do in this climate; it is now very frosty, and you are as thinly clad as if you were in India; let me not see your face again till you have been at the tailor's.' The young missionary was already an old Indian in this, that the fire of the tropics had made him indifferent to his first winter in Scotland, after which comes the reaction that often drives the sufferer to the sun of the south.

Where was there another like Chalmers or one worthy of him at that time in Scotland? Dr Inglis, the founder of the mission was gone. Dr Brunton had not then been appointed his permanent successor. He and the other members received the ardent advances of the astonished Duff with a polite indifference, or replied with congratulations on the fact that so good a conservative statesman as Sir Robert Peel had been placed at the head of affairs, as if to save and even extend to the Kirk which had been for years furiously assailed by the Voluntaries (those who believed that the Church should be supported solely by its members). More than once was Alexander stung into the warning that for the Kirk to trust any secular statesman, however respectable, was to lean on a broken reed. The transcendent interests of a great spiritual institution like the Church of Scotland, he said, must be placed only on Christ Himself, its living head.

There was one minister, besides Chalmers, who had watched the work done in Bengal and had genius to appreciate it. He at once invited Alexander to begin his crusade in Falkirk. That was John Brown Patterson, the marvel of the High School in Edinburgh, whom Pillans took with him to the university; the student who gained the hundred pound prize for the best essay on the character of the Athenians. The result of Alexander's preaching in Falkirk, and of a public meeting with formal resolutions to advance the Bengal mission, was not only a collection of money which surprised all in that day, but the lighting of a flame which, in coming days and years, Alexander was to fan and spread till it covered the land, and fired America and many other parts of Christendom. The glad report of this, made formally to the committee, was received with respectful silence.

Somewhat dubious now as to the attitude of the committee, the missionary received, with hesitation, the next invitation to tell the public of his work. Dr A. Paterson, who had been driven out of Russia by the intolerance of Czar Nicholas, asked him to address half a dozen godly folks who met once a month in the Edinburgh house of Mr Campbell, of Carbrook.

On finding the drawing-room crowded by a large audience Alexander remonstrated, and refused to remain. Explanation showed that no endeavour had been made to summon the audience, whom he therefore consented to address. The result was such an impression in many circles outside as well as within the Kirk, that an English visitor who had been present rode down to Portobello next morning to make a large donation to the mission, and Mr Duff was formally summoned, for the first time, to meet the committee in the rooms in the university which Dr Brunton occupied as librarian. Marvelling what the sudden cause could be, but delighted that at last he would have an opportunity of giving an account of his stewardship, he hurried to the spot with that punctuality for which, like all successfully busy men, he was ever remarkable.

Entering the room, he found that nearly all the members of the committee were present. After prayer the acting convener rose and, standing in the middle of the floor, in substance said that he had thought it right to summon a meeting to settle and determine the case of Mr Duff, who, in these days of agitation, turmoil, and revolutionary tendencies and irregularities of every description, had taken it upon himself to hold not exactly a public meeting, but at the same time a very large meeting in the house of Mr Campbell, of Carbrook, with a view of addressing it on the subject of missions. Now he regarded this as a very unwarrantable and irregular proceeding. Mr Duff had given him no intimation of his intention to hold such a meeting, nor had he any means of knowing what might be the leading subject of his address. He thought it therefore right to consult his colleagues, to induce them to lay down rules to regulate Mr Duff's proceedings on such matters in future, as it would never do, in unsettled times like these, to allow the agent of a responsible committee to adopt what measures he chose.

Immediately Alexander stood up and, taking possession of the middle of the floor, respectfully admitted that he was the agent of the committee, but of a committee guided by moral and spiritual influences and considerations. While in one respect therefore he was their agent, in another respect he must be considered on a footing of religious co-equality; co-responsibility with themselves; but not to insist further on this, he would soon bring the matter to a decisive issue. When he went to India originally, he declared that he would not go if hampered by any conditions which his own conscience did not approve; that, entering upon an entirely new field, full discretion must be allowed him within the limits of reason and sobriety to follow what courses he might deem most effective for the ends which the committee and himself had alike in common. This reasonable concession was at once cheerfully yielded by Dr Inglis and his committee; and now when he, Mr Duff, had returned, after several years of multiplied experiences, he thought that full discretion should be allowed him to adopt what course might seem best for awakening an interest in the Church's mission, so long as he was ready to take any counsel or advice which the home experiences of members of the committee friendly to missions might suggest.

He then explained how the recent meeting had not origi-nated with him; though when he came to understand it he fully approved of it, and thought that the successful result sufficiently proved its providential legitimacy. Of course, if the committee had any work for him to do of any kind anywhere, he would at once relinquish all other duty for the sake of taking up that; but beyond this he could not possibly go. He was an ordained minister of the gospel, and therefore supposed to be endowed with ordinary ministerial gifts, graces and attainments. He was in all respects therefore the free-man of the Lord; free to carry out whatever his blessed Master might indicate as His most gracious will. That liberty he would not and could not for ten thousand worlds relinquish.

The decisive issue, therefore, came to be this; if the com-mittee resolved, as they had a perfect right to do, to draw up some peremptory instructions to regulate his proceedings in purely spiritual, ministerial, and missionary matters, he must at once write out his resignation as their agent. If on reconsideration they came to the conclusion that it was better to allow things to remain as they were, and grant him full liberty of action within the reasonable limits stated by himself, he would rejoice in continuing as their agent, and do what he possibly could to create a deeper interest in the mission throughout the bounds of the Church, and thereby help to increase the funds and the number of agents to be sent abroad. For the people being profoundly ignorant of the whole subject, their being wakened to take a deeper interest in so spiritual a work as the evangelisation of the world would not only be carrying out more fully the last great commission of our blessed Saviour, but also tend in many remarkable ways to benefit their own souls. Having so spoken he sat down.

Instantly, all present, without any one of them uttering a single word, rushed out, leaving Alexander and the convener alone in the middle of the floor to look at each other in dumb amazement. 'Probably', said Alexander with great calmness, 'we have had enough of the subject for this day.'

So, on that memorable occasion, the uncompromising devotion to duty of the young missionary proved to be more powerful than all tact or ecclesiastical *finesse*, as it had done in more difficult circumstances among the Bengalis. Dr Inglis was gone. The country and the Church knew nothing of the Bengal mission save the meagre report printed once a year for a General Assembly which had not then become a popular parliament.

With the possible exception of Dr Brunton, it is evident that no member of the mission committee present at the meeting had the remotest idea of the importance of the mission in India; or rather what Alexander Duff had achieved to date. When Dr Brunton officially took charge on his appointment as convener, the scanty records of the committee meetings confirmed the apathy and total ignorance of the subject of the work in India. Alexander now knew he had a most difficult task ahead. He had to educate those in the West as he had done in the East and this battle would be no less difficult. The campaign in the East simply could not continue until he had the support at home to provide the ammunition.

After Falkirk the next call came from Dr Wilson of Irvine. Dundee followed, following a visit of Alexander to many of the ministers on his way to Moulin in Scotland to visit his mother and father.

In April, 1835, the convener of the mission committee in Edinburgh submitted to Alexander a letter from the Presbytery of London, expressing profound interest in the India mission of the established Church of Scotland, and inviting the missionary to preach to and address each of the congregations, which were ready to begin a system of contributions for the good cause. Alexander set off immediately for the congenial task which had been requested by the committee and duly successfully carried out the pleasant work.

He was about to set out for the final meeting when, as he raised a cup of coffee to his lips, he was seized with the violent shivering which marked the return of his old fever.

He was nursed in Alderman Pirie's house for three weeks, and insisted on returning to Edinburgh for the General Assembly, which he reached by steamer, apparently a wasted skeleton.

The reforming party in the Kirk had established the *Scottish Guardian* as their weekly newspaper, in Glasgow, and the editor, the Rev George Lewis, had formed a volunteer staff of reporters for the Assembly's proceedings. He instructed his staff to take down as full a report of the missionary's speech as possible. Monday, 25 May, 1835, had been assigned for what had up to then been the purely formal duty of presenting the annual report of the India Mission. The Assembly met in the Tron Kirk, Edinburgh. Though physically unprepared, and just risen from a sick bed, Alexander testified often after, that never during his whole life had he faced an ordeal like this with such divine help.

At first it seemed as if he could not go beyond a few sentences, and he was conscious that many were gazing at him, apprehensive, as they afterwards said, that he would soon drop on the floor. But, leaping by one effort into the very heart of his subject, he became unconscious of the presence of his audience save as a mass that was gradually warming to his heat. Advancing from stage to stage of what was, for him, 'a brief exposition', he whispered out his at that time unmatched peroration with an almost supernatural effect, and finally subsided drenched with perspiration as if he had been dragged through the Atlantic, to use his own expression. Then, for the first time, he marked the emotion of his hearers, many of them callous lawyers and Lords of Session, cool men of the world or antipathetic 'moderates'. Down the cheeks of even these the tears were trickling.

Returning to the report. With the unconsciousness of the highest art their first Indian missionary at once planted the General Assembly inside Bengal, as he set himself to 'the conversion of a hundred and thirty millions of idolaters'. Step by step he hurried them on from the first attempt, on the old system, to influence the educated Hindus, through the evidences of Christianity, of miracles, prophecy and the demand for the proof of the missionary's authority, till this conclusion was reached:

The power of conveying the necessary knowledge seems to me to be the only substitute we possess instead of the power of working miracles. But it is surely one thing to say, that a sound liberal education is greatly advantageous towards the establishment of the evidence and authority of the Christian revelation, and, consequently, towards securing a candid and attentive hearing, and quite another to say, that it is indispensably and universally necessary to the heart reception of the gospel remedy. The former position we do most firmly maintain, but in the solemnity of apostolic language, we exclaim, God forbid that we should ever maintain the latter! Instead of demanding your authority for the truth of Christianity, the Brahman may challenge you to invalidate, if you can, the claims of his system. You soon find that there is no common ground in logic, and you turn to the experimental principles of physical science to find the cataclysms of the Hindoo cosmogony exalted against the petty, the recent learning of the West. You turn to theology proper, only to find that the Vedic Shasters sanctify and render infallible all Brahmanism, secular as well as sacred.

'Do then', exclaimed Alexander, after pleading for the supply of missionaries 'qualified to silence the intellectually proud as well as to edify the spiritually humble':

Do then let me again crave the attention of this venerable court to the grand *peculiarity, that if in India you only impart ordinary useful knowledge, you thereby demolish what by its people is regarded as sacred*. A course of instruction that professes to convey *truth of any kind* thus becomes a species of *religious education* in such a land – *all* education being there regarded as religious or theological. Every branch of sound general knowledge which you inculcate becomes the destroyer of some corresponding part in the Hindoo system. It is this that gives to the dissemination of mere human knowledge, in the present state of India, such awful importance; it is this that exalts and magnifies it into the rank of a *primary* instrument in spreading the seeds of reformation throughout the land.

But effective preaching required indigenous Indian, not foreign, preachers. Appealing to the Highland ministers among his audience, the speaker used the same old analogy of the Gaelic and English which he had employed with such effect against the one-sided orientalists of Calcutta:

Oh, there is that in the tones of a foreigner's voice which

falls cold and heavy on the ear of the native, and seldom
reaches the heart! – whereas, there is something in the
tones of a countryman's voice, which, operating as a
charm, falls pleasantly on the ear, and comes home to the
feelings, and touches the heart, and causes its tenderest
chords to vibrate. Doubtless there have been, and there
may be now, individual cases of foreigners having in
some degree, or even altogether, surmounted this grand
practical difficulty. But these rare cases form such palpable
exceptions from the general rule, that they can scarcely be
counted on, in providing a *national* supply of preachers
of the everlasting gospel. Thus, again, is the *comparative*
inefficiency of *European* agency, when put forth *directly*
in proclaiming the gospel, forced upon the mind; and the
necessity of having recourse to *native* agents in the work is
once more suggested with a potency that is resistless. They
can withstand that blazing sun, they can bear exposure
to that unkindly atmosphere, they can locate themselves
amid the hamlets and villages, they can hold intercourse
with their countrymen in ways and modes that we never
can. And having the thousand advantages, besides, of
knowing the feelings, the sentiments, the traditions, the
associations, the habits, the manners, the customs, the
trains of thought and principles of reasoning among the
people, they can strike in with arguments, and objections,
and illustrations, and imagery which we could never,
never have conceived. How glorious then must be the day
for India when such *qualified native agents* are prepared to
go forth among the people, and shake and agitate, and
rouse them from the lethargy and the slumber of ages!

It is for reasons like the preceding, that a man of fervent
piety, going forth with the fullest intention of doing nothing but *directly* and *exclusively* preaching the gospel in the
native tongues, often finds himself, in such a country as
India, constrained to think of other and more effectual
means of ultimately accomplishing the same work, and
hastening the same consummation.

Then followed a graphic description of Alexander's own way
of overcoming such difficulties; a sad picture of the separation
of his third convert Gopeenath Nundi from father and mother,
from brothers and friends, for ever; and a contrast, which
time was unhappily only to prove both a prediction and a

justification, in the political results of the system which the Government of India alone of all ruling powers, civilized or barbarous, pursued – public instruction carefully divorced from all religion:

If in that land you do give the people *knowledge without religion*, rest assured that it is the greatest blunder, politically speaking, that ever was committed. Having free unrestricted access to the whole range of our English literature and science, they will despise and reject their own absurd systems of learning. Once driven out of their own systems, they will inevitably become infidels in religion. And shaken out of the mechanical routine of their own religious observances, without moral principle to balance their thoughts or guide their movements, they will certainly become discontented, restless agitators – ambitious of power and official distinction, and possessed of the most disloyal sentiments towards that Government which, in their eye, has usurped all the authority that rightfully belonged to themselves. This is not a theory, it is a statement of fact. I myself can testify in this place, as I have already done on the spot, that expressions and opinions of a most rebellious nature have been known to drop from some of the very *protégés* of that Government which, for its own sake, is so infatuated as to insist on giving knowledge without religion. But as soon as some of these became converts to Christianity, through the agency already described, how totally different their tone of feeling towards the existing Government? *Their* bowels yearned over the miseries of their countrymen. *They* now knew the only effectual cure. And their spontaneous feeling was, 'Ah! woe be unto us, if the British Government were destroyed and the Hindoo dynasties restored! The first thing would be to cut us off, and what would then become of our poor degraded country? We pray for the permanence of the British Government, that, under the shadow of its protection, we may disseminate the healing knowledge of Christianity among our brethren – that knowledge which alone can secure their present welfare and immortal happiness.' In like manner, and for the same reason, there are not more loyal or patriotic subjects of the British crown than the young men that compose the more advanced classes in our Institution. So

clearly and strongly did this appear to many members of
the present Government of India, that instead of regarding
us with jealousy and suspicion as enemies, they looked
upon us as the truest friends of the British Government,
the staunchest supporters of the British power.

Alexander went on to outline developments in English and
vernacular education, and concluded with a call for further
commitment to the cause:

> Whenever we make an appeal on behalf of the heathen,
> it is constantly urged that there are enough of heathen at
> home, and why roam for more in distant lands? I strongly
> suspect that those who are most clamorous in advancing
> this plea are just the very men who do little, and care
> less, either for heathen at home or heathen at a distance.
> At all events, it is a plea far more worthy of a heathen
> than of a Christian . . . I for one can see no contrariety
> between home and foreign labour. I am glad that so much
> is doing for home: but ten times more may yet be done
> for home and for abroad too. It is cheering to think of the
> overmastering energy that is now put forth in the cause
> of church extension in this land, as well as in reference to
> improved systems of education, and model-schools, and
> more especially the enlightment of the long-neglected and
> destitute Highlands. I know the Highlands; they are dear
> to me. They form the cradle and the grave of my fathers;
> they are the nursery of my youthful imaginings, and there
> is not a lake, or barren heath, or naked granite peak that is
> not dear to me. How much more dear the precious souls
> of those who tenant these romantic regions! Still, though
> a son of the Highlands, I must, in my higher capacity as a
> disciple of Jesus, be permitted to put the question; Has not
> Inspiration declared, that 'the field is the world'? . . . The
> sacrifice on Calvary was designed to embrace the globe in
> its amplitude. Let us view the subject as God views it – let
> us view it as denizens of the universe, and we shall not
> be bounded in our efforts of philanthropy, short of the
> north or south pole. Wherever there is a human being,
> *there* must our sympathies extend. . . .

Let us awake, arise, and rescue unhappy India from its present
and impending horrors. Ah! long, too long, has India been

made a theme for the visions of poetry and the dreams of
romance . . .

Let us arise, and resolve that henceforward these 'climes
of the sun' shall not be viewed merely as a storehouse
of flowers for poetry, and figures for rhetoric, and bold
strokes for oratory', but shall become the climes of a
better sun – even 'the Sun of righteousness'; the nursery
of 'plants of renown' that shall bloom and blossom in
the regions of immortality. Let us arise and revive the
genius of the olden time, let us revive the spirit of our
forefathers. Like them, let us unsheathe the sword of
the Spirit, unfurl the banners of the Cross, sound the
gospel-trump of jubilee. Like them, let us enter into a
Solemn League and Covenant before our God, in behalf
of that benighted land, that we will not rest till the voice
of praise and thanksgiving arise, in daily orisons, from
its coral strands, roll over its fertile plains, resound from
its smiling valleys, and re-echo from its everlasting hills.
Thus it shall be proved, that the Church of Scotland,
though 'poor, can make many rich', . . . that the Church
of Scotland, though powerless as regards carnal designs
and worldly policies, has yet the divine power of bringing
many sons to glory, of calling a spiritual progency from
afar, numerous as the drops of dew in the morning, and
resplendent with the shining of the Sun of righteousness
– a noble company of ransomed multitudes that shall hail
you in the realms of day, and crown you with the spoils of
victory, and sit on thrones, and live and reign with you,
amid the splendours of an unclouded universe.

May God hasten the day and put it into the heart
of everyone present, to engage in the glorious work of
realizing it!

The young missionary slowly turned and fixed his now
tear-filled eyes on the entire audience and with a thankful
upturned stare, slumped down on his seat. The man who
had not long since risen from the sick-bed did not need to
collect his notes. He had none. There was complete silence in
the hall as Alexander, now pouring with sweat, almost audibly
thanked his God for the divine help he had received in answer
to his prayer. The long-drawn sigh of the profoundly moved
hearers relieved the suppressed emotion which lighted up or
bedimmed every face.

Dr Gordon was called on to lead the devotions of the Assembly in praise and thanksgiving to God. Then one after another of the leaders of the house rose to give expression to his feelings. One said that Duff's 'lofty tone, thought and sentiment, its close argumentative force, its transcendent eloquence and overpowering impressiveness' was greater than any he had heard from Fox or Pitt in the House of Commons. The *Scottish Guardian* of the next day wrote thus:

Mr Duff's speech will be found at full length in our columns, occupying the most prominent place in the proceedings of the Assembly of yesterday. It has thrown a flood of light upon the christianization of India, and furnished principles and information for guiding our Church which will lead to an entire new model of missions, and give, we trust, a new direction to all the efforts of the Christians of Britain in behalf of India . . .

In his official biographer's view, more nearly than any of the speakers of the first half of the nineteenth century, Alexander thus realized that which Mr Gladstone had pronounced the supreme influence of the speaker, 'receiving from his audience in a vapour what he pours back on them in a flood'. But, while rejecting the mechanical or formally rhetorical preparation which would have cramped while it polished his utterance, Alexander did not neglect the careful and admiring study of the masters of English eloquence, from Chatham and Burke to Erskine and Canning. A little collection of their masterpieces published in 1827 seems to have been, at one time, his constant companion, but he did not learn more from these than from the great Dr Chalmers.

The new spiritual life which was to work itself out in the Disruptions of 1843 had asserted its power in the General Assemblies of 1834 and 1835. Alexander also sincerely believed that the Kingdom of Christ was not only spiritual but independent, and that no earthly government had a right to overrule or control it. He attached a great significance to this most important issue and would take such steps within his power to ensure compliance.

How was not only the Church but all Scotland to be organized for the permanent and progressive support, by prayer and by knowledge, by men and by money, of missionary work in India? That was the problem which had occupied the thoughts of Alexander on his homeward voyage, 'when rocked amid the billows of a tempest off the Cape of Good Hope', and again as he paced the deck on the return to health. His resolution was formed before he landed, only to be intensified by the early indifference of the committee which his first speech had dissipated, and by the return of the fever which had fired his spirit anew.

From his own mind the experience of Irvine, and from the Church his Assembly speech, removed every doubt. Generally preceding Dr Chalmers in the church extension movement at home, with a thoroughness and over an extent of country possible only in the case of one who devoted to it his whole strength and unique experience, Alexander went far to anticipate the greatest triumph in Christian economics, the Sustentation Fund for ministers. The parallel, the necessary balance and support of that fund, was the system of congregational associations under similar presbyterial supervision for the missionaries abroad.

But the essential preliminary to all success had to be made known – foreign missions are of no party. They are the care and the corrective, the test and the stimulus of all parties in the Church. The missionary who, as such, takes a side in ecclesiastical warfare, may gratify his own personal bias, but he imperils the cause in which he ought to be absorbed. Thus Alexander became the peacemaker, in one sense of the beatitude, at home, as in the higher sense his work in India of reconciling men to God won him abundantly the peacemaker's blessedness. He later described the success of his first campaign of 1835–37, and the cause of that success. As a question of mere statistics he raised the annual income of the foreign missions scheme from £1,200 to £7,589 in 1838.

Alexander started his crusade in Scotland by first taking his wife and baby son home to his beloved parish of Moulin in Perthshire. They boarded the Perth stage-coach which started from the Black Bull Inn at the head of Leith Street in Edinburgh. He leased the mansion house of Edradour at Pitlochry, all but a stone's throw from the cottage of his birth at Achnahyle, and was once again reunited with his parents and friends.

He rested briefly until he regained his energies which he would require for the work ahead. His purpose was simple. He wished to educate the people about missionary work and India in particular. He started in July, 1835, and visited not less than three presbyteries a week including Meigle, Forfar, Arbroath, Brechin, Montrose, Aberdeen, Old Deer, Peterhead,

Fraserburgh, Banff, Elgin, Forres, Inverness, Dornoch and very many others, and where appropriate, he preached in the Gaelic as well as English. During this time he had many repeated attacks of his illness, but retreated quietly to Edradour and his caring wife.

There were no doubts as to the popularity of the young missionary and he was in demand everwhere. Approximately two weeks after the 1835 Assembly meeting, the Rev Dr Gordon as secretary of the committee had put in force the short Act passed by the General Assembly recommending all presbyteries to give Alexander Duff a respectful hearing at meetings called for the purpose, and to form a presbyterial association to create in each congregation an agency for prayer and the spreading of information about the evangelization of the world. This Act had been drawn up by Mr Makgill Crichton, of Rankeillour, in the back-room of the publishing house of Waugh and Innes, next to the Tron Kirk, to give practical effect to the enthusiasm created in the Assembly by the great speech, and had been unanimously passed. Almost every parish in Scotland competed for a visit from him and this was not all. Zealously anticipating St Andrews and the other universities, Marischal College, Aberdeen, honoured itself and surprised the young divine, still under thirty, by presenting him with the diploma of Doctor of Divinity. He was now Dr Alexander Duff, D.D. LL.D.

Although not many, there were several instances when he encountered rudeness, and yet to Alexander this was a challenge and all part of the work. He had been requested by the General Assembly to visit the presbytery of Dunbar in East Lothian, some thirty miles east of Edinburgh, but had been advised by the Assembly committee that the parish minister, the Rev Mr Jaffray, was notoriously hostile to foreign missions and missionaries. This naturally did not deter Dr Duff, whose plain duty was to show courtesy to the man in whose Kirk he was to address the people and the presbytery. He called at the manse in Dunbar and after some hesitation, the servant admitted him. As Alexander entered the study, Mr Jaffray stood up and, glaring at the intruder with fury, shouted out in tones heard by passers-by in the street outside:

Are you the fanatic Duff who has been going about the country, beguiling and deceiving people by what they choose to call missions to the heathen? I don't want to

see you, or any of your description. I want no Indian
snake brought in among my people to poison their minds
on such subjects, so as I don't want to see you the sooner
you make off the better.

Alexander stood imperturbable. He replied that he was
merely showing him the courtesy due to an ordained minister
of the Established Church, as both of them were, and in any
case, he was there with the sanction of the General Assembly.
Alexander bowed and bade him farewell but in a parting
statement he said, 'The blessed Saviour's command was, "Go
into all the world, and preach the gospel to every creature"'. The
Rev Mr Jaffray became known as the 'Brahman of Dunbar', an
indication of his barbarous rudeness that was a great injustice
to the Brahmans of India, who were among the most courteous
and gentlemanly persons on earth.

Alexander spent Christmas and New Year with his family at
Edradour and was glad of the happy time to relax but repeated
attacks of his old fever made it impossible for the doctors to
allow him to even think of returning to India. This was not at
all what Alexander was planning and he knew that with God's
help, he would be given the health and strength to return to
his work. As can be seen from this official narrative of his
proceedings sent to the committee at the close of 1835, his
heart was still in India:

As nearly a twelvemonth has passed by since I reached
my native land, I naturally begin to look with a longing
eye towards the East. Summer is the best season for
leaving this country. But if it be resolved that I set
off next summer, medical opinion conspires with dire
experience in enforcing on me the conviction that the
intervening period spent in almost absolute repose would
be little enough so to recruit my frame as to entitle me,
with any reasonable prospect, to brave anew the influence
of a tropical climate. On the other hand much, very much,
might yet be done in this our native land in behalf of the
mission. Unless it be vigorously supported at home little
can be done abroad. But there is a disposition to support
it at home wherever its claims are freely and intelligibly
made known. The experience of the last few months, I
think, has amply confirmed this assertion. Of course the
grand advantage (and the only one to which I lay claim)
that I possess in advocating the claims of the mission at

home, is one that cannot be communicated to others, even that of having been on the field of labour, and having been an eye and ear witness of all that I happen to describe. It is this circumstance mainly, I must presume (for nothing else of an advantageous nature am I conscious of possessing beyond my fellows), that has made our brethren and members of our Church generally muster everywhere in such numbers and listen with such marked attention and resolve with such admirable unanimity. It was my own impression, months ere I landed on these shores, that good might result from visiting the presbyteries of our Church. But that impression has been deepened in a tenfold degree by the experience of the last four months, *i.e.* if professions without number do not turn out (which God forbid) like Dr Chalmers' exuberant shower of promises. About a third part of the presbyteries have now been visited, and clearly the other two-thirds could not be visited before next summer, or if so, such visitation would leave me in a condition the most unfit for resuming my labours in the East, but it seems most desirable that all the presbyteries should be visited. What then is to be done? As for myself I am in a strait between two. But after having thus stated the case I leave the matter entirely in the hands of the committee.

Dr Macwhirter settled the matter by promptorily deciding, on medical grounds, in favour of a less active and exciting visitation of the presbyteries.

By this time the effect of Dr Alexander Duff's work in Scotland had spread across the border, influencing churches and societies in England. When in the midst of his organization of associations in Perthshire, he was pressed by many and repeated invitations from the great missionary and religious societies in London to address them in the coming month of May. Even those who had most ignorantly objected to his Assembly oration of 1835, that it did not represent the operations of other Christians in India, had by this time discovered, both from his provincial addresses and the representations of their agents in Bengal, the catholicity of his spirit and the extent of his zealous co-operation with all the Protestant missionaries in Calcutta and the neighbourhood.

Especially was this the case with the Church Missionary Society, the evangelical organization of the Church of England, whose representatives, in Bengal, Dealtry, Corrie and Sandys, had been his most intimate fellow-workers. His response to that society's earnest appeal to address its annual meeting in May was the beginning of a relation which, as we shall see, became closer and more loving on both sides until the end. Never before had the directors deemed it expedient to go out of their own episcopal circle to find speakers, till Dr Duff was thus enabled to return, on a wider scale, the kindness of Dealtry and Corrie to himself when he first landed in Bengal. Alexander's wife Anne was expecting her second baby early in April and he decided to make no arrangements to travel south until some time after their baby was born. On 5 April, 1836, the baby was born. A girl who was named Anne.

In due course he made arrangements to travel to London to take up the kind offer to address the Church Missionary Society of the Church of England. At the meeting he found himself on the platform seated between the Bishops of Chester and Winchester. When the latter had spoken, the young Presbyterian apostle rose, and so addressed them that the interest and emotion of the vast audience continued to increase till he sat down amid a storm of enthusiastic applause. When all was over, among others the godly Mr Carus, one of the deans of Trinity College, Cambridge, introduced himself to Alexander, and at once exacted the promise that the missionary would accompany himself in a day or two on a visit to the university.

Other circumstances apart, the unique interest of this visit to Cambridge lies in the meeting for the first and last time of the aged Simeon and the young Duff. Simeon was within a few months of his death, but even after half a century's labours for his Master, in England and Scotland and for India, he was apparently in health and vigour. He and Alexander had what the latter afterwards described as 'a very prolonged sederunt'. As the guest of Carus at Cambridge, Alexander occupied the rooms in which Sir Isaac Newton made many of his most remarkable discoveries in optics. The old St Andrews student revelled in associations in which no college in the world was more rich. For Trinity, which Henry VIII founded and his daughters enriched, had been the nursery not only of the Church's most learned prelates and theologians, but of Bacon as well as Newton, of Cowley and Dryden and Andrew Marvell. But what interested him most of all, after the living Simeon, was the collection of Milton manuscripts in the college museum.

There he saw the list, in Milton's own hand, of the hundred titles, or more, which the poet had jotted down on returning from Italy, in his thirty-first year, as possible subjects of a great English poem, with *Paradise Lost* appearing at the head of them all.

At that time Mr Carus could not venture to call a public missionary meeting in the college, but the mayor presided over a great gathering of students and citizens in the town hall, whom Alexander addressed at length on India and its missions. From Cambridge he went to Leamington, where he gained some advantage from the treatment of the then celebrated Dr Jephson. Having avoided the excitement of the General Assembly in May of 1836, he thus spent the summer in England. On his return to Scotland in the autumn, to complete his organisations of the prebyteries and congregations, he was sternly ordered by his doctors to rest, but alas, there was to be no peace for Alexander and Anne. Their six-month baby Anne died.

Rest was impossible for Alexander and he made many calls throughout the country, in different directions radiating from his home at Edradour. He kept up a close correspondence with his colleagues Mackay and Ewart in Calcutta, and with other friends of the mission there. He was a keen observer of public affairs in the closing days of Lord William Bentinck's administration, and the opening promise of that of Lord Metcalfe, whom the jealous Court of Directors refused to appoint permanent Governor-General. Of how much that was most brilliant and abiding in these times could we not say that he had been a part? In July 1835 Alexander had spent a morning with Lord William Bentinck. Relieved of his responsibilities as Governor-General, Bentinck discussed the Indian situation with great frankness. One thing he said that Alexander never forgot was about the real location of power. His experience was that in the office of the President of the Board of Control, the chief secretary, through whose hands all official documents were sent out and sent home, for a long period – between forty and fifty years – exercised a power to which no President of the Board of Control, no director, no Governor-General or any other responsible official could pretend. A month later Bentinck, holidaying in Germany for his health, wrote to Duff:

I am much gratified to hear of your successful operations

in Scotland. It must be the result of great personal exertion alone, for though I have had ample reason to know the indifference and apathy that generally prevail respecting all matters connected with India, yet even with all this experience I was not prepared for the feeling of dislike almost with which any mention of India is received. But this conviction of a sad truth, this disgraceful proof of British selfishness ought only to have the effect of exciting those deeply interested in the moral and religious welfare of the people of India to renewed efforts in their behalf.

I have always considered the Hindoo College as one of the greatest engines of useful purpose that had been erected since our establishment in India; but that institution, in point of usefulness, can bear no comparison with yours, in which improved education of every kind is combined with religious instruction. I will not prolong this letter further than to say that I cannot be more gratified with any man's good opinion than by yours . . .

This, the greatest of the Bentincks, who thus expressed something like shame at a degree of English apathy to India still prevailing in spite of the first Afghan war and the Mutiny for which that iniquity was the preparation, died four years after, having represented Glasgow in the House of Commons. Born in 1774, he was sixty-five years of age when his ripe experience was lost to a country and a ministry which preferred to the wise Metcalfe, a place-hunter like Lord Auckland. The equally noble Lady William, renowned in the East for her Christian charities, was the second daughter of the first Earl of Gosford, and survived her husband till May, 1843.

The most real and fruitful result of Alexander's first Assembly speech and of those which followed it, in Scotland and England, was in drawing men to give themselves to India. The whole religious biography of the former country relating to that period was coloured by his influence or bore traces of his persuasive power. One who was then a youth of promise, and became the founder of the Edinburgh Medical Missionary Society, if not of medical missions, was profoundly impressed. We find the young Dr Coldstream, who had just settled in Leith as a physician, thus writing in 1837:

The missionary sermon and lesson of yesterday, by Dr Duff, were most impressive. I have no words to express their thrilling effect . . . I think I never felt so strongly the delightful influence of the bond of Christian love . . .

After a rest at Edradour, all too short, Alexander went up to London at the beginning of May, 1837, to take part in the anniversary of the Church of Scotland's Foreign Missions, held by the London Presbytery in Exeter Hall. Though weak, he was no longer the fever-wasted man who had excited the alarm of the Assembly in 1835. Nothing short of a reprint of the twenty-five pages of this rare address could do justice to this vein of the impassioned orator. Severed from its context, without the flashing eye, the quivering voice, the rapid gesticulation, the overwhelming climax, the few passages produced here seem cold and formal.

Beginning in the highest style of his art, this modern prophet, sent from the millions of Hindus to the very centre of Christian profession, congratulated London, especially its Scottish residents, on their recent response to an appeal to help Scots. Then after skilfully picturing the horrors of famine and pestilence among his own countrymen and within the narrow limits of their own island, and asking if imagination could conceive anything more harrowing, he replied that he knew a land that reminded people of Paradise:

But oh! in this highly favoured land – need I say I refer to India? – which for beauty might be the garden of the whole earth, and for plentcousness the granary of the nations – in this highly favoured land children are doomed to see their parents and parents their children perish – perish, not because there is no meat in the field, no flocks in the fold, no cattle in the stall, but because they are goaded on by the stimulants of a diabolical superstition to perish miserably by each other's hands.

Then followed word-pictures of life along the Hooghly – 'sons and daughters piously consigning a sickly parent, for the benefit of the soul, to the depths of a watery grave'; of 'the putrid corpse of the father and the living body of the mother' burning together, in every feudatory state at that time, and only in 1828 prohibited in the East India Company's territory; of the sacrifice of children by their mothers to the waters of Gunga and the jaws of the alligator; and of the systematic murder of female infants by the Rajpoot castes from Benares to Baroda. Rising from one scene of pitiful horror to another, every one of which an audience of 1837 knew to be living fact, the speaker reached the highest of all in the spiritual destitution and debasement which had made such crimes inevitable; and in the means which he had taken, through sacred and secular truth harmoniously united, to give India a new future. A far-seeing demand for pure English and vernacular literature, beginning with the 'Bible, the whole Bible, the unmutilated Bible, and nothing but the Bible', for those whom both state and church were educating. Dr Duff now came to the practical object of his address: the duty of every Christian man, woman and child in Great Britain:

> Look at men's acts and not at their words . . . For rest assured, that people would get weary of the sound of the demand 'Give, give', that is eternally reiterated in their ears, when those who make it so seldom give, or, what is the same thing, give in such scanty dribblets that it seems a mockery of their own expostulations – and of the sound of the command 'Go, go', when those who make it, are themselves so seldom found willing to go!
>
> How, then, is the remedy to be effected? Not, believe me, by periodical showers of words, however copious, which fall 'like snowflakes in the river – a moment white, then gone for ever'. No; but by thousands of deeds that shall cause the very scoffer to wonder, even if he should wonder and perish – deeds that shall enkindle into a blaze the smouldering embers of Christian love – deeds that shall revive the days of primitive devotedness, when men, valiant for the truth, despised earthly riches, and conquered through sufferings, not counting their lives dear unto the death.

We must not lose sight of Alexander's plan in the West. It was to inform his countrymen on India in order to obtain funds as ammunition for his battle in the East to Christianize the Indians by the use of the English language in educating the people in European science and literature. For the very reasons that he had already expressed to his audience relating to the unpopular image of 'Give, give' and 'Go, go', he would give them a mental picture of India, of lasting impression, which would strike at the heart of all who heard it. In this way, the listener would mentally link his request for mission funds to the more graphic picture in their minds. He then proceeded to inform his audience about India. Speaking first of its geo-graphical variety and then of the beliefs of its inhabitants:

You often hear India spoken of as if it was one enormous plain, covered with palm trees, and cocoa-nut trees, cotton and silk, sugar, indigo, rice and other tropical products. Now let me tell you that India is a country of infinite diversities. There are indeed plains in India the like of which, in natural resources and multiform associations, are not to be found in the whole world besides. At all events, sure I am with reference to the great plain which is watered by the Ganges, that, on the surface of our globe, you will not find another teeming with such multitudes of human beings, characterized by such varied and inveterate habits, manners and customs. It is a striking fact, that this single plain, or valley of the Ganges as it is called, contains twice as many inhabitants as to be found in the whole of North and South America. In addition to its plains, India has also the highest mountains in the world. In southern India towards Cape Comorin, and to the west along the declivities of the hills of Malabar, you have them densely covered by immense primeval forests up to the summits. In the north-east towards the Himalayan range, you see the mountains magnificently clothed in a like manner to the summits, with gigantic rhododendrons and other exotic flowers and flowering trees, interposed through many of the woods and diffusing a brilliant radiance over them, as if they glowed with roseate and purple hues of an orient morn, or bathed amid the illusive play of a thousand rainbows.

If you go to the north-west of India, across the river Indus, to that long range of hills stretching southwards from Afghanistan to the sea, and now constituting our boundary, you may look in vain for a tree there, you look in vain for a shrub there, you look in vain for a weed or a particle of soil there; the whole range seems as though it had been subjected to one grand conflagration which has burnt up alike, trees, shrubs, weeds and soil. You have the extensive flats of alluvial deposit in Bengal and a soil of inexhaustible fertility. One finds regions impregnated with, or strewn with salt as like a glittering mantel of hoar-frost, or regions of parched and burning sand; just as barren as the deserts of Africa.

The greatest part of the inhabitants of India consist of Hindoos, or followers of the Brahmanical system. They number upwards of one hundred and twenty millions and the variations are endless; in fact it would take whole days to go over them. You look at the upper classes of society and there you have thousands of men that are self-complacently wrapped up in an all pervading sense of their own superior dignity. Their genealogies, they can trace back through millions of years to one or other of the gods. They have immense masses of literature, science, philosophy and theology of their own, such as they are, and they are very subtle, very acute and very profound in their own way. Their paramount desire is, not only to rise up into the grandeur of conception, but into the actual feeling of self-identification that shall enable them to exclaim, 'I am a Brahma' the self existent, and whole existent, the universal whole and the absolute one.

Next look at the great multitudes and you will find them given up to idolatries and superstitutions without end, without number and without name. When they count their gods, it is not by units or by myriads, but by millions. Gods in whose characters and actions, all human vices and crimes will be found in a superhuman degree, and the abomination connected with their worship; who can describe, who can conceive?

He went on to outline the beliefs of the Khonds, a recently-discovered tribal people who lived in the hills west of Bengal. They were believed to offer four to five hundred child sacrifices every year to propitiate the Earth Goddess. After giving his audience graphic if not complete details of what happened on such occasions ('. . . their riot and orgies far exceed anything which it is possible to expose before a Christian audience . . .'), Alexander concluded:

These sacrifices go on to the present day despite the laudable efforts of the government to check them. As we are gathered here in this hall, preparations, or the very act itself could be being carried out. Such then is this vast country of India, teeming with such myriads of human beings, which has now become a province of the British Empire. Allusion has been made to the conquest of this great country. There is not, in the whole history of the world, anything to parallel it.

It was announced to the Assembly committee held a few weeks after, that £700 had been sent as a result of that meeting.

After again visiting some of the presbyteries in the south of Scotland, Alexander began his preparations for returning to India. But he was premature. His general health was suffering so greatly that he was detained, and was even forbidden to attend the General Assembly of 1838, by his medical adviser, Dr Macwhirter, who had been for years physician to the Countess of Loudoun, wife of the Marquis of Hastings, Governor-General of India. Dr Macwhirter, when in Calcutta, had the reputation of being an exceedingly skilful physician, while he was one of the most gentle and amiable of men. After full personal inspection and all manner of inquiries, the doctor lifted up his hands in astonishment, expressing the utmost surprise that, with a body so weakened by general as well as special disease, and so exhausted by the prodigious labours undergone, Alexander had been able to persevere, though at the same time he had done so, unconsciously to himself, not only at the risk of permanent injury but of premature death. Said Dr Macwhirter:

> You are not at all in a fit state to return to India. You must have months of perfect quiet under proper medical treatment with a view to recruiting. If you can really submit to this, since you are still but young in years and evidently have a singularly wiry and iron constitution, my medical judgment is that, after a reasonable time you will be so far recruited as to warrant you to return. My earnest advice to you, therefore, is at once to return to your quiet Highland home, where by correspondence I can perfectly regulate, from day to day if need be, your regimen and medical treatment; there you will have the tender, nursing care of the members of your family about you.

Thus most of the autumn, and a considerable part of the winter of 1838–39, was spent at Edradour.

The Duff's had now yet another daughter in addition to their first-born son, Alexander Groves, and their second child, named Anne, after herself. Mrs Duff was again pregnant.

While at Edradour, Alexander concentrated on writing and had many visitors. He frequently walked with his wife and children and probably for the first time began to realize the true pleasures of family love and life. He fished in the river Tummel and visited many local friends. He frequently preached in the church at Moulin, both in the Gaelic and English, but he was among his own people and found the experience both relaxing and indeed therapeutic.

Besides ever caring and nursing her husband, Anne had another problem which troubled her greatly. She knew that they would certainly return to India in 1839 and that her baby would be due early November 1838. It would mean parting with her children as there was no place for them in the climate and dangers of India. She realized that her baby, yet to be born, would not have reached the age of one year when she would be separated from it. Anne was paying, and would continue to pay, a high price for her brief period of happiness at Edradour.

Alexander, even at this time, had made arrangements for passage to India at the end of 1839. The young Queen Victoria was now on the throne and it therefore may have been significant that Alexander should turn his thoughts to the women of India. Female education in India had now to be considered most carefully and opportunities given to them if he wished to pursue his policy of rule for all under one God. Female education was already in progress, but on a very limited scale. He decided to examine the facts and take what action he could while still in the West.

The education of the women of India was begun by young ladies of Eurasian extraction, in Calcutta, under the Baptist missionaries as early as 1819. It applied to the higher caste girls only and Alexander decided that, as for the young men, he would wish to provide for all classes. In 1837, a Bombay officer, Major Jameson, began in Scotland 'The Ladies' Society for Female Education in the East' and Alexander thought it would be worth while to make inquiries. He made a visit to Penicuik, a small paper-making town some six miles from Edinburgh where the movement started. He addressed a meeting of the society and enlightened them of the situation in India and gave them encouragement for greater effort. He promised that he would do all he could to raise money for their noble cause, and this he did.

The young males of India were being taught English and were therefore starting to think in English. The existing systems in India were male dominated by their caste laws, and the males were now not only condemning the old systems, but trying to adopt a Christian-like approach to their way of life. A new way of life would give the women of India an equal opportunity in society like the Western women, but, like all women, they would have to fight for their case. For this reason alone, it was necessary to introduce the teaching of English and the Christian way of life to women of all classes in India.

Alexander set to work and made appeals in Scotland to help the cause of educating women in India, which he envisaged should be initially centred in Calcutta. He wanted a new College of Education for Girls. As soon as his new cause was announced, there came adequate proof of his popularity and powers of persuasion. A lady from London gave £500, the Misses MacIntosh of Raigmore House, Inverness, whose father had founded one of the six great commercial and banking houses in Calcutta, raised £1,000. These two donations alone paid for the site of the new ladies' college in Cornwallis Square, Calcutta, the cost of which was £1,600. Many other donations followed and the college was most fully equipped.

At this time, the income of the United Kingdom was estimated at five hundred and fourteen million pounds sterling, and of this, only a total of three hundred thousand pounds sterling was allocated to the world missions. This was but a fraction required for such a task, when one considers that the greatest part of the United Kingdom income came from the countries of the Empire, and India in particular. But even so, the money allocated for the missions did not come from the Government of the United Kingdom. It came from the churches themselves, since the original charter given to the East India Company by Queen Elizabeth in 1600 included a condition that the Company should in no way interfere with the religion of the country. This condition was again confirmed by Queen Victoria. The natives could be educated but not Christianized, but who else could, or would, educate the natives but the dedicated missionaries? Alexander and his fellow missionaries had no source for income other than from their Christian countrymen and women.

In 1839 the revenue of the Church of Scotland for missionary work of all kinds was fourteen times greater than it had been in 1834, so that Dr Chalmers exclaimed: 'We are planting schools, we are multiplying chapels, we are sending forth missionaries to distant parts of the world, we have purified the discipline, we are extending the Church and rallying our population around its venerable standard.'

So greatly had the Bengal Mission been extended under Mackay and Ewart, working out Dr Duff's system with his careful and constant support from home, that they were not satisfied with the mere addition of a third colleague in the person of Mr Macdonald. The three of them clamoured for a fourth to help them to overtake the special field in which no other mission had then followed them. To their demands, Alexander sent a letter to Ewart which said, in part:

. . . In December, my own health having much improved, I resolved to visit Edinburgh – *first*, to consult in person with my medical advisers as to my fitness for immediately returning to Calcutta; and *second*, in the event of that not being allowed, to enforce the appointment of another. As to the first point – though satisfied with the progress made on the whole, it was deemed utterly inadvisable to attempt to return till next summer. But, if the Lord will, I have now the certain prospect of turning my face eastward in June or July next. Meanwhile, I have laboured incessantly in pressing the second point, the immediate appointment of another. And I am sure you will rejoice to learn that yesterday, at a meeting of the general committee, not only was it resolved to appoint one, but the individual was actually nominated – and he will lose no time in setting sail to join you. The new colleague is Mr Thomas Smith, lately licensed to preach the gospel – one who has long pondered the subject of personal engagement in the missionary cause, though young in years. He has a fine missionary spirit, and in mathematics and natural philosophy was one of the most distinguished students of the session in Edinburgh. He will at once, therefore, be able to lend you effective aid, by taking up any of your own or Mr Mackay's departments in the scientific part of the course. He will thus relieve you of some of the most onerous duties that have devolved on you in consequence of Mr Mackay's lamented illness. We have given Mr Smith to understand that he may be called on by you to take up the very subjects which constituted Mr Mackay's share of instruction in the Institution. And I am happy to say that he will be prepared to, if deemed proper by you, to do so cheerfully.

. . . Now, my dear Ewart, there is at my disposal something above £1,000 in all. Do then send me by the first steamer a complete list of all your desiderata as to books, philosophical apparatus, etc., and I shall endeavour to have all supplied. Do not miss a steamer in sending me as complete a list as you can furnish, that it may reach in time to enable me to avail myself of it before returning to join you. . . .

The General Assembly of 1839 brought with it, for Dr Duff, the solemn but not sad duty of saying farewell to the country and the Church. As a member for his native presbytery of Dunkeld he spoke again, but with fresh power and new facts, 'on the subject of your great missionary enterprise'. Alexander would soon be returning to his beloved Calcutta where, in 1830, he stood as the first and only missionary of the Church of Scotland, and in which now there were eight.

He had served his Calcutta College well during his visit home and had provided much sorely needed finance from his appeals. He, himself, provided a sum which many to whom he had been blessed offered him in vain as a personal gift for his family. All that he would consent to, of a personal nature, was the publication of his portrait, painted by William Cowen, and engraved, in mezzotint by S. W. Reynolds. The original went to Calcutta.

The Duffs' fourth child had been born on 9 November, 1838, a boy named William Pirie, the second Christian name being after Alderman Pirie, their kind host and dear friend who had looked after them in London before their first departure to India. Alderman Pirie later became Lord Mayor of London and the first chairman of the Peninsular and Orient Steamship Company.

In the summer of 1839, Alexander and his wife made arrangements for their departure from Edradour. He preached his farewell sermon to his own people, in the Moulin parish kirk of his childhood, from the text, 'Finally, brethren, farewell.' The services, in both the Gaelic and English, lasted for five hours, and the crowded audiences were in tears. On the next day he met them again, and, after a short address, shook hands with the minister in the name of all the country people, who had flocked in from valleys and hillsides of Atholl. Then followed preparing for the living martyrdom of Indian exile, the parting of mother and father from their four children, the youngest of which was their son of a few months old, whose birth had been a source of new strength and joy to Alexander at the time of his depression.

The family moved to Bilston, by Loanhead, near Edinburgh,

until such time as they would sail for India. Alexander had heard of the widow of a clergyman of the Church of Scotland who had opened a boarding-house in Edinburgh for the children of parents who, like the Duffs, worked in India. The cost of caring for the four children was £100 per annum, a quarter of Alexander's income. The widow lady had been greatly fascinated by his appeals on behalf of India and said in substance;

> I shall esteem it a favour to have your children. The obligation is mine. I have the house, a noble one in Royal Terrace, Edinburgh. I have already the children of two distinguished medical officers serving in India, some ten in number. Your youngsters will add little to my outlay, and I will esteem it a privilege to look after yours as my contribution to the cause of missions.

The children's principal guardian, whilst their parents were in India, was Dr Brunton, Professor of Hebrew in the University of Edinburgh, at whose house the Duffs were now staying. Dr Brunton lived in the university itself, and had this small country retreat at Bilston. Dr Brunton stayed with his niece, Miss Stevenson, who was devoted to the children and became more than a mother to them. The children were taken to Greenside Church on Sundays, where the minister, Dr Glover, also took a kind interest in them.

At this stage it would be advantageous to follow the early years of the children, in order to set the scene for future events.

The happiness of the little band of four was tragically broken when Anne (or little Annie as she was called by her parents) died, in spite of the kind and unwearied attention of Dr Abercrombie (later Sir William Gull of Scotland). Later in 1844, Dr Abercrombie, together with Mr J. C. Kerr, of the then Edinburgh and Glasgow Bank, and Mr Charles Chalmers, brother of the illustrious Thomas, made arrangements for the youngest of the family, Alexander Groves, to enter Merchiston Castle Academy in Edinburgh. This matter was settled before his father had an opportunity of expressing an opinion; and being in Calcutta, he judged he could not go wrong when guided by such men.

In October, 1845, a crisis occurred in the affairs of the widow who took care of the children. The same kind gentlemen then arranged to send the youngest boy, William Pirie, to the same academy as his brother. The boy was almost seven years old. William later attended Edinburgh Academy, thence to university and followed his father into the church.

Alexander Pirie became a surgeon in the Army Medical Service. He was to serve in India and was the only officer to survive the mutiny at Meerut, but later died of the diseases with which he worked. Margaret, the surviving daughter, married Dr P. H. Watson and they both nursed and cared for Alexander in his latter days. But what of the parents? What domestic life did they have? Can we appreciate the sorrow of them losing two of their children, and not being present at her passing? Of the brave son they hardly knew? What would be the feelings of a mother, soon to be separated from her eleven-month-old baby, who she would not again see for eleven years? What did Anne and Alexander mean to each other?

Next to the life hid with Christ in God, Alexander found his solace and his inspiration in his wife. From her quiet but unresting devotion to him, and his excessive reticence regarding his most sacred domestic feelings, many failed to appreciate the perfection of her service not merely to her husband but to the cause for which he sacrificed his whole self. But something of what Anne meant to Alexander was revealed after her death, as we shall see.

9

Second Journey to India

The Overland Route, a phrase which was to cease to have any but a historical meaning after the opening of the Suez Canal in 1869, had just been made a fact when, in the autumn of 1839, Dr and Mrs Duff went out to India for the second time. On the ordinary roll of English martyrs of science the name of Thomas Waghorn is not to be found. It was left to the French to do justice to the memory of a man who, amid obstruction, obloquy and injustice ending in a pauper's death, first opened the British Overland Route to India in 1830. When M. Ferdinand de Lesseps created the consequent of that by cutting the canal between the Red Sea and the Mediterranean in 1870, his first act was to erect, at the Red Sea entrance, a colossal bust of Waghorn on a marble pedestal, with a bas-relief of the explorer on a camel surveying the desert, and this inscription: 'La Compagnie Universelle du Canal Maritime de Suez au Lieutenant Waghorn'.

In 1830, the former midshipman of the navy, who had become a Bengal pilot, sailed down the Red Sea in an open boat with despatches from Lord Ellenborough to Sir John Malcolm. He took four months and twenty-one days to make the journey from London to Bombay. All the authorities, except Lord William Bentinck scouted him as a monomaniac; yet he beat the Cape ships of the time, and his voyage was pronounced 'extraordinarily rapid'. For ten years thereafter he wasted his life and his means of living in attempting to convince the 'Company', which snubbed the Governor-General for sending the *Hugh Lindsay* steamer to Suez in a month; and to conciliate the king's government, which sent Colonel Chesney to discover a short way by the Euphrates and the Persian Gulf. The bluff English sailor triumphed, but only to see all the fruits of his victory snatched by the government which had scorned him.

At last, for shame, the government threw him a miserable pension which was at once seized by his creditors. Thomas Waghorn died in the misery of debt, while the Peninsular and Oriental Company sent its first steamers, in 1843, along the path he had persistently tracked out. To complete the scandal, less than seven years later his aged sisters were driven to ask the public for support, while the government which had so ruined their brother raised a revenue of fifty millions sterling a year from India and paid nearly half a million in subsidies for the postal traffic on his overland route.

When the Duffs resolved to return to India by what was, in 1839, still Waghorn's Overland Route, Alexander knew the story of the heroic pioneer so far, and he resolved to run the risk. He had been saddened that the eager life of Waghorn had been made a miserable tragedy by an ignorant country and an ungrateful government. Hotels in Egypt, swift horse vans instead of camels in the desert, and a steamer with cabin accommodation for twelve passengers, were the marvellous facilities provided. The journey between London and Bombay of nearly five months in 1830 had been reduced to a month and a half by 1839. Alexander had to find his way first to Bombay, at the request both of Dr Wilson and the Kirk's committee, that he might comfort and counsel his colleagues there.

His most rapid course thus lay from Harwich to Antwerp and Brussels, then south by Paris to Marseilles, and thence by steamer to Syra, there to join the mail steamer from Constantinople to Alexandria. They arrived at Antwerp on schedule and without mishap. Alexander observed the traces of the wealth created by the flow of the trade from India along the earliest overland route; by Solomon's cities in the desert, the Danube and the Rhine to the Dutch East India Company's docks. They travelled south to Chalons-sur-Saone. As they were driven slowly through the wine country, Alexander asked if they could stop a short while so that he could see the vines and the people who grew them. He later wrote:

In these countries, mantled with vineyards, one cannot help learning the true intent and use of the vine in the scheme of Providence. In our own land wine has become so exclusively a mere luxury, or, what is worse, by a species of manufacture, an intoxicating beverage, that many have wondered how the Bible so often speaks of wine in conjunction with corn and other such staple supports of animal life! Now, in passing through the vineyards in the east of France, one must at once perceive that the vine greatly flourishes on slopes and heights where the soil is too poor and gravelly to maintain either corn for food or pasturage for cattle. But what is the providential design in rendering this soil – favoured by a genial atmosphere – so productive of the vine, if its fruit become solely either an article of luxury or an instrument of vice? The answer is, that Providence had no such design. Look at the peasant at his meals in the vine-bearing districts! Instead of milk, he has before him a basin of pure unadulterated 'blood of the grape'. In this, its native and original state, it is a plain, simple and wholesome liquid, which at every repast becomes to the husbandman what milk is to the shepherd – not a luxury but a necessary, not an intoxicating but a nutritive beverage.

The sail from Chalons down the Saone took the travellers into the heart of scenery like their own Scotland, but with a climate more congenial to people used to living in India than the gloom and the grey of the cold north. They joined the rapid Rhone and were swept on two hundred miles in twelve hours to papal Avignon, thence to Marseilles.

The Marseilles steamer then called at Malta, passed within a hundred yards of the precipitous headland of Cape Matapan, and dropped anchor at Syra, the port of Europe which is nearest to India. The filth and the vice of a Levantine albeit Greek centre constrasted painfully with the glories of Homeric and even later days. The steamer from Constantinople had Colonel Hodges, the new British Consul-General for Egypt, on board, and also the Rev Mr Grimshaw, rector of Bedford, and known in his day as the author of a life of Cowper the poet.

On reaching Alexandria they found that the last act of the departing Consul-General, Colonel Campbell, would be to lay the foundation stone of the first English church of St Mark, which was to adorn one corner of the great square. Alexander learned that the ceremony was to be of a purely civil character, in this Islamic city, with its memories of Clement, of Origen and Athanasius, and sought an explanation of the anomaly. Colonel Campbell was a great favourite with the enlightened Muhammad Ali, the irresponsible ruler of Egypt. Being religiously disposed, the Consul-General had felt the need of a Protestant place of worship in the city like that of Alexandria, which was daily becoming a greater thoroughfare between West and East than it had been since the time of its founder. The colonel had repeatedly therefore asked his friend the Pasha for a piece of ground, outside the walls of Alexandria, on which a church might be erected.

Muhammad Ali frankly declared that personally he had no prejudice on the subject, but the religious heads of Islam at Constantinople would resist the attempt. However, he said, with a smile:

> Colonel Campbell, you and I have always been fast friends. You know that in the East the custom is for a ruler to make his friend a present of a piece of land, commonly called 'Jagheer', to be in perpetuity his own property, I will give you a small portion of the space occupied by the great square in Alexandria, very near its centre. It is my parting gift to you, only you must ask me no question as to what use you may make of it, as that may involve me in official trouble. But I tell you plainly, you may use it for whatever purpose you think proper.

Muhammad Ali went further. He could not himself be present, but he sent his chief officers and his bodyguard to honour his friend on the occasion of laying the foundation stone of the new church. How could a religious service be attempted in such circumstances? It was clear that in Eastern eyes the dedication of a site for the worship of God without the recognition of his presence would be a scandal or a cause of suspicion. Never or before had the Egypt of Fatimite caliphs and Turkish pashas heard publicly read in its greatest place Solomon's dedication of the first temple and the prayer of a Protestant minister from the West. On 14 December, 1839, Dr Alexander Duff of the Church of Scotland performed the religious part of the ceremony. In two interviews with Muhammad Ali thereafter, Alexander pressed upon the Pasha the importance, for industrial as well as for other reasons, of attracting the Jews back to Palestine, for the Pasha was at that time master of that part of Syria.

By *dahabieh* up the Mahmoodieh canal, excavated in 1820 by cruelly forced labour, and slowly up the Hooghly-like Nile of the delta, Cairo was reached, only to find that there were sixty passengers to fill the twelve berths of the small steamer to Bombay. This gave Duff a whole month, in which he not only visited the pyramids of Geezeh and Sakkara, and explored Memphis from the ancient cemetery, of which Sir G. Wilkinson's Arabs were busily laying bare the mummy pits, but carefully studied the condition of the unhappy fellaheen of Egypt, and afterwards went to Mount Sinai.

Alexander, drawing on his experience of British administration in Bengal, later wrote in the *Calcutta Christian Observer* of 1840, that the hope of a revival of Egypt under the Pasha was a delusion:

> That the Pasha is one of the most extraordinary men of his age – a man of uncommon talent and energy of character; a man, too, capable of being courteous and affable in the extreme – is universally conceded. But that he is, in any sense, the real friend or regenerator of Egypt, is belied by every one of his actions. Self, self, self, is with him the all in all. Personal fame, personal power, and personal aggrandizement, circumscribe the entire horizon of his policy. On the details of his well-known history it is needless to dwell. Born of humble parentage at Cavallo in Albania, in 1769, he for some time acted as an assistant collector of taxes, and afterwards as a tobacco merchant. Having been twice admitted to his immediate presence, it wonderfully struck us that his whole appearance still pointed very significantly to the lowliness of his origin. Of middle stature, inclined to corpulency rather than corpulent, he exhibited in his countenance nought of real greatness, dignity, or command. Indeed, the entire expression of it was decidedly of a sharp, harsh and vulgar cast; its chief redeeming quality being its venerable beard. But those eyes – were they not striking? Yea, verily; such a pair of flashing eyes we never saw. It seemed as if the possessor could penetrate through one's bodily frame, and at a single glance read the most secret thoughts and intents of the heart. Still it was not the piercing glance of a profound intelligence which mainly lightened through these eyes: it was rather the vivid flash of a tiger-like ferocity. Hence, doubtless, his favourite oath, when bent on some deed of more than ordinary horror, 'By my eyes!'. When he spoke, his voice had a peculiar shrillness which made one feel uneasy; and when he smiled, his very smile had somewhat in it of a savage grin.

Alexander showed in detail, in agriculture, in manufactures, in public works, in commerce, in military discipline, and in the aggravated horrors of the slave trade, that all the changes amounted to neither a reform nor a regeneration, but to the oriental art of squeezing the peasantry that the ruler might have a full treasury and a ruthless army. The solitary printing-press and polytechnic school were 'in point of fact, as much the mere instrument of an all-absorbing despotism as the drill ground, the cannon foundry or the powder mill'. While it was true that Muhammad Ali and his successors were capable of acts of generosity, it was an apt comment on their dynasty that 'the traveller sees with astonishment the richness of the harvests contrasted with the wretched state of the villages. If there is no country more abundant in its territorial productions, there is none, perhaps, whose inhabitants on the whole are more miserable.'

For the expedition from Cairo to the peninsula of Sinai a party of five Englishmen offered to join Duff. At Alexandria he had engaged an assistant at the British Consulate who was master of popular Arabic. The sheikh of the tribes of the Sinai range, who happened to be in Cairo, was engaged as guide of the caravan. Each of the travellers had three camels, for self, for tent and for provisions. One of the travellers was a Madras civilian, whose ideas of comfort in the desert proved to be those of the most luxurious 'nawab' that Thackery ever satirized. The route was the most southerly, from old Memphis to Jebel Attaka, believed by the scholars of that day to have been the line of the Exodus. Before sunrise on the morning after the first encampment in the desert, when all were up for a frugal breakfast and an early start, the nawab was heard shouting for his gridiron, and then for chops. He was pacified with difficulty, but only to call an early halt for 'tiffin' or luncheon in the blazing sun. Next day a sandstorm threatened to engulf the whole party and the unhappy gourmand demanded to be led back to the joys of the Waghorn hotel in Cairo. He was forced to proceed, but his troubles were not at an end. On the following morning, after the misery of the sand, he wanted their precious water for a bath, the colour of which, incidentally, was now the colour of London beer. The Arab guide eyed him from head to foot in astonishment, and picking up a handful of sand, said with great emphasis, 'That, sir, is the water of the desert!' The result was that, from Suez, Duff alone went on to Sinai, while his companions returned to Cairo.

The silence of the desert of Sinai for the next fortnight proved a time of refreshing to the spirit of the traveller, as passed from the toils of the West to the labours about to be renewed in India. He rode day by day along the track of the children of Israel, noting the wells, the palm trees, the acacias, the camel tracks and the desert landscape. As he left the Red Sea for the great plain at the foot of the Mount of the Law, he followed the eastern route and returned by the south-western, that he might cover as much ground as possible. It was evening when he came to the outer border of the great platform of the wilderness of sandy rock. The rays of the setting sun fell slantingly on the stupendous masses of grey granite which formed the Sinai range, as it stretched for forty or fifty miles along the sea and rose to a height of between eight and nine thousand feet. To Alexander's imagination the sight was that of a mighty fortress on fire, of blazing battlements and flashing towers. Next day at sunrise, while the ground was still bound by frost, the disintegrated granite seemed a mass of orient pearl and gold, and the plain looked as if strewed with the manna from heaven, which melted away as the sun rose in the sky.

The broad valley running along the north side, opposite the eastern portion of the Sinai range, was the Wady es-Sheikh. The wady ran eastwards for some distance, then turning to the south it entered the centre of the range, and proceeded westwards to the foot of Jebel Musa, the traditional Mount Sinai. Alexander considered that this was without doubt the route that would be pursued by any great caravan or large company of travellers, and more particularly by such a host as that of Israel. When the summit of the pass was reached, a lofty, perpendicular, conical-looking mountain suddenly rose up some miles in front. Immediately the guide and his fellow Arab porters dismounted and began to shout, 'Jebel Musa', showing the veneration they had for the mountain. They then entered on a very remarkable gently sloping plain, down to the foot of the mountain, but the surface as smooth as though it had been artificially prepared. Here was a plain quite capable of holding the entire encampment of the Israelites, for their ordinary tentage must have occupied very little space, somewhat like that of the Arabs in modern times.

Proceeding onwards, the party reached the base of a high peak. Here the first thing that astonished him was the literal truth of the scripture passage which spoke of the mountain that might be touched and, when the law was given with such awful solemnity from its summit, declares how means were used to prevent the people from touching it. Now when he saw Mount Sinai itself, the literal truth of the whole description flashed upon him.

A mile or two up the wady, on the east side of the mountain, was the celebrated convent, Justinian's St Catherine. The stately building was an irregular fortress, without any apparent entrance. For the sake of protection from the Arabs it was surrounded by a massive wall, forty feet high. In the centre of the eastern wall was a cupola, with a windlass inside; the ordinary rule was, when strangers appeared there, to let down a bag to receive any communication from parties known to the superior, who might accredit their character and position. Duff and his companions had received permission for six people to visit the monastery. But here was only one traveller, so the superior demanded an explanation from the sheikh guide. After that Alexander was hoisted into the convent, and was installed as a guest in all that was left of the great episcopal city of Paran. He was able to speak to his hosts in Greek and Hindustani. Next day Alexander climbed Mount Sinai. The impetuous missionary mounted upwards with a speed which alarmed his Arab guide and when the summit was reached, his heart was filled with gratitude to God for the favour with which He had visited him. Alexander read aloud, amid the awful silence of the mount, the Ten Commandments.

In early February, 1840, the little steamer entered the harbour of Bombay and Dr Wilson was waiting to receive Dr and Mrs Duff. This was the first meeting of the two missionaries of the Church of Scotland, Dr Wilson from the Scottish Borders and Edinburgh University, and Dr Duff from the Grampians and St Andrews University. They were both young men, Wilson was thirty-six and Duff was nearly thirty-four years of age. Like a bracing wind from the north, Alexander brought with him all the news of national and ecclesiastical affairs in Scotland, of the widening gap in the Church, of the work of Chalmers and other leaders, of the missionary spirit of presbyteries and congregations all over Scotland, soon to be checked for a time by internal disruption, but only to burst forth in home and colonial and educational movements as well as in foreign missions, along the lines marked out, as Dr Chalmers had said, by Duff himself.

This was Alexander and his wife's first visit to Bombay and they spared a little time to visit the city. The entrance to the spacious inlet which formed the harbour of Bombay was from the south, presenting to the eye a panoramic view that was both imposing from its vast extent and varied magnificence.

On the left was the long, flat, narrow but pleasant island of Calabak, with a lighthouse at its southern end, and its barracks for European troops in the centre. There were houses and gardens belonging to British residents. The island was formerly separated by a small shallow creek but was now united by a substantial stone causeway. The main extensive island of Bombay stretched north. Bombay was the oldest British possession in India; having been ceded by the Portuguese to the English in 1661 as the dower of Catherine, consort of Charles II, and transferred by the Crown in 1668 to the East India Company, on an annual rent of ten pounds.

The massive battlements of the fort lined the eastern shore facing the anchorage. The interior of the fort was over-crowded with private and public edifices, whose plain style of architecture and dark high tile roofs formed a perfect contrast to the corresponding metropolitan buildings, with their domes, flat balustraded roofs, their marble colonnades and green verandahs. Among the dense and dingy piles of masonry, the two most conspicuous were the gothic-looking tower of the English Cathedral and the spire of the Scottish Church. The esplanade formed a parade ground for the military and was the favourite resort of the British inhabitants for the oriental exercise of 'taking a drive'. Beyond was the native town almost buried in a forest of palm trees. To the south-west of the native town, the island shot out into a somewhat rocky promontory called Malabar Hill, picturesquely wooded and studded with neat bungalow cottages. To the north and east were finely cultivated rice fields and many county seats and gardens of the wealthy Indians and Europeans. Altogether the view from the entrance to the harbour of Bombay was one of some extent and magnificence.

The Duffs left Bombay and set sail for Calcutta, arriving at the Pilot Ground of the Hooghly river at almost the same time of the season as they arrived on their first visit. Again a rotary storm seemed to defy their advance. Before midnight the cyclone burst upon the ship with savage fury. For twelve hours the whirlwind raged with hideous violence and the captain had prepared to cut down the mast. The storm finally abated and they duly arrived in Calcutta harbour.

10

Second Term in India

Lord Auckland had been Governor-General for four years when, for the second time, the Duffs landed at Calcutta. His appointment to the most responsible office under the British Crown was felt, forty years later, to have been one of the most scandalous instances of the sacrifice of the good of the people of India and of the peace of the Empire to the intrigues and the self-seeking of political parties.

William Eden, younger son of a Durham baronet, and a barrister who entered political life, was created Baron Auckland for negotiating a treaty of commerce with France. His successor rendered services to the Whig party of a less evident kind, and in 1830 Lord Grey gave him a seat in the Cabinet. When sickness sent Lord William Bentinck home after an administration of nearly eight years, the Court of Directors of the East India Company would not allow the most brilliant servant they had had since Warren Hastings to fill the seat which he had previously occupied provisionally, because his honesty had been equal to his ability. They were willing to see the Hon. Mountstuart Elphinstone appointed, but he had had enough of office as Governor of Bombay and declined the high honour. On this the Tory ministry selected Lord Heytesbury, who drew the usual allowance for outfit, made the indispensable speech about peace at the Albion, and had taken his passage to Calcutta. But just as, under somewhat similar circumstances, George Canning gave place to Lord Amherst, and died Premier of England, so Lord Auckland was sent out instead of Lord Heytesbury.

The Melbourne ministry took office in April, 1835, with Byron's friend, Sir John Cam Hobhouse, as president of the Board of Control. Refusing their confidence to the Tory Governor-General designate, the Whig ministry, which was to hold office for six and a half years, sent out Lord Auckland to the seat which Bentinck had made more illustrious than ever, and for which Metcalfe and Elphinstone were better fitted than even he. In a word, the British Government had once again jobbed the appointment, and the whole Empire was to suffer the consequence in the military disasters, the financial losses and, greater than both, the political consequences in 1857 of the first Afghan war.

The best thing that George, the second Lord Auckland, did was to take to Calcutta and Simla with him his two clever sisters, one of whom, Emily, in her journals, not to mention her novels, has left us unconsciously the most vivid picture of the Governor-General's weakness of character. It was the Governor-General's vacillation – ending as is generally the case, in weakly following the evil – which brought Alexander Duff into conflict with Lord Auckland. The missionary had set out to return to Bengal, grateful to His Excellency for the interest which he and the Hon. Misses Eden had shown in the Institution during his absence, by frequent visits and occasional prizes. Up to the disasters of 1842, Lord Auckland – who had been made an earl in reply to the opposition of the Court of Directors of the East India Company – was personally respected for his amiability. His advisers liked a Governor-General whom they could lead and the public appreciated the social attractions of his court. But a question of great importance to the people had come down to him.

Lord William Bentinck's government had, in 1835, decreed that English should be the language of the higher public instruction, finally, as it seemed. Still the formal approval of the Court of Directors had not been communicated. Not only was Lord Bentinck out of office, but Dr Duff was far away, and of their coadjutors, Metcalfe was in Agra, while Macaulay and Trevelyan were soon to go. The defeated orientalists saw their opportunity with the new and weak Governor-General. They resolved to get rid of the reform of March, 1835, by a side-blow. Mr Thoby Prinsep and the Bengal Asiatic Society led the assault. Mr Colvin, the private secretary, was neutralised or so far talked over as to seem to consent to the undoing of that which he had formerly urged. On 24 November, 1839, Lord Auckland signed, at Delhi, a minute which is remarkable among Indian state papers for its bad style and worse reasoning. The contrast to Macaulay's and Duff's was painful. The minute professed to be a compromise of a dispute in which there could be no concessions by what was true to what the government officially had allowed to be false and therefore unworthy of being propagated by the public funds.

The evil which the minute had secretly attempted to do was

twofold. It reversed the decree of Lord Bentinck by restoring the stipends paid to Indians to learn Sanskrit and Arabic books, which their own learned men neglected where they did not teach them far more effectually in the indigenous colleges. Thus error was again endowed, while true oriental research was hindered. The minute finally shelved the plan for improvement of vernacular schools and teachers which Lord Bentinck had appointed the Baptist missionary Mr Adam to submit. Lord Auckland became the victim of what afterwards was mocked by his successors as the filtration theory – the belief that if only the higher classes are educated with the public money, the millions of the people who contribute that money may be left in ignorance till the knowledge given to their oppressors filters down to them. That continued to be the fact, if not the theory of the government in Bengal, at least, for the thirty years from Lord Auckland's minute to the time when Sir George Campbell was made Lieutenant-Governor of the province.

Alexander did well to be angry, for his experience and his foresight anticipated such a mistake. Lord Auckland thus became not only the foe of a righteous policy beyond the frontier but the reactionary enemy of the people of India. In the first of three letters on the subject, Alexander began with Wordsworth's lines:

> Oh! for the coming of that glorious time
> When, prizing knowledge as her noblest wealth
> And best protection, this imperial realm.
> While she exacts allegiance, shall admit
> An obligation on her part to *teach*
> Them who are born to serve her and obey;
> Binding herself by statute to secure
> For *all* the children whom her soil maintains,
> The rudiments of letters; and to inform
> The mind with moral and religious truth.

He then went on to suggest to the Governor-General that however great a statesman he might be, that did not necessarily qualify him as an expert on education. He concluded:

> Here are two systems of education, directly opposed
> to each other, and absolutely contradictory in their entire

substance, scope and ends. Reviewing these two systems, Lord Bentinck, with the straightforward bearing of British manliness and British courage in the spirit which fired the old barons of Runnymede, and with the decisive energy of uncompromising principle, thus pronounced his decision: 'Regardless of the idle clamours of interested partisanship, and fearless of all consequences, let us resolve at once to repudiate altogether what is demonstrably false; let us cleave to and exclusively promote that which is demonstrably beneficial, because demonstrably true.' Reviewing the very same system, my Lord Auckland, with what looks like the tortuous bearing of Machiavellian policy, in the spirit of shrinking timidity which heretofore hath compromised the success of the best laid schemes, and with the Proteus-like facility of temporizing expediency, thus enunciates his contrary verdict: 'Fearful of offending any party, wishing to please all, and anxious to purchase peace at any price, let us, dropping all minor distinctions between old and new, good and bad, right and wrong; let us at once resolve to embrace and patronize both, and both alike. . .'

In a word, 'Let us', says Lord W. Bentinck, 'disendow error and endow only truth'. 'Let us,' replies Lord Auckland, 're-endow error and continue the endowment of truth too.'

Such a decision could not be justified. Alexander's warnings might be dismissed as fanatical or impertinent, but Lord Auckland should remember his responsibility before God, and the religious public in Great Britain. Their influence had successfully stopped the prohibition against the free import of Bibles, and accelerated and ensured the abolition of suttee.

And rest assured my lord, that as certainly as the rising sun chases away the darkness of night, so certainly will the righteous agitation of this same British public eventually wipe away, as a blot and disgrace, from our national statue book, that fatal act, by which your lordship has restored the Government patronage and support to the shrines and sanctuaries of Hindoo and Muhammadan learning with all their idolatrous, pantheistic and anti-christian errors!

When the Duffs landed in Calcutta to begin the second period of work in India, even they were astonished at the outward signs of progress which ten years of English education had brought about. No one could doubt that, in the great cities and intellectual centres at least, as in Italy of the first three centuries, the Renaissance was a fact. Even on the way from the ship to his own college building and principal's or senior missionary's residence, which Alexander had yet to see, he noticed several pieces of evidence which he reported in his own graphic style to Dr Brunton.

The first object that caught his eye on landing was a sign-board on which were marked in large characters the words, 'Ram Lochun Sen & Co., Surgeons and Druggists'. Not six years had passed since the pseudo-orientalists had declared that no Hindu would be found to study even the rudiments of the healing art through anatomy. But here, scattered over the native town, were the shops of the earlier sets of duly educated practitioners and apothecaries who had began to find in medicine a fortune long before they were attracted to the rewards of going to law.

> When I gazed at the humble, yet significant, type and visible symbol before me of so triumphant a conquest over one of the most inveterate of Hindoo prejudices – a conquest issuing in such beneficial practical results – how could I help rejoicing in spirit at the reflection that, under Divine providence, the singular success of your Institution was overruled as one of the main instruments of achieving it? Oh! that a like energy were put forth – an energy like to that which characterized the Divine Physician – for the healing of the spiritual maladies of the millions around us! Holy Spirit! do Thou descend with a Pentecostal effusion of Thy grace. Come from the four winds, O breath, and breathe upon these slain, that they may live. Blessed be God that the better cause is neither wholly neglected, nor without promise.

After passing the Medical College itself, the next novel object which in point of fact happened to attract my attention as I approached Cornwallis Square, was a handsome Christian church, with its gothic tower and buttresses, and contiguous manse or parsonage. And who was the first ordained pastor therof? The Rev Krishna Mohun Banerjea, once a Koolin Brahman of the highest caste; then, through the scheme of Government education, an educated atheist and editor of the *Enquirer* newspaper;

next brought to a saving knowledge of the truth as it is in Jesus, and admitted into the Christian Church by baptism, through the unworthy instrumentality of him who now addresses you; and, last of all, ordained as a minister of the everlasting gospel by the Bishop of Calcutta, and now appointed to discharge the evangelical and pastoral duties of the new Christian temple which was erected for himself! What a train of pleasing reflection was the first view of this edifice calculated to awaken . . .

After passing the new church, which stands out to the eye so pleasing a monument of the incipient progress of Christian influence in this heathen metropolis, I came full in view of the Assembly's new Institution and Mission-house, on the opposite side of Cornwallis Square. Gratifying as some of the preceding spectacles were, this to me was the most gratifying of all. What a change since May, 1830, and how different the thoughts and feelings of the spectator! Then, almost the only thing determined on was, that Calcutta should not be my head-quarters and fixed abode; – now, I saw before me my head-quarters and permanent residence. Then, the precise line of operations to be adopted was not only unknown, but seemed for a while incapable of being discovered, as it stretched away amid the thickening conflict of contending difficulties; – now, there stood before me a visible pledge and token that one grand line of operation had long been ascertained, and cleared of innumerable obstacles, and persevered in with a steadfastness of march which looked most promisingly towards the destined goal. Then, I had no commission, but either to hire a room for educational purposes at a low rent, or to erect a bungalow at a cost not exceeding £30 to £40; – now, there stood before me a plain and substantial, yet elegant structure, which cost £5,000 or £6,000.

So Duff went on, contrasting past and present. He also wrote home about the contribution of his colleagues:

Our missionary brethren, Messrs Mackay, Ewart, Macdonald and Smith, have, in different ways, been labouring up to the full measure of their strength, and some, it is to be feared, beyond their strength. Of the rich and varied endowments and graces which all of these have been privileged to bring to bear upon this great missionary field it is impossible to think, without admiration of the disinterested devotedness wherewith all have been consecrated to the advancement of God's glory; or, rather, without adoring gratitude towards Him who bestowed the willing heart to regard such self-consecration as one of the chiefest of the privileges of the heirs of glory. How admirable the ordinance of Heaven! Diversities of gifts – yet one spirit! Here there are five of us, born, brought up, educated in different parts of our fatherland, in diverse circumstances and amid indefinitely varying associations. Still, when thrown together, in the inscrutable counsels of Divine providence, in a strange and foreign land, without losing any of our peculiar idiosyncracies, we find that we are one in spirit, one in the prime actuating motives, one in the grand design and end of our being! . . .

By 1841, too, Dr Duff's return enabled him to reorganize the Institution in all its departments, rudimentary school and college, English and oriental. He felt that all the gifts and varied energies of the five men should be utilised and directed to the one spiritual end of the immediate conversion of the students, as the test of a system which aimed at far more, even the ultimate subversion of the whole Hindu system and the substitution of an indigenous Christian Church. Alexander's earliest act was to propose the formation of a missionary council to meet regularly for consultation and prayer under the senior, or whomsoever the Church at home might recognise as the senior, on account of peculiar fitness for the presidency of a Christian college.

To no subject, when in Scotland, had Alexander devoted more of his little leisure than to the careful inspection of all educational improvements in school and college made during his absence in India. These he now proceeded to adapt to his Bengali circumstances. He had the buildings, the library, the philosophical apparatus for scientific and technical training – everything but the assistant native teachers. In all India there was no normal (teacher-training) school at that time. The Mission had raised its own subordinate masters, but on no regular system. He saw that his first duty was to devote part of his strength of his increased staff to the systematic training of native schoolmasters. He had introduced the gallery system, as it was called, into India for the first time. Every Saturday the Institution was crowded with visitors to see the novel sight of three hundred boys from six to twelve exercised after the most approved fashion of David Stow, beginning with gymnastics and closing with an examination on the Bible. Here was his practising department. Daily, since he lived in the grounds, Alexander himself persuaded all the native teachers to remain for an hour, when he taught them teaching methods with results which soon showed themselves in the increased efficiency of the school. Not only so, but he was continually called on to surrender his best teachers to other missions and to government, while he was consoled by the consciousness that he was thus extending a Christian, as well as educational influence, far and wide.

The General Assembly's Institution at that time was strongest in the two allied, though too often divorced subjects, of physical and mental science. The missionaries themselves were fresh from the highest honours in the classes of Chalmers and Jackson, Leslie and Forbes, Brown and Wilson. Of the five, four were masters in the field of mathematics, pure and applied. Dr Duff himself lectured on chemistry but his special delight lay in the exposition of psychology and ethics, leading up through natural religion to the queenly theology of revelation. Dr Duff lectured on the methods pursued in Scotland, in Switzerland, in Germany, in Prussia; and expounded the systems of Stow, Fellenberg, and Pestalozzi.

Two things were greatly insisted on throughout the classes – a clear conception of an idea in the mind, and the expression of that concept in words. Alexander did not think that a boy had thoroughly caught hold of an idea unless he could express it in his own words, however inelegantly. The students therefore took no notes of explanations given by the teachers; indeed, no notes were given in the class, for fear that they might contribute to cramming. Alexander was following the method of his own learning since his early schooldays at Kirkmichael in the Highlands of Scotland. He also opened a weekday evening lecture in his house. There, students who had completed their three year studies, returned to read morally and spiritually uplifting masterpieces of literature.

Alexander now turned his thoughts again to a subject dear to his heart. Female education. He, himself, was mainly responsible for the situation which had now arisen, in that, educated Bengali men would be looking for educated wives, and the increasing community of native Christians would seek the means of instruction for their children. The orphan refuge for girls, begun by Mrs Charles, was developed into an efficient

Bengali school under the Ladies' Society, and from that in later days, in its two branches, many young women went out to be zanana teachers, and the happy wives and mothers of a prosperous Christian community. The time for more public and direct aggression on the ignorance and social oppression of the women of Bengal, at least, was not yet. In a noble building planted just opposite Alexander's first college, and beside the church of his second convert, the Hon. Drinkwater Bethune, a member of the government, founded a female school. Yet the two enlightened Brahman landholders of Ooterapara, near Calcutta, had in vain asked the state to join them in opening a school for Bengali young ladies there.

But while Alexander sought, in the new orphanage, to prepare Christian teachers, wives and mothers for the future, as it developed before his own eyes, he was no less active in procuring the removal of legislative obstructions to the freedom of women within legitimate limits. In an official letter of 16 September, 1842, he expounded in detail the two evils of infant betrothal and early marriage – before puberty, often – and of the prohibition of widow marriage.

The characteristic disbelief of Hinduism, in common with all systems except Christianity, in the continence of man and the purity of woman, made widows for life of the infant girls whose betrothed had died. These, growing up despised, ill-treated and overworked, become the centre of the household and village intrigues which fill the records of the criminal courts of India, and the mainstay of the thousand great shrines to which pilgrimages were made from vast distances and amid incredible hardships all over the peninsula. Weary of life and dissatisfied with herself, allowed a freedom unknown to the wife and frequently never herself a wife, the Hindu widow vainly sought peace at the hands of the touting priest, who stripped her of her all, even of what honour she might have left, in the name of the Vaishnava Deity. Or she courted rest at the bottom of the village well. Add to this the state of wives who were no wives, of the Koolin Brahman's hundreds of wives, some of them whole families of mother and daughters, and we have an idea of the moral and spiritual problems which Christian education faced in even orthodox Hindus.

Alexander observed with satisfaction the discussion of these issues in the vernacular newspapers, and the formation, as early as 1842, of 'a secret society among the educated Hindus for privately instructing their young daughters and other female relatives'. The agitation against the legal prohibition of widow marriages, begun in these years, bore fruit in the Act of Lord Dalhousie and Sir Barnes Peacock, which, just before the Mutiny, removed all legal obstructions to the marriage of Hindu widows.

While thus sowing joy for generations to come, Alexander and Anne were called to bear bitterness worse than death. They were informed that their second child, Anne, had died. The shattering news came to them with no previous indication or warning of their child being in ill-health. It was not long since they had left their little band of four, and the baby that Anne had left was still only just over eighteen months old. The sad news came from Dr Alexander Brunton in Edinburgh, who at this time was mourning the death of their mutual friend Dr Briggs. In his letter of 2 June, 1841, he wrote:

> . . . Our heavenly Father has called little Anne to Himself. I need not detail the circumstances. I know that more than one affectionate friend intends to transmit them to you. Nor do I need to remind you what are the duties to which, after the first sore burst of anguish, you will feel yourself called. I write merely to assure you that the little sufferer had every human resource which you yourself could have desired. Mrs Campbell watched her with maternal care. The best medical skill of Edinburgh was promptly and affectionately bestowed on her. We have laid her in Dr Inglis's burial place, close to the spot of his own hallowed rest.
>
> I will mix up no other theme with this. The little which I had to say on business I address to Mr Ewart. I am sure you will not misunderstand me, as if I imagined that, even under this sore trial, you would cease for a day to labour in your Master's work. On the contrary, I know by experience that such labour is most wholesome medicine in human sorrow. But you are well entitled to judge for yourself at what precise time and in what proportion you are best able to bear the medicine.

Alexander replied to his dear friend on the 17 August and the following brief extracts indicate the great sorrow felt by him and his wife:

> . . . Even now, after the interval of nearly a month, the vivid realization of it brought about by my writing

this note scarcely allows me to to proceed. The tears flow now as copiously as on the day of the unexpected intelligence . . .

It was a kind thought of yours, and in beautiful harmony with all your other refined and delicate consideration for human feelings, to have our little one laid beside the man for whose memory beyond all others I cherish the deepest veneration. Kindest and best thanks to dear Mrs Inglis and family for their ready consent. Also my warmest thanks to the committee for their tribute of respect. I think far more of their act of favour in behalf of the departed than if they had bestowed thousands on the living. May the Lord reward you all . . .

While the college, in spiritual influence and intellectual force, with its nine hundred students and three branch stations, was thus advancing to the state of efficiency in which it had to close for the last time in 1843, due to the Disruption of the Church, of which we shall deal later, all around there was disaster and confusion in public affairs. Thus longingly did Dr Duff dwell on the triumphs of peace, and on the way which it opened for the Prince of peace, into the lands beyond British frontiers, then on the Sutlej and the Yoma mountains of Arakan. How hopefully, in the Punjab, the Karen country and China, were his anticipations realized:

For the last three years all India has been in a state of suppressed ferment and smothered excitement, by the desolating warfare in Afghanistan and China. A permanent peace with Afghanistan may prepare a way of access to the vast nomadic hordes of Central Asia, who, from time immemorial, have been the conquerors and desolators of its fairest and richest provinces. The last few years have served to prove that, though the sword of war may destroy, it cannot tame or subdue any portion of these wild and lawless races. What fresh glory will this shed on the triumphs of the gospel, when, by the peaceful 'sword of the Spirit', these very tribes are brought into willing subjection and endowed with meek and lamb-like dispositions! A permanent peace with China may open up an effectual door of ingress to more than 300,000,000 of human beings – one-third of the entire race of mankind! – hitherto shut up, and, as it were, hermetically sealed against the invasion of gospel truth. How mysterious, and yet how wisely beneficent the ways of Divine Providence! China being sealed against the intrusion of Bible heralds, the last thirty years have been chiefly devoted by the lamented Morrison and others to the study of that unique and solitary lingual genus, the Chinese tongue – to the investigation of Chinese antiquities, literature, mythology, and other such like subjects as tend to throw light on the genius, the character, the mental and religious habitudes of so singular and multitudinous a people, to the preparation of grammars and dictionaries, and tracts, and above all, to the translation of the Word of life, that Book of books, the Bible. And when the requisite apparatus for an effectual spiritual warfare has been fully prepared, suddenly and unexpectedly the immense field for their practical application has been thrown open, by the instrumentality of one who 'meant not so, neither did his heart think so'. (Isa. x. 7.) What a striking coincidence! Who dare say that it is fortuitous? Oh no! It is altogether the ordination of Him who 'knoweth the end from the beginning'. It is one of those marvellous points of confluence among the manifold streams and currents of Providence, which may flow, for years or even ages, unseen beneath the surface, till the 'set time' hath come for their springing forth visibly, to bespeak the presiding presence of Him, who 'doeth according to His will among the armies of heaven and the inhabitants of the earth'.

11

The Disruption of the Church

Alexander Duff might have spent the rest of his career in quietly developing the principles and extending the machinery of his system on its India and Scottish sides, but for two forces, in church and state, which the shrewdest took long to foresee. His Kirk had to work its way back to the purity and spiritual independence of covenanting times, and in so working it became broken in two.

Foreign missions being of no ecclesiastical party but the privilege of all; we have seen how Alexander, during his first visit to Scotland, had kept himself aloof from even the most vital controversies. To him, as charged with the conversion of a hundred and thirty millions of human beings, Whig or Tory, Voluntary or State Churchman, even 'Intrusionists' or 'Non-Intrusionists', were of little account save in so far as they could promote or hinder his one object. Even in India, on his return in 1840, he was so silent regarding his relation to parties and the course he would follow if rupture took place, that some doubted how he would act. In truth, the approaching cataclysm so weighed him down, in reference to its effects on his own mission, that he refrained from speech, in public, till the issue could be fairly put before him and his colleagues for decisive settlement. But not one of the clerical combatants in the thick of the fight knew its meaning, historical and spiritual, better than the missionary. His youth had been overshadowed by the 'cloud of witnesses'. His heroes had always been the men of the Covenant. His hatred was that of the patriot rather than of the priest, to the Stewarts who, down to the last Act in Queen Anne's time, had robbed the Kirk and its people of spiritual freedom. He waited only for the right time, the time of duty to the Mission as well as to his principles, to declare himself with an energy and an uncompromising thoroughness, hardly equalled by the ecclesiastical leaders who headed the host of disruption heroes on the memorable 18 May, 1843.

But not only had the education of the Highland boy, under such a father and teacher as his, early fed his young life with the history of his Kirk, which is that of his country. In his three years' wanderings over every presbytery and almost every parish of Scotland, from the Shetland Isles to the Solway, he had become acquainted with the actual state of religious and social life in a way unknown to Chalmers or the young Guthrie, or the most experienced Lowlander of the time. To the highest test which can try a Christian or a Church, the Christ-like philanthropy of missions, he had jealously brought the Church of Scotland from 1834 to 1840, its ministers and people, its parties and their professions, its policies and aims. He thus learned, as no one else could, the wrong, religious and political, done to the country by the dishonest legislation of Queen Anne's advisers all through the eighteenth century, even to the Reform Act in the state and the Veto Law in the Kirk. And a happy experience taught him, and Chalmers through him, that the heart of the people was sound in spite of the torpor and retrogression of a century and a quarter, that the Scotsmen of 1834 to 1843 were the true spiritual descendants of their fathers of the first and the second Reformation. This had been his experience of the ministers of the 'moderate party', who had formed the majority in the Kirk down to the year 1834 and who called in the civil courts to drive out the evangelical majority ten years after.

Alexander was accustomed to declare that, personally, he had received everywhere at their hands the most courteous and friendly treatment, with the two exceptions of Peebles and Dunbar. Seeing that he kept himself and his cause aloof from parties, moderates as well as evangelicals invited him to their manses, placed their conveyances at his disposal, passed him from presbytery to presbytery, and loyally obeyed the Assembly of 1835 in promoting meetings and subscriptions.

Many stories circulated about the behaviour of the clergy. It was almost incredible to what extent not only heterodoxy but profanity, intemperance, and other immorality found a place among the moderate ministers in the rural districts, especially in the Highlands and Islands to which the public opinion rarely penetrated.

At the upper end of a long strath in the Highlands lived a parish minister who was scarcely ever known to be sober. Business took him frequently to the other end of the valley, where he had to pass a distillery. It was the frequent sport of the owner to tempt the poor wretch, and then, placing him on his pony with his head to the tail, send him back amid the derision of the people, a man supporting him on either side.

Another parish was a preserve of smugglers, whose rendez-vous was the kirk, where the little barrels of Highland whisky were concentrated before despatch to the south. The isolated spot was the terror of the gaugers (Customs), for whom the hardy inhabitants, banded together, were long more than a match. A new minister was presented to the parish, a man of great promise and considerable scholarship. His one weakness was a passion for the violin. Through that he fell so low, that when his parishioners assembled at the inn they sent for the minister to play for them, and even carried him off when well drunk to a house of doubtful repute where the revelry was continued. On one occasion he fell into the peat fire, where his limbs became so roasted that for six months he was laid aside and he was lamed for life. His brethren resented the scandal only by refusing to allow him to attend the presbytery dinner, and by denying him all help at communion seasons. Brooding over these insults, he resolved to adopt that form of retaliation which would be most disagreeable to colleagues, some of whom differed from himself only by being bigger hypocrites. He sent to the neighbouring cities for the most evangelical Gaelic ministers to assist him on fast and sacrament days. The result was that the smuggling parish became not only a new place, such as all the success of the excise could never have made it, but the centre of the light to the whole presbytery. The people flocked from a great distance to hear the grand preaching in their own tongue. The drunkard's successor, appointed under the Veto Act, was a godly man, and when the disruption came the whole parish left the Established Church.

When farther north still, Alexander found himself the inhab-itant of a room in the manse which was curiously stained. On asking the explanation he was told that, as the most secure place, the attics had long been the storehouse of the smugglers and among other illegal produce, there were stacked small sacks of salt. So soon as the brig appeared in the harbour of Stromness, with flying colours, the minister at the beginning of the century promptly went on board. Even if the day were Sunday, he would go in the face of all the people, before or after doing pulpit duty! The manse had actually been built for the purpose of receiving contraband articles, which were hoisted up by a pulley swung on a hook projecting from a window in a high-pointed gable. The plaster of the ceiling of the room below was saturated with salt, which gave rise to severe staining in damp weather.

The mass of the common people, who did not turn for spiritual life to the seceding churches which were to form the vigorous United Presbyterian Church, found it in the study of the Bible and of writers like Rutherford and Boston, Bunyan and Doddridge. But this degeneracy of the Kirk had affected the upper classes of society in a way incredible in later times. The literature of the day, scanty as it be, revealed not a little of the truth.

Nor were English visitors to the Highlands in these early days any better than the moderate ministers whose kirks they rarely entered. Sir Robert Peel and a party of his friends had leased the shootings around Kingussie. To most of them all days were alike for sport. The peasantry, finding themselves in a sore strait between their conscience and the temptations held out by the Sunday sportsmen, waited on their minister with entreaties for advice. He at once wrote to Sir Robert Peel a letter, read by Dr Duff, which acknowledged all the kindness of the great statesman to the people, and asked him to respect their conscientious convictions. A week passed and no reply came. But on the next Sabbath the practical answer was given when, somewhat late, Sir Robert Peel and his whole party took possession of the great pew belonging to the estate they had leased. On the next day the minister received a long and kindly letter from the Premier, declaring that it was he that should apologise for not ascertaining his duty to the people, and expressing a wish that all clergymen would act with similar faithfulness.

Such reminiscences of his study of the inner life of the Church of Scotland, bad and good, lighting up his intimate knowledge of its history and his sympathy with the spiritual and civil patriotism of its people, made the disruption when it came, a very real and joyous event to Alexander, though far away from all its controversies and its triumphs. His enthusiasm burst forth the more impetuously that, for three years in India as during the five which he had spent in Europe, he had maintained an unbroken silence on the great spiritual-independence controversy. The chivalrous honour of the man prevented him from making any allusion to it in his official correspondence. Nor was Dr Brunton, on the other side, less thoughtful. Neither could prevent the result; so long as that was doubtful or had not been precipitated by providence, it might have been perilous for either to link to a temporary struggle, however great, the abiding principles of catholic missions to the non-Christian world. They would have been less than men if, in the intimacy of private correspondence, such sentences as the following, had not occurred. But from first to last (in Duff's official biographer's opinion) and in every detail save the very serious questions of rights of property, legal and equitable as between Christian brethren, no controversy in all Church history had ever been conducted so free from the spirit condemned by Christ and his Apostles, as the missionary side of the Disruption of 1843.

After Alexander's return to Calcutta in 1840 Dr Brunton thus confidentially wrote to him on 2 April:

Your clerical friends are well; as well, at least, as Non-Intrusion fever will allow. The excitation and the embitterment are by no means abating. Government declines to attempt any legislative measure. Lord Aberdeen has given notice of one without saying what it is to be. Matters are getting more and more embroiled. Oh that peace were breathed into the troubled elements by Him who 'stilleth the noise of the seas, the noise of their waves and the tumult of the people'. Amidst the other lamentable consequences of this turmoil it swallows up every other interest in some of our fairest and purest minds, and the sweet call to missionary enterprise is too passionless to gain a hearing, where once it was pleasant music. Send us better tidings from the lands of the South than we can transmit to you from this dwelling of storms.

By 28 January, 1843, Dr Brunton wrote of 'the really appalling schism in the Church which seems now inevitable, and which may most lamentably affect all her great and glorious "schemes". May God avert it! In man there is now no help or hope.'

So rigorously did Alexander carry out his official duty to the committee and his sense of what was best for the mission, that when his most intimate friends privately pressed him to say how he would act in the event of an actual disruption, he told them why he could not reply to such a question. What Lord Cockburn called 'the heroism' of 18 May, which made Francis Jeffrey declare that he was 'proud of his country', was not officially intimated to the now fourteen Indian missionaries till October. Not till the end of July had the preliminary letters from Dr Brunton, and from Dr Charles J. Brown representing the Free Church, reached them, declaring that each Church was determined to carry on the Foreign and Jewish Missions.

Dr Brunton wrote:

> We are most anxious to retain the co-operation of those whom we have found experimentally so thoroughly quali-fied for their work and so devoted to its prosecution. We earnestly hope, therefore, that you will see it to be consistent with your sense of duty to remain in that connection with us, which to us, in the past, has been the source of so much satisfaction and thankfulness. I write to you collectively, not individually, because we have no wish that personal considerations should influence your decision.

Dr Chalmers was not present at the meeting of the provi-sional committee of the Free Church, for which Dr C. J. Brown wrote a letter, which thus delicately concluded: 'The committee do not of course presume to enter into discussion with you on the subject, or to say one word as to the course which you may feel it right to follow.' To that Dr Chalmers added this postcript: 'I state my confident belief that, notwithstanding the engrossment of our affairs at home, the cause of all our missions will prove as dear, and be liberally supported as ever by the people of Scotland.' With such faith, in such a spirit, did the second Knox and his band of 470, soon increased to 730 and later to some 1,100 ministers, commit their Church to extension abroad no less than at home. In this respect the third reformation was more truly Christ's than the second or the first.

For himself alone, Alexander published an 'Explanatory Statement, addressed to the friends of the India Mission of the Church of Scotland, as it existed previous to the Disruption in May, 1843'. This passage takes up the narrative at the reception of the official appeals from Dr Brunton and Dr Charles Brown:

> We were now laid under a double necessity openly to avow our sentiments. Was there any hesitation when the hour of trial came? None whatsoever. So far as concerned my own mind, the simple truth is, that as regards the great principles contended for by my friends and champions of

the Free Church, I never was troubled with the crossing of a doubt or the shadow of a suspicion . . . But though there was not a moment's hesitation as to the rectitude of the principles, and consequent obligation in determining the path of duty, there was a sore conflict of natural feeling – a desperate struggle of opposing natural interests. Many of my dearest and most devoted personal friends still adhered to the Establishment . . . All the most vivid associations connected with my original appointment, – the ardours and imaginings of inexperienced youth – the exciting hopes and fears unseparable from an untried and hazardous enterprise – anxieties felt and removed – trials encountered, difficulties overcome, and success attained – were all indissolubly linked with the Established Church of Scotland. The revered projector of the Mission, Dr Inglis, and his respected successor, Dr Brunton, had, each in his turn, throughout the long period of *fourteen* years, treated me rather with the consideration, the tenderness, and the confidence of a father towards his son, than with the formal but polite courtesies of a mere official relationship. When I looked at the noble fabric of the General Assembly's Institution, so very spacious and commodious, and so richly provided with library, apparatus, and all other needful furniture; and recalled to remembrance the former days, when we had to toil and labour in close, confined, and unhealthy localities, without the aid of library or apparatus, and but with a scanty and ill-favoured assortment even of the necessary class books . . . I reflected on the high probability, or rather moral certainty, that separation from the Establishment must be followed by an evacuation of the present Mission premises, I could not help feeling a pang somewhat akin to that of parting with a favourite child. Again, when I looked at the still nobler fabric within – a fabric, of which the other was but the material tenement – the living fabric, consisting of so many hundreds of the finest and most promising of India's sons, beaming with the smiles of awakening intelligence, and sparkling with the buoyancy of virgin hopes; when I considered this fabric, so closely compacted through the varied gradations of an all-comprehending system whose organization, discipline, and progressive development, it had required thirteen years of combined and incessant labour to bring to the present point of maturity and perfectness; and when I thought how, in the present crisis of things, separation from the Establishment might prove the dissolution and breaking up of the whole into scattered fragments; I could not help experiencing a sensation somewhat equivalent to that of beholding a numerous and beloved family engulfed in the deep, or swallowed up by an earthquake. Once more, when I thought of the doubtful and inadequate prospect of our support in the new relationship of a Free Church Mission . . . the loss and alienation of many of the great and mighty, who hitherto had smiled propitious on our labours – the disadvantage and disparagement to our credit, cause, and good name, which might accrue from our abandonment of premises with which had been associated so much of what was reputable and successful in our past proceedings – the certainty that, by numbers of the more bigoted natives, such forced abandonment would be construed as a retributive visitation from the gods, on account of our persevering attacks on their faith and worship – the confusion and disgrace which might thus, in their estimation, redound to Christianity itself, and the corresponding triumph to an exulting heathenism – the dread of anticipated rivalries and collisions between the agents of Churches so violently wrenched asunder, and the scandal and stumbling-block which these might occasion or throw in the way of the struggling cause of a yet infantile evangelisation. When I thought of all this, and much more of a similar character, it seemed as if a thousand voices were ringing in my ears, saying, 'Pause, pause; cling to the Establishment, and if you do so, you will advance, without interruption, in the gorgeous vessel of Church and State, which so majestically ploughs the waves over a sea of troubles.'

In opposition to such a muster and array of antagonist influences, what had I to confront? Nought but the blazing apprehension of the truth and reality of the principles at issue – their truth and reality in Jehovah's infal-lible oracles, their truth and reality in the standards, constitution, and history of the Church of Scotland – nought but the burning monitions of conscience, relative to the morally compulsive obligation of walking in the path of apprehended duty. It seemed as if a thousand counter-voices kept peeling in my ears, loud as the sound of great thunders, or the noise of many waters, saying, 'Let pride or prejudice, self-interest or natural feeling, be allowed to obscure the apprehension of truth, or stifle the directive energy of conscience; and then, though your dwelling be in the palaces of state, and your refuge the munition of rocks, there will be inward misgivings, that ever and anon shall cause the heart to melt, the hands to be feeble, the spirit to faint, and the knees to be weak as water. But, be fully persuaded in your own mind. Let no sinister influences be suffered to interfere. Let the apprehension of truth, derived from the Fount of Revelation, be steadfast and unclouded, and the beckonings of conscience, illumined by the Word, meditation, and prayer be unreluctantly recognised and implicity followed . . .' With views and sentiments like these, however powerful might be the counter-inducements, how could I decide otherwise than I have done?

On 10 August, the five Bengal missionaries of the Church of Scotland united in a despatch to both Dr Brunton and Dr Gordon, forwarding eight resolutions in which they declared their reasons for adhering to 'the Free Protesting Presbyterian Church of Scotland', as Christian men and ministers. They formed a provisional church committee, which held the first public service of the Free Church in Calcutta, in Freemasons' Hall, on 13 August. Alexander preached the sermon, afterwards published, and announced that the Rev John Macdonald would, in addition to his daily missionary duties, act as minister till the congregation could call a pastor from Scotland. A missionary character was given to the congregation from the first, by the baptism of a convert, Behari Lal Singh. But now, where was a church to be found?

Alexander went so far as to apply to Lord Ellenborough's government for the temporary use of a hall belonging to it, but the authorities evaded the question by professing inability to understand the nature of the case. Then the Eurasian committee offered their Doveton College to the man who had done so much for them. Six lay elders and six deacons were duly elected by the congregation, who at once prepared for the erection of a proper ecclesiastical building. After some five thousand pounds had been spent in erecting one designed by Captain Goodwyn of the Engineers, it fell down the night before it was to be entered for worship. Undismayed, the members constructed, at a total sum of some twelve thousand pounds, another building.

The Church at home made an immediate appeal for congregational collections and the result was that £6,402 was sent to the India mission before the end of the year. With the consent of both parties the Calcutta missionaries continued their work in the Institution and mission-house built and furnished by themselves, to the close of the session of 1843. But what then?

Morally, equitably, the whole belonged to Alexander and his colleagues, who had called it into existence. The college, its library and its scientific equipment, were the fruit of personal legacies and gifts made to Alexander himself chiefly, and on the express understanding that he was to use the funds as he pleased. Alexander proposed that the honourable and gentlemanly solution would be for the missionaries to purchase back from the Established Church the premises which were morally their own, if required; and that the Church, desiring to begin a new mission, should break fresh ground in Upper India. The once imperial cities of Agra and Delhi had, for years, been pleading for extended branches of the Calcutta Institution.

The Established Church committee, in an evil moment for themselves and the cause of truth and charity, put forward a 'Mr Thomas Scott' as auditor of accounts and allowed him to make the decision that the whole of the Institution and its furnishings belonged to them and therefore Alexander and his colleagues would lose all. Alexander replied to the decision by the Established Church committee in a letter of eighty octavo pages, but they would not budge. The only solution was to build their own establishment in native Calcutta.

A Colonel Dundas and some Indian friends, in Scotland, presented Dr Duff with about four hundred pounds as 'a mark of respect' and for personal uses. This too he devoted to the mission. Adjoining the Institution in Cornwallis Square were three acres of unoccupied ground belonging to the government, but not enclosed and therefore filled with refuse. In vain had he asked the local financial board to purchase it in order to meet the needs of the increasing number of students and converts. The price was £3,500. He received another legacy of £1,000 and added this to the Dundas gift. He then sought the consent of Lord Auckland himself to the sale of the land for this total sum, but the proposal had first to be sanctioned by the Court of Directors. By the time that the deed of conveyance was ready, the Disruption controversy was approaching its close. Mr Macleod Wylie, a barrister who wrote a pamphlet on 'The Scotch Law of Patronage and the recent Secession' proving the Free Church right in law as in scripture, advised Dr Duff to keep the deed in his own name, the property being his own, until the issue of the conflict became clear. This he had done, and on this spacious open ground he might, naturally and conveniently, have erected the new college.

Alexander decided that while the site would have been ideal for the new Institution, he considered that they should not be seen to be activated by vindictive or retaliatory motives, or animated by a spirit of hostile rivalry. He and his colleagues decided that the land could be let and the proceeds wholly and exclusively applied to missionary purposes. The new mission-house was erected there long after.

The whole college vacation of 1843–44, extended to two months, was spent by the missionaries in exploring every nook and corner of the native city for a site and home for the new Institution. The renown of the Disruption sacrifice, which had gone out through all lands, had in India been increased by the decision to evict the missionaries from their college, even though they had offered to purchase their own. From all sides, Hindu as well as Christian, Anglican and Congregationalist as well as Presbyterian, in America no less than in Asia and Europe, came expressions and proofs of indignant sympathy. The year 1844 opened with spontaneous gifts amounting to £3,400.

The hunt for a college building, aided by good men of all creeds, concentrated itself on one place. In obtaining that, Alexander was helped by an orthodox Hindu, the father of the most distinguished medical Bengali, Rai Kanye Lal Dey Bahadoor. There was one house in Neemtollah Street which was large enough to accommodate an institution like the Free Church Institution, but it was in an untenantable condition, the joint owners were not agreed among themselves and they had no mind to let the house for the use of a college. With the help of Rai Kanye Lal Dey Bahadoor, the owners were persuaded to let the building on terms favourable to both parties: a rent of two hundred rupees a month, and the defrayal of the whole expense of a thorough repair at a heavy outlay involving additions and alterations. The missionaries had the gift of £3,400 and now had the rent from the ground purchased next to the old college and were therefore well able to proceed.

Here on 4 March, 1844, the General Assembly's Institution of the Free Church of Scotland met for the first time, and here it grew till on an adjoining site its successor was built. There were the same missionaries, the same staff of teachers and monitors, the same converts to begin with, and more than a thousand students and pupils. The spacious hall, formerly devoted to idol revelries, became the common place of worship of the living God in Christ. The shrine of the family image received the gallery class of children, who there learned to spell out the words of the Divine Teacher. From all parts of Eastern India and Scotland friends sent supplies of books for the new library. Dr Mackay, who had built his usual rooftop observatory, was gladdened by the donation of a Herschel ten-foot telescope from the son of Captain Alexander Stewart, of Moulin memory.

Even when in the depths of the darkness, Alexander knew he could not slacken with his policy in the West, in order to obtain funds and personnel to enlarge work in the East. Here is an extract of a letter which he sent to Dr Gordon in Edinburgh on 20 January, 1844:

. . . Connected with this subject, allow me to hint that a new Professorship in the Free Church College in Edinburgh, of missions and education, would tend mightily to impart life, energy, wisdom and consistency to all her missionary and educational schemes, domestic and foreign. So far as I know, it would be the first Professorship of the kind that has ever been established, and would tend more than anything else to stamp the Free Church as the introducer of a new era in the history of this world's christianization. I have purposely conjoined 'missions and education', as both united would comprehend a discussion of the best modes of imparting all useful knowledge, human and divine, to old and young, of all classes and of all climes, founded on the constitution of the human mind, history and experience, and above all, the Word of God.

Little did Alexander know that he would raise the first endowment and be himself the first professor.

12

Continuing the work in the East

Having thus founded and organised his second college, the Free Church General Assembly's Institution, Alexander's next care was for the branch schools by which the educated catechists and converts were evangelising the rural districts. Takee, the first, was the property of the Chowdery clan of Hindu landholders. They too remained faithful to their alliance with Dr Duff. To secure a healthier position in which European missionaries could live without serious risk, they moved the school from the somewhat inaccessible rice swamps to their town residence in Baranuggur, a northern suburb of Calcutta. The mission at Culna was retained by Alexander and his colleagues as their second rural station. Then followed Bansberia, Chinsurah, and Mahanad in Lower Bengal. Alexander had now crossed the river Hooghly to its right bank, leaving the whole country on the left to the Established Church.

He then discovered a schoolhouse near the country town of Hooghly district, closed and for sale. Alexander secured the perpetual lease of the grounds as well as the large bungalow and his first object was to erect substantial buildings for a Christian high school. For this there were now little funds, but a Mr Lennox of New York, and his two sisters, sent £500 to him and he sent a share to the missions at Madras and Bombay. The other two missionaries sent the money back to Alexander, stating that they had enough for their needs and that he should use all the money. Alexander wrote home of this noble act.

Soon a fine college building of their own was to take the place of the hired house in Calcutta, and that would exhaust their resources. It was Sir James, then Major, Outram who came to the rescue. He wrote to Alexander stating that he had six thousand rupees and asked, 'Have you any object on the banks of the Ganges to which this can profitably be applied?' Instantly Alexander replied:

> Oh, yes! I want an educational institution in a populous locality on the banks of the river in an excellent situation,

and have been waiting a considerable time to secure the means of erecting a suitable building. Now singularly enough the minimum sum fixed on in my own mind was exactly Rs 6,000, and if you approve the idea you may send that sum to me, and we shall commence at once the erection of the building.

The mission-house was erected. Major Outram was delighted and spent a day at the Institution.

Another of Alexander's supporters was Sir Henry Lawrence, then a young lieutenant of artillery at Dum Dum, who used to spend his whole income, beyond a bare sustenance, on Christian philanthropy in India. He concentrated his energies on the Hill Asylums for soldiers' children, but sent four hundred pounds each year to be distributed among the missionaries.

With the support which the missionaries now received from their kind friends and supporters, they made great progress in their object of spreading the word of God and educating the native population of Bengal. The battle continued with even greater enthusiasm, but like all battles, there had to be both risks and casualties. In July, 1844, there came to Dr Duff's house one Gobindo Chunder Das, who had been removed from the old Institution by his father. After the usual persecution by his family and relatives, he finally, after six years of misery, returned to Alexander for help. He was received into the church and became a useful teacher in the college. He thus became the first convert of the Free Church Mission. The conversion and baptism of young men of marked ability and high social or caste position now followed so fast on Gobindo's that, once again, the Hindu community of Calcutta was deeply concerned.

The year 1845 opened with the public confession and admission of Gooroo Das Maitra. He was later ordained as a missionary minister and called by the Bengali Presbyterian Church in Calcutta, to be their minister. At the same time Umesh Chunder Sirkar sought baptism. But he was young, only sixteen, and longed to instruct and take over with him, his child-wife of ten. His father was a stern bigot, of great authority and influence as treasurer to the millionaire Mullik family. For two years, therefore, the boy-husband and his wife searched the scriptures diligently in the midnight hours snatched from sleep, when alone, in the crowd of the great Bengali household, they could count on secrecy, though ever suspected. After much reading of the Bengali Bible, Umesh Chunder taught her the Bengali translation of *Pilgrim's Progress*, the most popular Christian book after the Bible.

On the next idol festival, when even Hindu married women were allowed to visit their female caste friends in neighbouring houses in closed palankeens, Umesh conducted his true-hearted little wife to Dr Duff's house. They came to the missionary's house on the Sunday afternoon, at the close of a prayer meeting which one of the elders of the Free Church congregation, Mr. J. C. Stewart, son of Dr Stewart of Moulin, used to hold with the converts. Now began a commotion such as no previous case had excited. Dr Duff's house was literally besieged. The Mulliks as well as the Sirkars, both families or clans, and their Brahmans, beset the young man. They attempted violence, so that the gate was shut next day to all but the father, the brother, and the wealthy chief of the Mulliks. For days this went on, for the missionary would not deny to the new convert's family that which was the only weapon he claimed for Christ, persuasion. At last the scene changed to the Supreme Court. The Chief Justice, Sir Lawrence Peel, knew that Dr Duff was not holding the youth against his will, and did not grant a writ of *habeas corpus* to release him. There was no question raised as to his wife. Mullik's followers still raged outside the house while the young couple were baptised.

Some of the students were invited to join the Duffs for breakfast. Mrs Duff liked the company of the young in her house as she missed her own children. Alexander was as punctual as clockwork; exactly at eight o'clock in the morning, the prayer-bell rang and they joined the Duffs in the breakfast-room. Alexander was always observant of the forms of politeness, and never forgot to shake hands with his guests. His hand-shake was different from that of other people. It was warm and earnest and he would go on shaking, catching a fast hold on the hand, and would not let it go for several seconds. Anne played a significant role at the school in teaching and many other duties too numerous to mention. She took a motherly interest in the boys, and from her the boys learned a great deal which might otherwise have been glossed over in the usual teaching. She led all the singing, as although Alexander always joined in he never ventured to start it off.

By the end of 1845, the number of resident converts had increased to thirteen, and four of them were married. Alexander was at his wits' end in making even a temporary provision for their proper accommodation. No sooner was the necessity known, than twelve merchants and officials, nine of them of the Church of England, presented him with a thousand pounds to build a home for the Christian students in the grounds beside his own residence, which, with wise foresight, he had long ago secured. To this, as the Bengali congregation developed and, according to Presbyterian privilege, 'called' its own native minister, he added a church and manse with funds entrusted to him for his absolute disposal by the late Countess of Effingham. In the same year, Mr Thomson, of Banchory in Scotland, and other friends in Aberdeen, unsolicited by him, sent Alexander a library and scientific apparatus for the college, which completed its equipment.

As Alexander reviewed the situation to date, he was well pleased at the progress which had been made in Calcutta and Bengal. Even the Disruption position had been satisfactorily overcome, and now promised even greater prospects for the future. The work he had done in the West, as part of his plan, was now paying dividends for his work in the East.

The successive but contrasting administrations of Lord Auckland and Lord Ellenborough, raised questions in the minds of all Britons in India, official and non-official. The civil and military services were placed, temporarily, in a heated antagonism. The disasters in Afghanistan, followed by the evacuation of the country after a proposal to sacrifice the English ladies and officers in captivity, and by the follies of a public triumph and the Somnath proclamation, had roused Great Britain as well as India.

The annexation of Sindh and the war with Gwalior further stirred the public conscience in a way not again seen till the Mutiny, of which the Auckland-Ellenborough madness was the prelude. And the whole was overshadowed by a new cloud in the north-west, far more real, at that time at least, than the shadow cast by the advance of the Russians from the north. The death of Runjeet Singh, who from the Sikh Khalsa, or brotherhood, had raised himself to be Maharaja of the Punjab, from the Sutlej to the Kyber and the glaciers of the Indus, had given the most warlike province of India six years of anarchy. It was time, if India was not to be lost, that someone who was both a soldier and a statesman should sit in the seat of Wellesley and Hastings.

The new Governor-General was found in the younger son of a rector of the Church of England; in the Peninsular hero who, at twenty-five, had won Albuera, had bled at Waterloo, and had left his hand on the field at Ligny, and had become a Cabinet Minister as the Secretary-at-War. Sir Henry Hardinge went out to Government House, Calcutta, at sixty, and he returned to England in four years as Viscount Hardinge of Lahore. Before he left England he took the advice of Mountstuart Elphinstone, never to interfere in civil details. All through his administration he consulted Henry Lawrence, and saw himself four times victor in fifty-four days, at Moodkee and Ferozeshuhur, at Aliwal and Sobraon. Like his still greater successor, his victories were those of peace as well as war. He opened the public service to educated Indians. He put down suttee and other crimes in the feudatory states. He stopped the working of all government establishments on the Christian day of rest, Sunday. He fostered the early railway projects, and carried out the great Ganges Canal. For the first time since, ten years before, Lord William Bentinck resigned the cares of office, it seemed that India was being wisely governed.

Almost the first act of the new Governor-General, in October, 1844, was to publish the resolution directing that the public service would be thrown open to educated Indians. This step, for the first time, acknowledged the value of the college and schools. The order was received with such enthusiasm by both Indians and Europeans, and even the bureaucratic Council of Education, which had adopted all Alexander's educational plans while keeping him and his Christianity at arm's length, burst into the unaccustomed generosity of notifying that the measure was applicable 'to all students in the lower provinces without reference to creed or colour'. True, this was only interpreting the Hardinge enactment according to the Bentinck decree, but now being the order of the government in India, it marked a decided advance towards the measure of toleration and justice to Indian and missionary alike, which Alexander fought for till Parliament conceded it in 1853.

Alexander now felt it was time to add yet another dimension to his primary task of Christian enlightment and education in India. It had been on his mind for a considerable time that the press would be a most important ally, and the opportunity now arose to achieve this goal. The editors of the existing newspapers were Captain Kaye of the daily *Hurkaru* and Mr Marshman of the weekly *Friend of India*. They were the first to urge the importance of establishing a magazine or review to which men of all shades of religious and political union could contribute. The former, afterwards Sir John Kaye, had been led, by ill health, to abandon a promising career in the Bengal Artillery for the sedentary pursuits of a literary life. Mr Marshman had come to India with his father at the close of the previous century. He had received an intellectual and spiritual training of unusual excellence; he had made the grand tour of Europe, he had discharged professional duties in the Serampore College with great ability, and he had become the first Bengali scholar and established the first newspaper in that language, and had succeeded Carey as the Government Translator. He installed the first steam paper-mill in the East and produced excellent law and school books for all Bengal. From first to last he contributed sixty thousand pounds for the enlightment and christianisation of India. To these two, and to Alexander, we owe the *Calcutta Review*.

The first number appeared in May, 1844, and at once leaped into popularity. A second edition was called for, and then a third was published in England. Alexander wrote an article on 'Our Earliest Protestant Mission to India', and from that time he became an indefatigable and able contributor. The *Calcutta Review* was a quarterly publication. In the second number he chose the subject of 'Female Infanticide among the Rajpoots and other Native Tribes of India'. Next came 'The State of Indigenous Education in Bengal', followed by 'The Early or Exclusively Oriental Period of Government Education in Bengal'. He was preparing other articles of a similar kind when the editorship came to him. Mr Kaye himself saw the fourth number through the press then Alexander took over, and continued to hold the editorship until he returned home in 1849.

Mr Kaye insisted on Alexander taking some adequate remuneration but he peremptorily declined. He looked upon the work as one calculated in many important ways to promote the vital interests of India, and in endeavouring to promote these, he felt there was no inconsistency between devoting a portion of his time to it, besides the more direct mission work. The grand object was to raise up the whole of India from its sunk and degraded position of ages, in every aspect of improvement, political, social, civil, intellectual, moral and religious. He felt, however, that the Institution ought to derive some benefit from the *Review* and, accordingly, a sum of five hundred rupees a year would be taken for scholarships and prizes. This arrangement lasted until

1856, when the periodical passed into other hands. Not long afterwards, Mr Kaye, now Sir John Kaye, published a book on the history of Christianity in India and dedicated it to Dr Alexander Duff.

A succession of sickly seasons, followed by an epidemic of fever during the latter rains of 1844, had filled Calcutta and its neighbourhood with thousands of sick, diseased and destitute natives, Hindu and Muslim. It killed off tens of thousands. The sanitation in Calcutta and elsewhere at the time was almost non-existent, and in fact, they had to wait another forty years before waterworks and drainage were provided. Alexander was shattered by what he saw. He wrote a sermon, later published, describing the horrors of the epidemic so that it would be read by those, like himself, who until then could not have imagined what it was like.

In paragraph after paragraph of graphic description, he asked his listeners or readers to consider the plight of the poor who came to Calcutta from all parts of the country in search of employment or to beg for charity:

> Think of them, in hundreds and thousands, with scarcely any clothing to cover their nakedness by night or by day . . . exposed at different seasons to pinching cold or scorching heat, or drenching rain, or stifling dust, or steamy vapour, or suffocating smoke . . . surrounded by accumulated deposits of filth and rubbish . . . not merely without the means of personal or domestic cleanliness, but often parched with thirst, without a drop of water to cool their burning tongues . . . craving for some cordial to soothe, or assuage, or mitigate inward agonizing pain . . . with cries and tears imploring the kindly offices of medical aid . . . Think of them in hundreds and thousands . . . unceremoniously handed over to the heartless officers of death.
>
> Ay, and what is most affecting of all – think of them, in hundreds and thousands, enduring these countless and untold sufferings in the present life, without any support or consolation drawn from the anticipated glories of the future. The humble disciples of Jesus, however poor or despised, neglected or scorned here below, can well afford to endure groans and griefs and agonies and tears; because the hope, full of immortality, renders the light affliction which is but for a moment, not worthy to be compared

with the eternal weight of the glory that is to follow. But these unhappy victims of a degrading superstition have to bear the unmitigated burden of all their sorrows, not only unvisited by earthly joy or uncheered by heavenly hope, but scared and haunted by ghastly spectres and images of terror that flit portentously around the portals of death and the grave . . .

And if the constant state of disease, suffering and death, even in ordinary years, points to the necessity of establishing such a sanctuary of health, what shall we think of that necessity as enhanced by those extraordinary seasons of raging epidemic which, as in the months of March and April last, occasionally visit and scourge this devoted city and its neighbourhood? Surely, surely, if the suffering and mortality of ordinary years plead so impressively and resistlessly for the necessity of providing an asylum for the thousands of hapless sufferers, that necessity is augmented and enhanced a hundred, yea, a thousand-fold, by the return, in almost periodic cycle, of an extraordinary season of smiting, all-devouring pestilence.

May I not then, dear friends and brethren, confidently call upon you, as professing disciples of the Lord Jesus to come forward now, and vigorously support this great and philanthropic undertaking?

In his greatest style, from pulpit, to press, to people, Alexander made this passionate plea for the creation for a place of healing. Thereafter, the missionaries and the members of the Bengal Medical Service united with some of the wealthy Bengali in the plan of building the great Medical College Hospital for the poor of all creeds and classes. A member of the Seel family, who at one time actually threatened Alexander's life and work at the time of the case in the Supreme Court, gifted the land on which the hospital was to be built. Other natives of means gave large sums. The British residents showed their usual liberality, and the medical professors offered their services without charge. Hence, Dr Alexander Duff's sermon and publication, which is in some respects the most characteristic he ever preached, showing the breadth of his charity and the comprehensiveness of the Christianity which he came to plant and to water in Bengal till it should become there also a tree whose leaves are for the healing of the nations.

Soon there arose, by the side of the Medical College, what was for long after the largest single hospital in the world, where people of all religions and classes found Christian medical care and not unfrequently spiritual healing in Christ. The opening of the hospital marked a new development of medical education in the East, for the course of the Medical College was reorganized in 1845 so as to qualify its students for the diplomas of the British licensing bodies. From then onwards, in Calcutta and its suburbs alone, the number of patients treated in this institution, ultimately made up of ten hospitals and dispensaries, rose to a third of a million human beings a year. In 1877 there were 25,358 in-door and 300,204 out-door free patients.

Hardly had the Medical College Hospital been completed when the generous Scotsmen of Calcutta turned to Alexander to represent them in national movements of their own. One was, in 1846, the prospect of raising a monument to John Knox, which resulted in the purchase of his house in the High Street of Edinburgh, and the erection of the church which bears his name.

13

Notice of recall to Scotland

It was early on a Friday morning in July, 1847, while Alexander and Anne were enjoying on the house-top, as usual, the too brief hours of coolness before the tropical sun should rise high in the heavens, that the government express mail brought them the news of the death of Dr Chalmers. To Alexander the loss, suddenly announced, was not that of a father and a friend alone. Nor was his sorrow the offspring of gratitude merely to the memory of one of whose lectures and training and personal influence for five years had done more to make the Highland student what he had become than any other single influence. Nor did he think chiefly, moreover, of the solemn hour of his ordination at St George's, and the second charge given to him in the same place by Chalmers as by Paul to Timothy. Alexander in the fullness of his own experience of the wide arena of India and the East, and of his knowledge of the men who make the history alike of the Church and the world, thought of Thomas Chalmers as the earliest Scottish apostle of evangelical missions, as the preacher who, before even Dr Inglis, had in 1812 and again in 1814, dared to tell his countrymen that they stood alone of all English-speaking peoples in their contempt for the missionary cause, and that the time was at hand when they must become the foremost of missionary nations. Even educated Hindus were moved at the sad loss, as they were familiar with his writings and had been taught by his greatest students. Alexander replied to Dr James Buchanan on 7 August, 1847, in a long letter that ended:

> Standing, as we do, in this great metropolis of Asiatic heathenism, surrounded by myriads that are perishing for lack of knowledge – myriads amounting, in the aggregate, to more than half of the race of man – it need not be wondered at that the mind should rapidly pass over all other features, however brilliant, and instinctively fasten on the missionary element in the character of our late revered father and friend.

Who could succeed him? not indeed as national leader of the third Reformation, but as a theological teacher and as a missionary influence at the head of the New College, which had been founded for the Free Church in Edinburgh. Many a heart turned instinctively to his greatest student, who had created two colleges of his own in Calcutta, and not a few elsewhere in imitation of these. While, after their orderly fashion, presbyteries and synods, unanimously or by large majorities, and then the General Assembly itself, in commission, called on Dr Alexander Duff to come home as the successor of Chalmers, every mail deluged him with private appeals to sacrifice his own 'predilection'. It was the old story of 1836, when every vacant charge with a large stipend thought to tempt him. Remembering that time, and with a conviction of the paramount claims of India more like that of Alexander himself, two leaders of the Free Church only were found to plead publicly that he be let alone, Dr Gordon, secretary of the Foreign Missions Committee, and Thomas Guthrie.

Alexander gave serious thought to the whole question of leaving his beloved India, and his active missionary work. It was as he was deep in thought over the matter, that he was given a letter from eleven of his Brahman students:

The all-merciful, omnipotent, just, and impartial God, compassionating the wretched people of India, first sent the eminently holy Dr Carey and others as missionaries. But, in the vast firmament of this country, they appeared as little stars and fireflies, and were consequently unable to dissipate the encompassing gloom. Then came Reichardt, and Wilson, and Piffard, and Ray, who have returned home, and a multitude of others, all of whom have done much for the real welfare of the truly wretched people of this country. But these have not done what they desired. They have not been very famous. Not only are their names unknown to most of the people of India, but even in the city of their habitation a few persons only know the names of some of them. After making these prefatory remarks, we the undersigned Sanskrit Pundits, submit as follows:

We have spoken of the success of some missionaries, and presently we shall speak of the eminently pious and learned Dr Duff. The Rev Doctor has been greatly blessed by Almighty God. His name is in the mouth of every

Hindoo because of his transcendent eloquence, learning, and philanthropy. As to his eloquence; from his mouth, which resembles a thick dark rain-cloud, there do issue forth bursts of incessant and unmeasured oratory; so that he fills his audience with rills of persuasive eloquence, just as the rain of heaven fills rivers, streams, brooks, valleys, canals, tanks, and pools, and, dissipating the dark delusions of false religion, he makes rise on their souls the light of true religion. This illustrious person, in order to the accomplishment of his object, has devoted his head and heart, and spent large sums of money. If some husbandmen, after ploughing, sowing, and watering a field, which held out to them the near prospect of a golden harvest, were to be stopped in their agricultural pursuits by one who, without considering either the labour bestowed upon the field, or the certainty of speedy gain, were to say to them, 'you must engage in something else', how, we would take the liberty of asking you, would the husbandmen feel, and how would the corn flourish? We leave it to your cultivated understandings to apply this example to the case in hand.

Such a man as the Rev Doctor was never seen in this country before. Now, alas! the object of our devout wishes is far from being realized. That which never came to our minds even in the visions of the night is suddenly about to happen. Oh! what must be the magnitude of the sin of this people to merit such a catastrophe! Consider how difficult it is to reform the ignorant; to remove mountains is, we think, a far easier matter. Consider again, how almost impossible it is to break down the barriers of caste, and open up social intercourse between the highest and lowest classes of the Hindoo community; to make sun and moon rise in the west is more practicable.

With the illustrious Duff India weighs heavy, but the mere report of his recall has made her light. With his recall the grand net which has been spread in this land for the establishment of the true religion would seem to be taken away. Good men have become sad, and bad men are rejoicing. The friends of true religion are praying that God would change the minds of the people of Scotland, and prevent Dr Duff's recall. If you are determined to blast the fruits of all missionary efforts that have been and are being made in this country, then our solicitations are like shedding tears in a forest, where there is none to sympathise with us. But, should you fulfil the object of our desires, we would then be extremely glad. What need is there to write more to such wise and considerate men as you are? Be pleased to excuse the length of this letter, and overlook all mistakes either in the matter or manner. Praying that we may be enabled to avoid the path of gross delusions, walk in the way of true religion that confers lasting benefits on all, and meditate on God with sole earnestness, we, with much humility, subscribe our names . . .

[This letter was a translation from the Sanskrit and written to the College Masters.]

It was necessary for Alexander to act before the meeting of the General Assembly in May, 1849. He accordingly wrote to Dr Tweedie. Tracing all the way by which the Lord had led him, from his own father's teaching to Chalmers' death, he declared that he must remain – must die as he had lived – the missionary:

I trust, therefore, that Dr Candlish, Dr Begg, Dr Buchanan, and other revered and beloved men will readily excuse me for not entering more minutely into the 'merits' of the question. They meant to honour me, and truly did honour me far more than I am conscious of deserving.

The men of the world, too, he wrote:

Whenever I met with such, as well as their organs of the public press, uniformly congratulated me on what they are pleased to designate as my contemplated 'elevation' or 'promotion' to the Edinburgh theological chair. I deem it, therefore, an unspeakable privilege to have it in my power to do anything, however humble, towards magnifying my much despised office. The conclusion of the whole matter is this, that in some form or other, at home or abroad or partly both, the Church of my fathers must see it to be right and meet to allow me to retain, in the view of all men, the clearly marked and distinguished character of a *missionary to the heathen* abroad, labouring directly amongst them; at home, pleading their cause among the churches of Christendom . . . For the sake of the heathen, and especially the people of India, let me cling all my days to the missionary cause.

The other Free Church missionaries and friends, Drs Wilson, Mackay, and Ewart, Messrs Anderson, Hislop, and MacKail, and Mr Justice Hawkins, united in the same request. But they agreed with Drs Gordon and Guthrie at home, that it was desirable for Alexander to return to Scotland for a time, to consolidate, in the Free Church, the work of missionary organisation to which he had given the years of his visit previous to the Disruption. When it became known that he would not sink the missionary in the divinity professor, the General Assembly urged his temporary return.

The Swiss Rev A. F. Lacroix, of the London Missionary Society, indeed went so far as to urge that the Free Church should found a chair in its new college:

> to be called the 'missionary or evangelistic' chair, having for its object to impart information and instruction regarding that most interesting and important portion of the Christian system – the universal spread of our Lord's kingdom over the earth. To such a professorship, if ever it be established, I should hail to see you appointed, but to no other. May the day soon come when the Free Church of Scotland will deem it its duty, *in this manner*, to complete the good work it has begun, and which has already produced such beneficial effects in various parts of the pagan world!

It is most significant that the Rev Lacroix made this proposal at this stage, as it prepared Alexander for the inevitable time when health or other reasons would prevent him working in the field. The outlook did not seem so bleak, and surely, by holding such an elevated position and giving lectures to the Universities of Edinburgh, St Andrews, Aberdeen and Glasgow, he would be in a most advantageous position in helping to secure new men for the field. This indeed is what came to pass.

Dr Nicholson pronounced it most desirable, on medical grounds, that Alexander should return to Europe after ten years' labours which had evidently shattered his constitution. At this stage Alexander did not know what his health would allow him to do. He did not know precisely how his Lord and his Church would direct his future activities, but of one thing he was certain. While in India, of all countries in the world, this was surely the great missionary field, he determined that he should visit all its evangelical and many of its Roman Catholic missions, south and north and west, before he took his message from the front of the battle to those at home. Dr Nicholson agreed that this would be possible, 'provided you take the common precautions necessary in travelling in this country, and avoid all needless fatigue and exposure'.

From April to August 1849, Alexander suffered fatigue and exposure, he underwent risks and toil, such as no motive lower than the missionary's could justify, and few others could have borne after a decade of exhausting duties in Bengal. He foresaw that should he be destined to serve the remainder of his missionary work at home, then he must have a much wider knowledge of the country of his work.

He parted from his wife for the first time, leaving her at the college to carry out her very many duties which comprised of helping the other missionaries with education of the young, supervising the general domestic duties of the establishment, taking care of the welfare of the pupils and students, providing motherly care to all, a task which to her, with her own children in Scotland, was a blessing, and to lead the singing!

The steamer which took him from Calcutta to Madras also took Mr Anderson and his first ordained convert, Rajahgopal, to Scotland. From his diary, we are able to trace the incredible galloping journey, travelling by night, and almost every night, with only broken and unrefreshed snatches of sleep in his palkee.

May 11, 1849. This evening, about eight o'clock, left our kind friends of the Mission, Madras, after addressing shortly the girls and young men and praying with all. Spoke about the necessity of self-denial and self-consecration; devoted lives are a more powerful preaching than burning words. Friends loaded me with kindness.

Heard the gun at eight o'clock on the Mount Road . . . Towards midnight the moon rose brightly. The road excellent, but few villages to be seen, and little real cultivation. Jungle everywhere instead of corn-fields. What is the cause? It must be investigated. Land-tax partly, no doubt; but the villainous exactions of underlings also. The system of interminable sub-division of land among children allows of no accumulation of capital. Hence no means of improvement; poverty everywhere increasing. The Gospel the only effectual remedy.

At daybreak found myself within five miles of Chingle-put. Feverish from want of proper sleep, and the disturb-ance of the system by the shaking and jolting of the palkee. Stepped out to take a walk. The basin where I stood was flat. One or two large tanks or reservoirs of water – fresh, clear water – were in view. These . . . are used for . . . irrigation. They looked like small Scotch lakes at the foot of hills. Close to one of these I passed; from it issued a small, clear, purling brook. It was the first of the kind I had seen for years, for in Bengal proper, clear, crystalline streams are nowhere to be found. . . . My emotions and fancy were vividly excited. I felt as if transported to the Grampians. I thought of the water of life, pure as crystal. I stepped from the roadside, and with the palms of the hand refreshed my dust-covered face and parched lips from the sparkling, gently murmuring brook, lifted up my soul to God, and took courage . . .

So much for what was then called the Middlesex of South India, the first principality acquired by the East India Com-pany, which the devastations of Hyder Ali and the worst ravages of famine had thus marred, and the old ryotwaree system of land tenure and tax had prevented from recovering. The fort was taken by Clive from the French in 1752.

At midnight he set out for Sadras, and continued to take the coast road by French Pondicheri, Cuddalore, Chillumbrum, Mayaveram, Danish Tranquebar, Combaconum, and Nega-patam. After an unsuccessful attempt to cross by boat from Point Calimere to Jaffna in Ceylon, he struck inland to Trichinopoly and Madura, by weary, dust-laden roads. From Madura he made a second vain attempt, by Ramnad, to reach Ceylon, and therefore again struck inland to Palamcotta, just north of Cape Comorin. From that centre he went round the chief Christian stations of Tinnevelli. Thence to Trevandrum, on the west coast, by Nagercoil. Having studied the flourishing mission settlements in the intensely Hindu state of Travancore, and its northern neighbour of Cochin, he went up the Malabar coast, by its picturesque backwaters, crossed the Western Ghauts by the Arungole pass to Palamcotta and Tutticorin, from which he sailed to Colombo, the capital of Ceylon.

At Point de Galle he took the mail steamer to Calcutta, where he delivered two lectures and a powerful sermon on his remarkable tour. The first described the missions at Tanjore and Tranquebar, the root of all Protestant evangelising in South India. The second discussed the condition of the Roman Catholic and Syrian Churches, and of the black and white Jews in Cochin. During his tour he was particularly thoughful for his dear wife and daughter, and his boys in Edinburgh. He made sincere reference to this in his diary, when at Aulamparna. Indeed it had been the first parting from his protecting angel and the mother of his children.

Hardly had Alexander returned to Calcutta in August, the worst part of the Bengal rainy season, when he made his preparations for the completion of his missionary survey of India. Early in October, when the first breath of the delightful cold weather of Northern India began to be felt, he took the steamer up the Ganges. At Benares he could contrast the Hinduism of the Ganges with that of the Coleroon and the Cavery countries. At Agra and Futtehpore Sikri he saw the glories of Akbar and Shah Jahan.

Zigzagging up the Ganges and Jumna valleys, and visiting all the mission stations as well as historical and architectural sites, Alexander reached the then little frequented sanitarium of Simla, in the secondary range of the Himalaya. But he would not rest until he had penetrated five marches further, to Kotghur, near the Upper Sutlej. That was then the most far-flung station of the Church Missionary Society. While in this region he took careful note of an incident which he often afterwards recounted.

When on a narrow bridle path cut out on the face of a precipitous ridge, he observed a native shepherd with his flock following him as usual. The man frequently stopped and looked back. If he saw a sheep creeping up too far on the one hand, or coming too near the edge of the dangerous precipice on the other, he would go back and apply his crook to one of the hind legs and gently pull it back, till it joined the rest. Though a Grampian Highlander, Alexander saw for the first time the real use of the crook or shepherd's staff in directing sheep in the right way. Going up to the shepherd, he noticed that he had a long rod which was as tall as himself, and around the lower half a thick band of iron was twisted. The region was infested with wolves, hyenas, and other dangerous animals, which in the night-time were apt to prowl about the place where the sheep lay. Then the man would go with this long rod, and would strike the animal such a blow as to make it at least turn away. This brought to the traveller's remembrance the expression of David, the shepherd, in the twenty-third Psalm, 'Thy rod and thy staff they comfort me' – the staff clearly meaning God's watchful, guiding and directing providence, and the rod his omnipotence in defending his own from foes, whether without or within. The incident showed that the expression was no tautology, as many of the commentators made it out to be.

Lord Dalhousie had become Governor-General before he was forty, and was then entering the Punjab. Sir Henry Lawrence had returned from his shortened furlough and was at the head of the new administration, with his brother John and Sir Robert Montgomery as his colleagues. The second Sikh war had been fought, and the most triumphant success of British administration in the East was just beginning. Alexander became Sir Henry's guest in Government House at Lahore, of course, and they had many conversations on affairs public and private, missionary and philanthropic. On the last day of 1849, Alexander wrote:

> Yesterday I had the privilege of preaching the everlasting gospel to an assembly of upwards of two hundred ladies and gentlemen, civil and military, in the great hall of the Government House, now worthily occupied by Sir Henry Lawrence, whose guest I have been since my arrival. And, as indicative of the *radicalness* of the change that is come over the firmament of former power and glory in this city, I may state that I had the option of holding public worship either in the Government House, formerly the residence (though now greatly enlarged) of the redoubted Runjeet Singh's French generals, or in the great audience or Durbar Hall of the Muhammadam Emperors and Sikh Maharajas. What a change! The tidings of the great salvation sounding in these great halls – once the abodes of the lords-paramount of the most antichristian systems and monarchies! Surely, the Creator hath gone up before us, though in the rough and giant form of blood-stained war. God in mercy grant that in these regions, so repeatedly drenched with human blood, men may soon to learn to 'beat their swords into plough-shares and their spears into pruning-hooks'; and thus cultivate the arts of peace, and make progress in the lessons and practice of heavenly piety!

In Bombay at the end of April there was a rush of home-going

Britons eager to escape the worst of the hot season. Duff could secure only 'a den in the second lower deck', and he had a fall on board. But the end of May, 1850, saw the Duffs once more in Edinburgh.

14
Moderator

The Duffs arrived at Waverley station in Edinburgh at the latter end of April, 1850, and their younger son William Pirie had been given leave from Merchiston Castle School to meet them. A knot of friends, including Dr Lorimer and Mr Kerr were also there. In the *Memoirs of Dr Duff*,[1] his son describes the meeting with his father:

> It is difficult to recall my first impression. A modest income did not allow of a very striking domicile, and we took up our residence for the first year in Middleby Street, Newington, a southern suburb of Edinburgh . . . I remember distinctly the supper that night. My father looked wearied, and his coat indicated much travel and much wear. My mother said 'Had —— your old bearer been with you, he would not have allowed you to wear your coat in such a state'. The next morning I was away to Merchiston before any one was up. On Saturday I was allowed leave of absence till Monday. I walked with one of the Merchiston tutors to Newington by way of the Grange. Presently a worn gentleman was seen, coming feebly along. I did not know him. He did not know me.
>
> The tutor said, 'Dr Duff', and sure enough father and son were then introduced.
>
> It was on the following Sunday evening he catechized me. He evidently expected great things, though I was not yet twelve. Had I not for five years enjoyed the exceptional advantage of tuition at a great Christian school, presided over by the brother and nephews of his own illustrious and beloved teacher?
>
> In an agony of spirit he delivered his judgment. 'The heathen boys in my Institution in Calcutta know more of the Bible than you do.' . . . Those who remember Dr Duff can understand there was something of restraint and

[1] W. Pirie Duff, *Memorials of Alexander Duff, D.D.* (London: Nisbet, 1890).

reticence when he found his son more ignorant than the native lads in the Calcutta Institution.

Anne's reaction was one of unrestricted joy at being with her own darling children once more. Her young son, almost twelve, was a baby of eleven months when she last fondled him.

The missionary found that he had returned to Scotland not a day too soon. There was urgently wanted for the Foreign Missions of the Free Church a financier in the best sense, one who could create a self-sustaining and self-developing revenue, as well as control of expenditure so as to make it produce the best possible results. It was felt a lesson to all philanthropic agencies, that he who was the most spiritual of men and most fervid of missionaries, with a Celtic intensity of fervour, was at the same time most practical as an economist and far-sighted as an administrator. He had shown this in the establishment of his first school and college in Calcutta; he had proved it in his first home campaign of 1835–39, to which Dr Chalmers had publicly acknowledged his indebtedness. It was now necessary that he should repeat, in Scotland, the organizing toil of his previous campaign, if the Foreign Missions of the Free Church were to be worthy of its history and of the professions of its duty to the one Head of the Church Catholic.

Not that the Free Church had been illiberal, even to the missions abroad, in the first seven years of its operations. On the contrary, while contributing to church history a new fact since the Acts of the Apostles, in what then appeared to all Christendom the marvellous contributions of a million of comparatively poor people, it had added to the original twenty Indian and Jewish missionaries with which it started, new fields in South Africa, in Central India, in rural Bengal and in Bombay. But while Chalmers, Guthrie and Dr R. Macdonald created sustenation, manse and school funds, there was no one to put the foreign mission subscriptions on an organized and self-acting system. Now there was such a man.

During the ten days and nights of the General Assembly of 1850, of which the Rev Dr N. Paterson, of Glasgow, was the Moderator, Dr Duff delivered five addresses. Published separately because of the crowds whom they drew to the great Tanfield Hall of Disruption memories, and of the interest which the imperfect report excited throughout Scotland and the evangelical churches, these orations covered eighty pages. As a whole they were marked by a condensation of style which the very fullness and variety of the speaker's experience, drawn from the wide extent of India, forced upon him. He began:

This time twenty-one years ago, when I was set apart by the Church of Scotland to proceed to India, all the world seemed to be in a state of calm; there might be said to be a universal calm at least in the world of politics. Many, however, regarded it as the calm which was to precede the storm and earthquake; and truly the earthquake speedily came – the French Revolution and its convulsions, and social changes in this land in connection with the Reform Bills and such like. So that, on returning four or five years afterwards, it appeared as if something like an earthquake had passed over the social fabric of this country; as if the accustomed manners and habits of the people had exhibited somewhat the aspect of social chaos, and to it might figuratively be applied the words of a national poet –

'Crags, rocks, and knolls confus'dly hurled,
The fragments of an earlier world.'

Since returning the last time, and looking about expecting to find greater social changes from the still greater earthquake which had passed over this land, especially in the Church department, it was the delight not only of myself but of others from abroad, to find that instead of such a chaos all things had quietly settled down and were progressing in harmony and in order; that the old Church in its new and free form had risen up entire in all its organisms and complete in all its parts.

Now that the machinery is perfect, he urged, apply it to foreign missions.

When addressing the General Assembly fifteen years ago, my knowledge of India was comparatively limited. It is so no longer. I feel this night, if there there were time and patience on the part of the House, and if strength on my part were vouchsafed, that it would be easier for me to speak for six hours than for one. If the Lord spare me and I am allowed to visit different parts of the land, all I have gathered in connection with India shall be poured throughout Scotland in good time.

His first speech, on the first business day of the Assembly, was on the report of the committee for the conversion of the Jews. As a missionary to the Gentiles he sought to express the intensity of his sympathies with a cause which is emphatically that of foreign missions. He told of his own Jewish converts; he described the last hours and Christian confession of the rabbi whom, and whose family, he had baptised. He sketched the condition of the three Jewish settlements in Western and Southern India, and he pleaded for 'harmony and earnest co-operation in promoting the spiritual and eternal welfare alike of Jews and Gentiles'. On this the first occasion of addressing a General Assembly of the Free Church, he then asked the vast audience to bear with him while he poured out his testimony to the principles of spiritual and civil liberty for which the missionaries and ministers of the Disruption had sacrificed their all.

Two days after, 'as a Colonist', he moved the adoption of the report on colonial and continental missions, telling the story of the Calcutta congregation, and advocating the claims of the Eurasians on the brotherhood of Englishmen as they had 'never yet been pled before an ecclesiastical court in this land'. He had still to sweep away another prejudice against the cause he represented. Reminding the Church that he had, from the banks of the Ganges, long since volunteered the assertion that Dr Chalmers' Sustentation Fund for ministers 'is the backbone of the whole ecclesiastical establishment', he said:

> With the same intensity with which I wish to see all nations evangelised and the gospel carried to all lands, I would wish to see this and other sustentation funds augmented vastly beyond their present measure, so as not only to uphold the existing ministry at the present rate, but in the way of vastly greater competency; yea, and to see the fund increased so that it may maintain double the number of ministers, and overtake not only the existing religionism but the existing heathenism of the land.

Then in his fourth and fifth speeches he came to his own special subject of the India Mission. This was claimed to be oratory at its best. On each night, now swaying his arms towards the vast audience around and even above him, on the roof, and now jerking his left shoulder with an upward motion till the coat threatened to fall off, the tall form kept thousands spellbound while the twilight of a northern May night changed into the brief darkness, and the tardy lights revealed the speaker bathed in the flood of his impassioned appeals. As the thrilling voice died away in the eager whisper which, at the end of his life, marked all his public utterances, and the exhausted speaker fell into a seat, only to be driven home to a rest barely sufficient to enable his fine constitution to renew and repeat again and again the effort, the observer could realize the expenditure of physical energy which, as it marked all he did, culminated in his prophet-like raptures.

In the midst of the speech of 29 May, Dr Tweedie took advantage of a pause to interrupt him. In truth, the leading men around Alexander trembled for his life if he were to go on when it was near midnight, and in an atmosphere which could scarcely be breathed, and must be particularly oppressive to the eloquent speaker. The alarmed friend begged that the conclusion might be postponed. Alexander was roused by the applause of the House to declare that he must go on; and he did so for two more hours, while not a hearer moved save to catch the almost gasping utterance towards the close. Night after night had been devoted to the considerations of missionary objects. As a Scottish audience addressed by a Highlander, no speech had greater effect on the Assembly than the following:

> In days of yore, though unable to sing myself, I was wont to listen to the Poems of Ossian, and to many of those melodies that were called Jacobite songs. I may now, without any fear of being taken up for high treason or for rebellion, refer to the latter, for there never was a Sovereign who was more richly and deservedly beloved by her subjects than she who now sits on the throne of Great Britain – Queen Victoria – and there are not among her Majesty's subjects any men whose hearts beat more vigorously with the pulse of loyalty than the descendants of those chieftains and clansmen who a century ago shook the Hanoverian throne to its foundation. While listening to these airs of the olden time, some stanzas and sentiments made an indelible impression on my mind. Roving in the days of my youth over the heathery heights, or climbing the craggy steeps of my native land, or lying down to enjoy the music of the roaring waterfalls, I was wont to admire the heroic spirit which they breathed; and they became so stamped in memory that I have carried

them with me over more than half the world. One of these seemed to me to embody the quintessence of loyalty of an earthly kind. It is the stanza in which is said by the father or mother –

'I hae but ae son, the brave young Donald;'
and then the gush of emotion turned his heart
as it were inside out, and he exclaimed –

'But oh, had I ten, they would follow Prince Charlie.'

Are these the visions of romance – the dreams of poetry and of song? Oh, let that rush of youthful warriors, from 'bracken, bush and glen', that rallied round the standards of Glenfinnan – let the gory beds, and cold, cold grassy winding-sheets of bleak Culloden Muir bear testimony to the reality, the intensity of the loyalty to an earthly prince; and shall a Highland father and mother give up all their children as a homage to earthly loyalty, and shall I be told that in the Churches of Christ, in the Free Church of Scotland, fathers and mothers will begrudge their children to Him who is the King of kings and Lord of lords? Will they testify their loyalty to an earthly prince, to whom they lie under very little obligation, by giving up all their sons, while they refuse, when it comes to the point of critical decision, even one son for the army of Immanuel, to whom they owe their life, their salvation, their all?

He went on:

From one end of India to the other the soil is strewn with British dead. There is not a valley, nor dell, nor burning waste, from one end of India to the other, that is not enriched with the bones, and not a rivulet or stream which has not been dyed with the blood of Scotia's children. And will you, fathers and mothers, send out your children in thousands in quest of this bubble fame – this bubble wealth – this bubble honour and perishable renown, and will you prohibit them from going forth in the army of the great Immanuel, to win crowns of glory and imperishable renown in the realms of everlasting day? Oh, do not refuse their services – their lives if necessary – or the blood of the souls of perishing millions may be required at your hands.

The Assembly instructed the committee to take steps for bringing the subject of foreign missions fully before the mind of the Church, and that in such a way as may be arranged between the committee and the synod or presbytery which Dr Duff or the other brethren may care to visit. The Assembly appointed these visitations to begin with the synod of Perth, and after that had been undertaken, to be extended from synod to synod, as circumstances might direct, until they shall, if possible, have gone over the whole bounds of the Church. Alexander's plan in the West was surely under way and the whole power of the Assembly was behind him and his cause.

For the next three and a half years Alexander gave himself to the creating of his new organization, an organization for prayer, information, and the quarterly collection of subscriptions for the missions in every one of the then seven hundred congregations of the Free Church of Scotland. He now considered that what was wanted was such knowledge on the part of the new race of ministers and elders that the freewill offerings of the Scottish nation, Highland and Lowland, might systematically flow out beyond the bounds of sect and party into the wider and truly catholic region of their Indian and African fellow-subjects. He had to teach his own countrymen, and especially his fellow-ministers, a lesson in Christian economics.

In his own country, as in India, separated from his family then requiring most of all a father's care; in winter and in summer; in weariness and often in pain, the first missionary of his Church pursued his work, inspired by an enthusiasm before which the most repulsive and exhausting work was sweet. His almost daily letters to his wife include passages which reveal the man and his work.

As during his first furlough in 1835, Alexander's campaign included England, Wales and Ireland, in addition to Scotland, though the first three rather that he might tell the Church of England, Wesleyan and Welsh societies, and the Ulster Presbyterians, how worthy their Indian agents were of more generous support. He also had another object in view. The time for the East India Company applying to Parliament for a renewal of its twenty years' charter was at hand, and he desired to create among the governing as well as missionary classes, and the directors, such an intelligent interest as would, without public agitation, in the first instance, secure justice to non-government education in India, whether Christian, Hindu, Parsee or Muslim. We shall see later, that the very effectual pressure of Parliament and prolonged public discussion were required to secure the concession of justice.

In the four months between the close of the General Assembly and the meeting of its commission in November, 1850, he visited every congregation of what might be called his own synod of Perth. From this point he travelled far and wide, accepting invitations requesting his presence for addresses on missionary work. The following passages are quoted from his letters giving dates and places, so that we may follow the path of this most extraordinary man:

Cernarvon, 10 September, 1851. On Tuesday forenoon I had a long and animated interview with the celebrated Dr McNeile, of Liverpool. We both harmonized famously on the whole subject of Popery, and so had an exhilarating conversation. Missions too, and prophecy, the preparatives to the millennial glory, were fully discoursed of – agreeing fully on all points, but agreeing to differ as to dogmatic views on the personal advent and reign of Christ; Dr McNeile seeing his way to be very positive on that head, while I do not. But he spoke with exceeding candour and forebearance, and so we parted full of warm expressions of mutual regard and goodwill . . . This morning . . . attended a meeting of the Welsh Conference [and was asked] to address them . . .

Bangor, 13 September. Yesterday, at two o'clock, I preached to the largest audience I ever addressed in this world – amounting by computation to between fifteen and twenty thousand people! At the synod meetings of the Calvinistic Methodists of Wales there are open-air preachings, at which some of their more popular men officiate. On the present occasion the place chosen was a green park behind the city of Caernarvon – being a continuation of the upward acclivity on which the town is built. It looks to the west on the Menai Straits and the Isle of Anglesey – the small hill of Holyhead, whence the Irish packet sails, in the distant west. To the north-east, east, and south-east, are the lofty Welsh hills, Snowdon distant only eight or nine miles. At the foot of the park a temporary stage is erected for the preacher and fifty more, covered over with canvas above, and all around except the front. The people assemble all around and beneath this platform, stretching out some hundreds of yards on either side of it, and from this extended base line crowding up in front to the upper end of the park, like a compacted cone or pyramid of living heads. From the platform the spectacle exhibited is a very exciting and wonder-striking one.

On Wednesday there were two sermons here in the afternoon. But yesterday was the great day. Never was there a clearer sky in these British isles, nor a warmer sun at this time of the year, than yesterday at Caernarvon. From ten to one o'clock – prayer, psalms and two sermons. Then an hour's interval for the people to retire for refreshment. A little before two, the broad street leading up to the park was a living, moving stream of human beings; every second person carrying a chair aloft – holding it by the back, the four legs pointing to the zenith, to prevent accidents. At two o'clock the great living cone or pyramid was formed. It is astonishing how densely they were packed, and more men than women, making allowance for the hat-wearing women. Considering the busy season of the year – the thick of harvest – it was surprising to see such multitudes congregated from the districts all around. And such quietude and fixedness of attention and general decorum!

It was not willingly that I ventured to address such a throng. First, I felt as if my voice would not reach the twentieth part of them. Second, not above a twentieth part of them could understand English. But the synod unanimously requested me to preach, saying there were many sprinkled over the mass who could understand, and that the testimony for the great truths of the gospel from a stranger would tell on all who understood, and through them, on others by interpretation. So I reluctantly yielded. But I was really glad I did so. From the stillness of the multitude, and the absence of even a breeze, it seems that my voice reached the outer skirts of the amazing throng – one of the ministers having walked gently round on purpose to ascertain the point. And what I was enabled to say appeared to cheer greatly those who understood, for I heard the responding groan loudly sounded from individuals in all directions.

What astonished me was the fixed look and marked attention of the thousands who understood not a single word of what I uttered. Beforehand such a phenomenon might seem incredible. Almost all were seated, generally two on a chair. The psalm-singing, with its singular plaintiveness and richness of tone and depth of heart-melody, was the sublimest thing of the kind I ever listened to. About half-past four the Welsh sermon ended, then a few verses of a psalm, short prayer and blessing. In a moment the prodigious mass was on the move. Thousands of chairs were upheaved, with legs high in air – a perfect forest in quick motion . . .

Woolwich, 22 September. Yesterday I officiated for Mr Thomson, who is very unwell. The congregation consists in a large measure of officers and soldiers, a very interesting and affecting spectacle. . . . I believe Colonel Anderson and others mean to make a private subscription and send the amount to me, as a token of goodwill towards our Mission. At the close of the forenoon service a person sent word to the vestry that she wished to speak to me. On my going out, she began by saying that she was a servant; that, being a nurse in an officer's family, she could not get out at night; that the Lord had done much for her soul, and she desired to be grateful by remembering His cause; that she happened to be in Edinburgh and heard me at last Assembly, and she concluded by begging me to accept of her mite for sending the gospel to the perishing heathen. So saying, she put a sovereign in my hand. I looked with some degree of wonder. She noticed my surprise, and simply in substance remarked, 'Oh, sir, what is that compared with what He has done for my soul!' . . .

Whitehaven, 29 November. Reached Carlisle at quarter to ten o'clock, a hundred miles in three hours including all stoppages! What a revolution in travelling since that awful weary night when you and I left Edinburgh, 1st. Nov. 1839, at nine p.m., reaching Carlisle to breakfast next morning between eight and nine, with bones and back half-broken with jamming in a box of a coach, and eyes half-blind with attempts (alas, how vain!) at sleep; and hearts filled with sadness at the thought of those left behind! And yet, after *twelve* years, we have three of them still with us – as if the Lord by His goodness were rebuking our faint-heartedness. One is gone – gone from us; but oh, I do live in the hope that she has only gone before us to hail our arrival (if we are upheld faithful to the end) in a better world. I seldom allude to the dear child that bore your name, but the sweet image of her often crosses my mind. She was a perfectly lovable one; and I know not whether I ever felt any stroke so acutely as her unexpected death. And even still, when alone by myself, the thought of her cheerful animated countenance, with its sweet expression and lisping tongue, often brings the tear to my eye, as now . . .

Manchester, 24 December. Our great meeting came off last evening, and by God's blessing, nobly. It was much owing to Barbour's skilful management. No such platform has been seen here, on any occasion. Pastors of all churches present, and several clergy of the English Church; Hugh Stowell, etc., speaking, making motions. Some of the leading laity. The meeting was quite an enthusiastic one. Before breaking up nearly a thousand pounds were announced as subscriptions, in hundreds and fifties; Barbour himself giving £500. After a rather restless night I feel this morning tolerably well; but, on the whole, it must be confessed to be too much for me. Oh that the Lord may come down among us in showers of blessing! I have to address a meeting tomorrow.

Glasgow, 19 February 1852 . . . to Hope Street Church, the largest Free Church in Glasgow . . . crowded . . . a noble audience . . . This morning, joined Miss Dennistoun, sister of Mrs (Dr) Wilson, Bombay; and Mrs Wodrow (widow of Wodrow the great advocate of the Jews, and descendant, I believe, of the historian) at breakfast. Thereafter a succession of callers.

Paisley, 16 March. I came here yesterday forenoon, met with the presbytery, and addressed a public meeting in the evening. All very cordial in this quarter. But I am nearly done up. Last week I delivered five addresses at Greenock and two at Dumbarton, besides the Sabbath services before and after. Here I gave two addresses yesterday, I have another tonight, and one tomorrow.

Wick Bay, 19 June. [After a stormy passage] 'Oh for more real inward life in the midst of this endless tumult and turmoil!'

Thurso Castle, 12 July. This morning your anxiously looked-for communications reached me at Wick, dated 8th and 9th I hope that on the 9th, at least, you would have received two letters from me, one dated 6th, on board the steamer in Kirkwall Bay, and the other of the same date after arriving at Wick. Be so good as to tell me specially in your next whether these came to hand. Truly the 9th July, 1829, [their marriage day] was a memorable day in our eventful history. The Lord be praised for its abounding mercies. Our cup has been made to run over, goodness and mercy following all our days and through all our steps . . .

Golspie, 17 July. What I long for is a little repose, to get mind and body brought back to some degree of equilibrium. What with incessant travelling and speaking, for the last two nights I have had, on one only two hours sleep, and the other three, that I might now almost sleep standing. I have, however, experienced much of the loving-kindness of the Lord; and that makes up for all the fatigues, so far as the spirit is concerned.

Alness, 24 July. Your two most welcome letters were awaiting me. For them, and especially the long and affectionate letter of the 19th, I return my warmest thanks. Truly the 19th July, 1834 [the day of their first departure from Calcutta] was an ever-memorable day in our history . . .

Near the Foot of Ben Nevis, 12 August. I am seated at a window looking across on Ben Nevis, which has not yet uncovered its brow from its nightcap of clouds. But the whole scene is elevating and imposing. On Tuesday morning I came from Culloden House to attend the meeting of presbytery at Inverness; besides members a large body of elders and deacons attended from different congregations, town and country. In the end all very cordially agreed to work out the association plan . . . I went up, as others did, to the fall of Foyers as the morning was fine – going, seeing, and returning to the steamer all within the hour. I will not here, even had I time, indulge in the ordinary poetic sentimentalisms about cataracts. The whole scenery is certainly very rugged and grand. I had no previous adequate idea of the beauty here, and ruggedness there, and towering grandeur yonder, of the scenery along the Caledonian Canal. But the gem in the whole was Glengarry House and woody heights, while the sublime (next to Ben Nevis) was in the Glengarry hills. I do not now wonder that your youthful fancy was fired in these regions. I thought, as I passed, that I saw you, in mental vision, skipping along these beautiful lawns and banks and sloping acclivities – in all the gay and buoyant vigour of eighteen. And I trow that among the gazers on that scene of inspiring and exhilarating joy, there would be no one more joyously elastic than my own beloved partner. But then, probably, this world, with its phantasmagoria of fleeting dreams, may have occupied the chief place in her affections; while now, praised be God, the enduring realities of the everlasting future in the realms of day, have acquired their proper ascendancy; and so the sober pursuits of 49 Minto Street, Newington, may be not only more profitable, but in reality more prolific of pure joy to the spirit, than the gaysome lightsome buxom joyousnesses of Glengarry in the days of blooming and elastic girlhood.

Portree, Skye. The *élite* of the whole Free Church population of the island were there, from end to end – many from fifteen, twenty, twenty-five and even thirty miles distant; several too of the leading, would-be great men still connected with the Establishment; and the moderate minister's own wife. It was a great day at Portree and Skye. So it was felt, I do believe. The services beginning about eleven did not end till about six. And all that time the great bulk of the audience sat still without once moving from their seats. Feeling myself in much weakness and not a little mental depression, I could scarcely tell from what, I found more than ordinary freedom in addressing sinners, and could see from the countenances, and the tearful eyes, that impressions were produced. God grant that they may prove not ephemeral impressions on the mere sensibilities of nature, but living impressions, inwrought by the power of the Holy Ghost. After sermon old Mrs McDonald came forward to embrace me. She had remained purposely for a fortnight to witness the opening of the church . . .

Huntly Lodge, 13 October. A most delightful meeting yesterday with the presbytery of Strathbogie; and in the evening a grand public meeting. One of the presbytery elders, Mr Stronach, a gentleman of property, who, as magistrate, was called in to quell the disturbance at the ever-memorable Marnock settlement, publicly declared that it was what dropped from me, on my visit to this place, seventeen years ago, which first gave him the impulse towards missions, an impulse which has sustained him ever since . . .

Kincardine O'Neil, 24 November. Before leaving Rhynie this morning I wrote a short note to W[illiam]. It was piercingly cold. A keen hard frost, with a cloudless sky, and icy wind. Since I left the pulpit on Sunday I have scarcely yet got into anything like warmth, either by night or by day. I have felt as if the cold was oozing through my whole body, from head to foot . . .

Banchory-Ternan, 25 November. In crossing from Alford I had a magnificent view of the massive and lofty mountain of Lochnagar – reminded thereby of the unhappy Byron. Had a very delightful meeting with the presbytery of Kincardine O'Neil; and tonight, with the congregation here. I have still an oppressive cold on my chest – nostrils running without ceasing, with cough. In my bedroom shut up all day, till I went out to the meeting at six. Unable to speak very loud; but the people were so still and attentive, that a whisper was almost heard by them. I am more than ever convinced that if only I could visit *all* the congregations in person, associations would at once be organized in every one of them. This was once the parish of the celebrated Principal Campbell, who wrote the famous essay on Miracles in answer to Hume. The ruins of his manse are still here. The whole of Deeside was wont to be a regular preserve of the Moderates. It is cancered all over with Moderatism still. Oh, for a life-breath from heaven to stir up the dead! . . .

Banchory House, 6 December. The loving-kindness of the Lord in directing me hither has been unspeakable; and I do desire to cherish a deeper sense of gratitude towards Him, who is the Author of all these mercies. I have been terribly beset by all sorts of applications from all sorts of persons and societies for all sorts of objects. From the shortness of my sojourn, it has been utterly impossible for me to attend to the great bulk of them. But as a specimen of the way in which I am sometimes captured, in spite of every effort to escape, I shall briefly narrate the facts of a case.

Some weeks ago I received a letter asking me to preach a sermon on behalf of a school established in a very destitute locality for the children of a colony of poor fishermen. I wrote to say that, with so many engagements before me, which must be compressed within so short a time, I could not honestly, commit or pledge myself in any way to preach such a sermon; but that if, after coming to Aberdeen, I found my strength equal to it, I had all the heart to respond to such a call . . .

. . . The public meeting of Thursday, attended, they say, by at least 2,000 jammed into an immense edifice, well-nigh felled me. Still I had to go to Skene, twelve miles distant, to hold a public meeting there on Friday evening. Returning to town on Saturday, I addressed a large body of the students of all the colleges, at 2 p.m.!

He had agreed to take a double service in the Free Church on the Sunday morning, and therefore said he was unable to take an evening service as well. However, Alexander's hand was forced when he discovered that the evening service had already been advertised in two Aberdeen newspapers: '. . . I despatched a special message . . . to say, that though under no moral obligation in the matter, but rather the contrary, after such fraudulent usage, I would for the sake of preventing scandal, and therefore for the sake of Christ's cause, endeavour to do what I could in the evening.'

Ayr, 5 February, 1853. I was more than delighted with my visit to Kilmarnock . . .

Wigtown, 10 February. Our meetings at Stranraer were very pleasant . . .

Alexander continued on his seemingly endless journeying, in pursuit of his great cause, but he was fully aware that it was taking toll on his health. In the last of this series of letters to his wife, writing to her from Ayr in December 1853, he said:

> . . . No one can ever fully know how much I often suffer, both in mind and body, in the midst of these frequent, prolonged, and violent exertions. And to none but yourself can I ever moot the subject except in the vaguest and most general terms. In the excitement of speaking, the spirit forgets the fragility of the body; and therefore, people think me strong. Ah, if they could see me in my solitary chamber, all alone, after such meetings as last night, their congratulations on my supposed strength would be exchanged for downright commiseration. The whole frame feverish – the whole nervous system, from the brain downwards, in a state of total unrest. The very tendency to sleep gone. Going to bed, as this morning, at half-past one, not from sleepiness but from inability to sit up longer through exhaustion. Turning and tossing from side to side, and longing for sleep. Then drowsiness, and half-sleep, and horrid dreams, and longing for the morning's dawn. Getting up disquieted and unrefreshed, to meet a company at breakfast – with aching head besides,

and sorish throat. Necessity for appearing as pleasant as may be, so as not to damp or discourage others; and every effort in this way only increasing the pain. But enough; I must say no more on this subject . . .

These passages from letters to his wife reveal the inner self of Alexander. They reveal his deep love for his wife and his family, yet this love was only known to Anne as he had been parted from his children for most of their lives. His love for them was there, but there was little opportunity to demonstrate it, or to enjoy their love in return.

The period over which these passages are quoted extends from the General Assembly in 1850 to the end of 1853, but we must now look back to the earlier part of this work period, when in May, 1851, Dr Alexander Duff was appointed, as the first missionary to sit in the Moderator's chair since the first General Assembly in 1560. Not only that, almost without precedent, he sat there twice, as we shall see.

At the unusually early age of forty-five Alexander Duff was, in 1851, called by acclamation to the highest ecclesiastical seat in Scotland, that of Knox and Melville, Henderson and Chalmers. His immediate predecessor had declared that what the Preacher of the Old Testament calls 'the flourish of the almond tree' had been the chief recommendation in his case. The still young missionary found his qualification in 'the office which it has been my privilege, however unworthily, amid sunshine and storm, for nearly a quarter of a century, to hold – the glorious office of evangelist, or that of making known the unsearchable riches of Christ among the Gentiles'. He went on:

Wholly sinking, therefore, the man into the office and desiring to magnify my office, I can rejoice in the appointment. In the early and most flourishing times of the Church, the office of the apostle, missionary, or evangelist, who 'built not on another man's foundation', was regarded as the highest and most honourable. Those who thus went forth to the unreclaimed nations were the generals and the captains of the invading army in the field, while bishops or presbyters were but the secondary commandants of garrisons planted in the already conquered territory. And even in later times, when, in the progress of degeneracy and amid the increasing symptoms of decrepitude and decay, the bishop came to mount the ladder of secular ambition over the more devoted and self-denying missionary, the office of the latter still continued to be held in considerable repute. Hence we read of Augustine, and Willibrord, and Winifred, and Anscharius, and many more besides, who fearlessly perilled their lives in labouring to reclaim the Saxons, Frieslanders, Hessians, Swedes, and other pagan and barbarous tribes, being afterwards created bishops and archbishops, in acknowledgment of their arduous and successful toils. But in more recent times, when the office of the missionary fell into almost entire desuetude among the leading Reformed communities of Christendom, and the attempt to revive it was at first denounced as an unwarrantable intrusion and novelty, the name, once so glorious in the Church of Christ, came to be associated with all that is low, mean, contemptible, or fanatical; but, praised be God, that of late years the name has been rescued from much of the odium, through a juster appreciation of the grandeur, dignity, and heavenly objects of the office that bears it. For the office's sake, therefore, wholly irrespective of the worthiness or unworthiness of the individual who may hold it, I cannot but hail this day's appointment as a sure indication that, whatever the case may be with others, the Free Church of Scotland has fairly risen above the vulgar and insensate prejudices of a vauntingly religious but leanly spiritual age.

When in London, in 1851, Alexander was called on to commit to the grave the body of his dear friend Sir John Pirie. His widow's house was ever after Alexander's home in London until her death in 1869.

As the time approached for the renewal of the charter to the East India Company in 1854, the governing classes both in India and England prepared for conflict. As official advocate of the venerable corporation, Sir John Kaye took credit for all that had been done not only by the directors, but in spite of them, by governor-generals, missionaries and those whom they used to denounce as interlopers. So the Company was spared from extinction once more, by the Whigs under Sir Charles Wood as President of the Board of Control. But several compromises were effected by the Cabinet and Parliament, most happily for both India and the mother country. The two greatest in reality, though they appeared little at the time, were, the concession of nearly all of Dr Alexander Duff's demands for a truly imperial, catholic, and just administration of the educational funds, honours and rewards; and the transfer to the nation, by competitive examinations, of the eight hundred and fifty highly paid appointments in the covenanted civil service. And then, as if to prepare the way for the Company's coming extinction in 1858, the new charter was passed subject to the pleasure of Parliament, and not for the almost prescriptive period of twenty years.

The evidence and suggestions presented to the select committees of the House of Lords and Commons on Indian territories by Dr Duff, Mr Marshman, and Sir Charles Trevelyan, were carried out even in detail. But it was Duff who succeeded in placing the keystone in the arch of his aggressive educational system by the famous despatch of 1854. There is no duty more delightful to a statesmanlike reformer as that of convincing a parliamentary committee. Nor intellectually are there many feats more exhausting than that of sitting from eleven to four o'clock, and on more days than one, indeed for several weeks during the sessions of 1852 and 1853, the object of incessant questioning, by fifteen or twenty experts, on the most difficult problems, economic and administrative, that can engage the statesman. This was Alexander's position, and he was moreover one of a band of witnesses of rare experience and ability.

On the Indian side were judges and civilians of such distinction as Sir E. Ryan and Sir E. Perry, Messrs R. M. Bird and Mangles, Sir J. P. Willoughby and Sir F. Halliday, and of such promise as Sir George Campbell. Among soldiers, besides Gough and Napier there were Cotton, Pollock and Melville. Scholars like H. H. Wilson, lawyers like N. B. E. Baillie, bishops, missionaries, and priests, and finally Parsees submitted their evidence. Among the members of the Lords Committee were peers of the official experience of Ellenborough, Tweeddale and Elphinstone, Broughton and Glenelg, Powis and Canning, Lord Monteagle of Brandon, Lord Stanley of Alderley and Lord Ashburton. The Commons Committee included Mr Joseph Hume, Mr Baring, Sir Charles Wood, Mr Cobden, Mr Vernon Smith, Mr Lowe, Mr Gladstone, Mr Disraeli, Lord Palmerston, Mr Macaulay, and Mr James Wilson.

Alexander's evidence on the purely judicial and administrative questions decided by the charter proved to be of unexpected value. Not only had he been conversant, personally, with the reforms of Lord William Bentinck and the experienced civilians who advised and assisted the most radical statesman who ever filled the Governor-General's seat; the missionary had for six years been the head of all the reformers in India, who, in the *Calcutta Review*, discussed in detail the measures which were successfully pressed on the attention of Parliament. Lord Halifax introduced the new India Bill. Lord Northbrook, then the president's private secretary, sent out the state paper to the Marquis of Dalhousie as the memorable despatch of the 9 July, 1854, signed by ten directors of the East India Company. Alexander's handiwork can be traced not only in the definite orders, but in the very style of what was afterwards pronounced the great educational charter of the people of India.

15

America and Canada and return to India

Among the visitors to the General Assembly in Edinburgh in May, 1851, was a Mr George H. Stuart, a merchant of Irish descent from Philadelphia in the United States of America. He sat spellbound by Alexander's addresses. He approached the young missionary and invited him to America saying, 'We want to be stirred up there.' How could Alexander refuse such an invitation? It was not until 1854, when Alexander's extensive tour of Britain came to a close, that the Assembly Foreign Missions Committee sent him to the United States and to the colonies, that were to become the Dominion of Canada. The time was not particularly favourable for a kindly reception in the West of public men from the Old Country, not even ecclesiastics. The young republic was then very resistant to criticism. In Dr Duff, however, there was a great man who represented Asia as well as Europe, and much could be learned from him.

He arrived at the mouth of the Hudson on 13 February, 1854, having set sail from Liverpool on Saturday 28 January in the steamship *Africa*. The journey had been extremely rough. The vessel was capable of thirteen knots but at times struggled like a giant ox against the gale at a bare one and a half knots. The ship rolled and pitched with creaking and doleful straining sounds, thumping off the waves like the sound of artillery. On 6 and 7 February, snow and sleet added to the general turmoil, the temperature being sixteen degrees Fahrenheit. The ship was a huge mass of ice, encrusting ropes, spars and rigging. The sail masts had an accumulation of two to six inches of ice, and the exposed woodwork two to three feet. The ship lay nearly a foot deeper in the water than she would otherwise have done. All through the night, sleep was completely out of the question, with such thumping, creaking, horizontal tremors and vertical quiverings, and momentarily the mighty hull was submerged by the surging waters breaking over her bulwarks. In daylight, the spectacle of sea, one mass of boiling foam rolling in mountains, was grand beyond description. The captain remarked if it had been a sailing vessel, they would have been utterly helpless. The storm finally abated and a comparatively smooth sea with a favourable breeze followed.

At last the vessel came within three miles of New York, but due to dense fog had to drop anchor at a sandbank. Eventually the fog cleared and the rising tide carried the ship off the sandbank, and they were all happy to see Staten Island on the port side. Alexander was met in New York by Mr Stuart and his brother and the Rev Mr Thomson, one of the Presbyterian ministers of New York. Alexander was carrying government despatches and this gave him precedence before all others, and his luggage was hurried ashore in a few minutes. For the remainder of the passengers, it could be several hours before they cleared the strict port regulations.

On the way to Mr Thomson's house, he could not but be amazed at the posters promoting all manner of things and in particular, the press advertisements, publishing all manner of extravagancies about him and at this he was somewhat distressed. He had landed in the land of 'Go-a-headism' as he put it. From New York, he boarded the train to Philadelphia where he arrived on 1 March, in a terrific snowstorm, the like of which the local people had not seen for twenty years. Having travelled in a long railway carriage, crammed full of people, and with the foul air and noise, he was somewhat fatigued and looked forward to retiring to a quiet, warm room. His hopes were completely dashed when he arrived at the house. Before entering, he was told that about sixty to seventy ministers were waiting to welcome him.

It was now between ten and eleven o'clock at night, with a snowstorm raging outside. The ministers comprised Episcopalians, Presbyterians of every school, Congregationalists, Methodists, Baptists and Dutch Reformed; in short, all the evangelical ministers of every church in Philadelphia and its neighbourhood. He stood in dumb amazement at what all this could mean. He was introduced to all with a warm handshake and a most cordial greeting. They then adjourned to a large room, where a long table was laden with the most luxurious food, which he thought was fit for an Asiatic prince. He was asked to say grace, as they all wished to hear his now most famous voice. Although exhausted with his journeying, his spirit was lifted by the extraordinary welcome which he received. He circulated among the warm-hearted men of God and spoke to as many as he was able. He eventually retired after one o'clock, when the last of the guests had left, wondering what his unprecedented reception meant. The guests now had to find their way home on foot because of the blizzard, and it was many hours and near daybreak when some of them finally arrived at their homes.

The first hall where he gave an address could contain three to four thousand people, who came by invitation only. Alexander had been warned that an American audience was always sober, stern and sedate. It therefore took him by surprise when he was greeted with tumultuous applause from the representatives of the most influential families in the city, to whom the tickets had been distributed. The manifestations of enthusiasm on the part of the audience took Alexander utterly aback. This was indeed a contrast to an Exeter Hall audience, which never exhibited any of these noisy symptoms, either of approval or disapproval.

When he alluded to America and Britain shaking hands across the Atlantic as the two great props of evangelic Protestant Christianity in the world; and to America's not standing by and see the old mother country trodden down by the legions of European despotism, whether civil or religious, it seemed that the great audience was convulsed, and heaved to and fro in surging billows, like the Atlantic Ocean in a hurricane. Nothing like such a scene had been witnessed here before at any religious meeting whatever, according to the later press reports.

The next day, being cold and dry, Mr Stuart took him on a sleigh drive through the city, and it was by this method that he spent the next few days visiting the city in detail.

He visited 'Independence Hall' in which the leaders of the revolution, in 1776, signed the Declaration of Independence, by which they were declared rebels and traitors against the British monarchy; this led to the war which was won by them in 1784. He visited the mint and saw the processing of the Californian gold. He visited the penitentiary, the first ever built with separate rooms for each inmate; male and female. He saw them in most excellent quarters and engaged in weaving, shoe-making, and carpentry. He visited the centre of the city, a district as low, sunken and debased as the worst he had yet seen anywhere. He entered many of the awful dens; some underground with darkness only made visible by a few smouldering cinders and heaps of rags and bones and filth all round. In the midst were men, women and children, who filthy, haggard, savage-like, and drunken, lay cursing and blaspheming. This was the 'City of brotherly love', but 'in short, such utter hellishness', he confided to his wife, he never saw surpassed'. He wrote many letters to Anne in Edinburgh, and in one he wrote, relating to the exhausting programme:

> . . . You may say, why allow yourself to be done up in this way? Indeed I have fought and struggled and toiled to prevent it. But all in vain. The kindness of these people is absolutely oppressive; their importunity to address here and there and everywhere so absolutely autocratic, that I am driven, in spite of myself, to do more than I know I can well stand. Bad as the state of things in Scotland was in this respect, it is ten times, yea, a hundred times worse here. Here the applicants for my services are legion, and their dinning impetuous as the Atlantic gales. Ministers in all directions ask me to preach for them; committees of all sorts, of a religious, philanthropic, or missionary character, do the same; managers of schools entreat me to visit and address their pupils; young mens' associations and all manner of nondescripts beleaguer me. Indeed if I could multiply myself into a hundred bodies, each with the strength of a Hercules, and the mental and moral energy of a Paul, I could not overtake the calls and demands made upon me, here and from many other quarters, since my arrival . . .

He made a short visit to Elizabeth Town in New Jersey and on his arrival back in New York, hundreds of reporters were waiting. He informed them that he would speak to them at his first meeting. At the meeting that evening, many of the reporters simply laid their pens down. They might as well have tried to report a thunderstorm. Never had they heard such a man as Dr Alexander Duff from Scotland. In one of the newspapers next day it was reported, 'Never before did we so fully realize the overwhelming power of a man who is possessed with his theme.'

The next places on his invitation list were Baltimore and Washington.

In Washington he preached to Congress, in the Hall of Representatives, and there he had a prolonged interview with the President. The Speaker sat to the left of his official chair, the President, Franklin Pierce, to the right. Emblems of mourning for the late Vice-President, covering the canopy, surrounding the portraits of Washington and Lafayette, and 'enveloping the Muse of History in her car of Time over the central door', seemed to intensify the stillness of the dense congregation of public men from all parts of the States. After devotions led by the chaplain of the Senate and ministers of several churches, he spoke from the inspired words of Paul to the dying Roman Empire: 'By one man sin entered into the world, and death by sin, and so death passed upon all men, for that all have sinned.'

After a day with the President, and another at the tomb of George Washington, at Mount Vernon, he turned westward, across the Alleghany Mountains to Pittsburg in the Ohio valley. He travelled along the singularly beautiful valley of the Ohio, with its meadows and groves, and cultured plains and rolling wooded hills, by Cincinnati and Louisville on to the junction of the Ohio and Mississippi; from that to St Louis, then northward to Chicago, on to Lake Michigan; thence crossing eastward to Detroit he entered Canada, visiting the principal places there as far as Montreal. Travelling in those days, by whatever means, was not as reliable as it later became, and the following incident was recorded in a letter to his wife:

Between 12 and 1 p.m. went to the railway station to proceed to New London, about 100 miles west of Hamilton, towards Lake Huron. We started with a very heavy train of between six and seven hundred passengers; and as the first fifty miles west is a gradual ascent, we proceeded very slowly. Like all American railways it is but a single line, and very recently opened. Well, on we went till we passed a small station, some thirty miles distant, within half a mile of a town ambitiously called Paris. There our engine slipped off the rail; but the steam being instantly let off, and the engine happily breaking down, none of the passenger trams were overturned, though the shock and collision were such as to break the panes of glass in the backmost one in which I sat. A *second* more – yes, a single second more, and the whole would have been overturned. What lives then would have been lost; what limbs fractured – it is fearful to contemplate. God be praised for the marvellous deliverance! At that wretched little station, with a cold biting frost, where neither food nor shelter could be had, we had to wait on in expectation of the train from the west. As it turned out, it too had met with an accident and so was delayed. Meanwhile, another train arrived from the east with 300 more passengers. But the rail was broken up by our mishap, and so no passage for it. Towards dusk the western train came up; then passengers and luggage were reciprocally transferred from the eastern train to the western train, and about half-past 8 p.m. we were afloat again, very weary, cold and hungry! It was between eleven and twelve before we reached London. The congregation had assembled at seven, waited patiently till half-past nine when a telegraph conveyed the news of our disaster, and they dispersed. By 1 a.m. I tried to get to rest, praising God for His wondrous goodness.

Next day:

Up early to breakfast; a new circular issued, inviting the congregation to assemble at half-past ten, and, singular to say, a full church we had by that time. As the train was to leave between 1 and 2 p.m., I went to the pulpit with the watch before me, and spoke on till near the train time. From the church went to the railway terminus, and proceeded eastward . . . when within three or four miles of the accident on the preceding day, our engine again slipped off the rail, and buried itself in a steep clay bank, without (most mercifully) overturning the passenger carriages. We had all to get out, climb the wet clay bank, and walk about on the crest of it, waiting for the arrival of a train from the east. Mr Buchanan, being a leading director of the railway, sent on to the next station for an engine. It came; but after trial, could do nothing for us. Then we got into the engine, amid the coal and wood, and posted back to the station, the cold (there being no shelter) piercing us through and through. My shoe soles had also given way, and my feet were wetted. From all this I contracted a heavy cold, which has been generally oppressing me ever since. At the small, wretched station, without shelter or food, we had to wait on till nigh midnight before we started, so that instead of reaching Hamilton at 6 p.m. on Friday, we only reached it at 3 a.m. on Saturday morning. The Lord be praised, we arrived at last, with unbroken limbs.

In Toronto he addressed the assembled students of the Knox College. Another day, after a full programme of visiting public institutions, he addressed a great public meeting in the largest church of Toronto at 7 p.m. It was crammed to suffocation with 3,000 people who listened to him for nearly three hours. Home at eleven and up in in the morning for a public breakfast, the thing he hated most. Five hundred ladies and gentlemen were present, but Alexander knew it was the greatest possible compliment to him. He addressed the guests for an hour. At noon he boarded the steamer for Kingston, about 180 miles east of Toronto. Several hundred gathered on the pier and gave him three cheers on departure.

About halfway to Kingston, the steamer stopped at Coburg. He was soon in a carriage and off for a mile, and ushered pell-mell into a church crowed and crammed with people, and without delay taken to the pulpit, where he addressed the large audience. He went on until the loud tolling of the steamer bell warned that it was time to get on board. At 6 p.m. on Thursday 13 he arrived in Kingston; there was a cold, sharp frosty wind; masses of ice all around. A city of 12,000 inhabitants, it was once the seat of government, and a very handsome and beautiful town, with many fine stone buildings. He visited the castle, the strongest next to Quebec in Canada. He met many of the chief inhabitants. At night he addressed a great public meeting in the City Hall; ministers of all denominations attended and among the rest two or three Kirk or Establishment ministers and professors, as their theological college was at Kingston. He gave a long address. There was much heartiness and goodwill, and apparent good was accomplished. From there to Ogdensburgh, thence to Montreal.

The city of Montreal is at the east end of a large island surrounded by the waters of the St Lawrence and Ottawa rivers, and had at that time a population of 60,000 people. The French called the place Mount Royal, corrupted later to Montreal. The city was rich in endowments, establishments, cathedrals, churches, colleges and convents. Alexander was unwell, still suffering from a severe cold and painful throat, and decided to rest until it was time for the public meeting in the evening. It was a vast one of 3,000 people, densely packed together, who were greatly impressed by what he had to say. The following morning, a great public breakfast was given to him, and he had to speak again. There were several hundred guests, and he saw them so interested, he spoke on and on. Looking at his watch, he found it was 1 p.m. Although most of the guests were business people, not one stirred. They seemed greatly moved and impressed, and the varied replies delivered by several of their numbers were quite thrilling. They declared his visit to them an 'angel visit'; that he must have been sent by Christ to rouse them from their apathy.

Alexander intended to visit Quebec and was fully bent on going but was disappointed to find that the river was not yet open for steamers. Sir James Alexander had written him from Government House, and other important individuals, pressing him to visit Quebec, but it was not to be. He returned to New York as his final call in the West. He wished to attend a catholic missionary convention, the first of the kind that had been held in the United States. Throughout 4 and 5 of May he gave addresses in the Broadway Tabernacle to the young men of the city on religious education, and to a select circle of its leading men on his own work in India. He guided the deliberations on foreign missions of nearly three hundred evangelical clergymen, from all parts of the West. He finished with a two-hour address of high-toned fervour.

During his entire visit to the USA and Canada he had not made a single appeal for funds for for his missionary work. He had decided that the whole purpose of his tour was to inform and educate the people in the West of the need for greater effort in missionary work, and in that, as later events would prove, he was highly successful. On 13 May, 1854, he embarked on the *Pacific*, bound for Liverpool. At the quayside there were several thousand people to bid him farewell. The University of New York enrolled him on its honour list as LL.D. He was quietly given an envelope containing £3,000 for his mission fund, from New York and Philadelphia. It is interesting that a similar sum had been given by the congregations of the City of Glasgow in Scotland while he had been on his tour; a result of the work he had done at home. Canada also sent a sizeable sum to help his work.

Alexander reached Edinburgh just in time to take part in the Foreign Mission proceedings of his own Church's General Assembly, and to tell Scotland something of his experience in the USA and in Canada. The money now collected allowed a new college to be built for him and his colleagues in Calcutta, ready for his return eighteen months afterwards. But now the physical and mental penalty for all this effort had to be paid. Did any man, in any profession and under any stimulus, ever spend his whole being as Alexander had done, in travel, organising, in writing and speaking, under the extremes of heat and cold, in east and north and west?

Alexander had lived many lives before he was fifty.

He had planned to return to India in the autumn of 1854, but the doctors ordered his careful treatment to be followed by absolute rest in the sunny south of Europe. Congestion of the brain, inflammation in some of the membranes and other infections, the most alarming of which was mental prostration from the reaction, kept even Alexander from defying the doctors. When, by the middle of June, he was able to travel by easy stages, he went south by Lancaster to Great Malvern. The water treatment and regimen were then, and there, beginning to attract such cases as his. The first gleam of improvement at the end of July led him to reason with the doctors thus: 'Let me travel slowly to India through southern Europe, and I need not begin work until February next.' The plea was in vain.

While in Malvern he met Lord Haddo, who was receiving the treatment. His father, the fourth Earl of Aberdeen, was the Premier at that time of the preparations for the Crimean War. Lord Haddo had been told that he was soon to die, and found great comfort in Alexander.

Alexander's recovery proceeded slowly. The beginning of winter, however, forced him south even from Malvern. After a residence at Bayonne, under the care of Anne and his eldest son, Alexander Groves, who had completed his medical studies, he turned aside to Biarritz, where the winter was spent in seclusion in a mild invigorating atmosphere, favourable to the still congested brain. His son acted as his doctor and his secretary, answering the many communications from home and abroad. His son's professional view was that his father's intellectual powers were wholly unimpaired, and the substance of the brain was unaffected.

At last he was able to journey on, going by Pau and Montpellier, he was able to sail from Marseilles to Civita Vecchia, so as to reach Rome by Easter. There the papal police daily visited his lodgings, and all his applications for the return of his passport were ignored. At last, on appealing to the British Consul, he was told, 'Go where you please; just say you are an Englishman; Palmerston is in power.' The wisdom of this advice he often proved.

At Rome he had a severe relapse. Seeking a region of purer warmth at that season, he resolved to sail from Genoa to Syria. He then journeyed by Alexandria to Beirut, where he visited the American Presbyterian Mission. He crossed the Lebanon by easy stages to Damascus, and thence doubled back to Jerusalem. Jaffa was the port of departure for Constantinople, whence he took the steamer to Marseilles again. He came to England and reported at Malvern, thence back to Edinburgh.

The glorious autumn quiet of an Edinburgh September was all he could give to his boys, then demanding a father's personal care more than ever. He at last obtained consent that he could leave for India, provided he took six months' rest from all work, and the doctors suggested that the Mediterranean or Egypt would be ideal. Alexander reasoned that the dry and embracing air of Northern India would do him just as much good, and made his plans accordingly!

Their younger son, William, then seventeen years of age, described the departure of his parents to India on their third tour:

In the autumn of 1855 his home work was completed, and on the 13th October, with my mother, he left Edinburgh for his third visit to India.

He explained to me in touching language the almost hopelessness of his position as regarded the completion of my education. In some such words as these he said, 'To the best of my ability, I have given you, W., the best education Edinburgh affords, and had I seen any indication of your going forward to the Church, I would have felt it an imperative duty to stint and scrape to enable you to complete your studies.' I told him I perfectly understood his position. and was willing to accept the sacrifice of foregoing a career on which lustre had been shed by more than one of my class-fellows at the Edinburgh Academy.

I accompanied my parents to London. Mr H. M. Matheson received us at his beautiful seat of Heathlands (Hampstead), and in the course of a day or two my parents left for Alexandria, by way of Trieste. It was in the old days, before Charing Cross Station or Victoria existed, and I well remember the toilsome drive from Hampstead to London Bridge; I also well remember how my mother's and my own heart were well nigh breaking, and how at London Bridge my father possessed himself of the morning's *Times*, and left us to cry our eyes out in mutual sorrow. In passing, and apart from passing controversies, I may say my father was never happy without his *Times*, and frequently contributed letters under the signature of 'Indophilis' . . . A sadder parting as between mother and son there never was. The father buried in the *Times*, and controlled by his stern sense of Carlylean duty, parted from the son without any regret on the latter's part.

Setting out from Trieste, the Duffs joined the mail steamer at Suez. They travelled down the Red Sea, then they parted. Anne went on by Ceylon and Madras to Calcutta, charged with the care of more than one expectant bride. Alexander joined the government steamer at Aden for Bombay. Seeing his beloved friend, Dr Wilson, 'soon operated with a reviving effect'. From Poona by Ahmednuggur, Aurungabad and Jalna and hence by Kampthee, Jubbulpore and Mirzapore, he came to Benares and Calcutta, having followed a chain of Christian fortresses across the whole breadth of Northern India. Just before Sunday 17 February, 1856, he entered his own city, to begin the third and last period of his evangelising work in India.

16

Last Term in India

Lord Canning took the oaths and his seat in Government House on the last day of February, 1856. There was much sadness when, at the historic ghaut a few days after, the great Marquis of Dalhousie left the East India Company's metropolis. In extent, in resources and in political strength he had developed its territories into an empire able to pass triumphantly through the ordeal of mutiny and insurrection, which the government at home had invited, in spite of his protests against a reduction of the British garrison in inverse proportion to the addition of a province like anarchic Oudh. Because of the Crimean War, followed by the Persian expedition, provinces as large as France were almost without a British soldier, and predictions of the extinction of the Company's Raj the following year were current.

Lord Dalhousie had protested in vain against the suicidal withdrawl of so many Queen's regiments and had urged reforms in the sepoy army which the jealous Sir Charles Napier resented. Henry Lawrence had predicted a collapse of some kind if military reorganization were longer postponed.

Lord Charles Canning, the son of George Canning, now held the highest office in the Empire, at a salary of of twenty-four thousand pounds a year. He was now forty-four years of age and married to Charlotte, a former lady-in-waiting to Queen Victoria, and a woman of great talent in writing, painting, and later in photography. Lord Canning gave the appearance of being cold and aloof and had few close friends. He was an awkward, stiff, public speaker and generally had a rather gloomy, pessimistic character. Despite this he was a handsome man with fine eyes, and like Alexander, had extraordinary powers for continuous work. He had no illusion of the apparent serenity of the India sky. On his appointment he foresaw that a cloud might arise which could threaten British India with ruin. How true this was to be in 1857.

When Lord Canning formally took over from Lord Dalhousie, he was shown around the house by Lord Dalhousie, he observed that the house did not appear to have a single water-closet. The former occupier laughed heartily, 'You would not find even one in the whole of Calcutta, and another thing, the native servants move about so silently, and when still, are virtually invisible.' Lord and Lady Canning took a considerable time to get used to this behaviour. Even after a considerable time, Charlotte Canning could enter a large room and be unaware of the presence of several servants, because of their stillness and their attire blending in with the colourful surroundings.

When Canning took office, the East India Company's profits had been dwindling since the early eighteen-forties, due to the troubles in the north of India. With many yearly losses, the Company was at present in debt to the sum of about fourteen million pounds. For that reason, Lord Canning was expected to show a revival in the economy but, unfortunately, this would have to wait as his first major step was to mount the Anglo-Persian War of 1856–57.

His instructions came from the Prime Minister, Lord Palmerston, who was always obsessed with Russian motives. In this instance Persia, with Russian backing, had invaded and occupied the province of Herat in the far north, two hundred miles north-west of Kandahar, which the Afghans considered as theirs. To warn off this threat, the secret committee of Parliament authorised the East India Company to wage war. The Persians were defeated and a peace settlement was concluded in Paris, in time for Charles Canning to attend the annual Old Etonian dinner in Calcutta!

At the same time there was increasing unrest among the Hindu sepoys. They were mostly from Amoudh and high-caste Hindu. Thousands more were employed in the Company's defence service. Their complaints were many and, for them, justified. The sepoys were not allowed to bathe as frequently as their religion demanded. They were issued with sheepskin jackets to protect them against the cold of the mountains, but were told that they would be used for overseas service; all against their religion which did not permit them serve abroad. Even the flow of the sacred Ganges river had been tampered with to make a canal, but worse than this was the statement made in the House of Commons:

Providence has entrusted the extensive empire of Hindustan to England, in order that the banner of Christ should wave triumphantly from one end of India to the other. Everyone must exert all his strength that there be no dilatoriness on any account in continuing the grand work of making all Indians Christians.

The East India Company had its own 'Ecclesiastical Establishment' of clergy paid out of Company revenue. There was now a rumour spreading throughout India that the British were determined to forcibly convert all to Christianity, and thus destroy their own customs, beliefs, and way of life; and for this purpose, a great army was on the way from England. Such a rumour was easily spread and impossible to stop.

Lady Charlotte, in one of her many letters to Queen Victoria at this time, wrote:

There is an odd, mysterious thing going on, still unexplained. It is this. In one part of the country the native police have been making little cakes – 'chuppatiis' – and sending them on from place to place. Each man makes twelve, keeps two, and sends away ten to ten men, who make twelve more each, and they spread all over the country. No one can discover any meaning to it.[1]

This system of warning from village to village had been a practice long before Europeans came to India. It was a warning to people that some great calamity was about to happen. People put different meanings to the warnings and the rumours thus took hold.

More fuel to the fire had been added by the law which had been introduced permitting Hindu widows to re-marry, and a law to preserve the ancient Indian property rights of converts to Christianity. Common messing in jails betrayed the sacred caste rights. Native orphans were to be brought up as Christians. Education was to be provided for females. Religious fears now reached panic pitch. All that was needed now was a spark to ignite the explosive situation. The spark came on 12 May, 1857, when a telegram was received in Calcutta from the North India garrison town of Meerut, thirty-six miles from Delhi. Trouble had been brewing for several months. It started when the Indian Infantry had been issued with the

[1] Quoted in Charles Allen, *A Glimpse of the Burning Plain: Leaves from the Indian Journals of Charlotte Canning* (London: Michael Joseph, 1986), p. 52.

new Enfield rifle to replace the now obsolete 'Brown Bess', musket and in order to make the loading of the new rifle easier, the cartridges were lubricated with animal fat, which was exceedingly offensive to Hindus and Muslims. They had been ordered to bite off the grease-covered end of the cartridge, before inserting it into the rifle. The authorities, realizing the problem, discarded the animal fat and substituted a mineral fat, and gave notice of the fact to all. It was, however, too late. Unrest began in January, with the 2nd Native Infantry, at two places, Dum Dum and Ranigang, over a hundred miles apart. There were further incidents between February and May, involving troops in Bengal and Lucknow, but the Mutiny proper started at Meerut.[1]

On Saturday, 9 May, the entire garrison at Meerut was paraded before the divisional commander, Major-General William H. Hewitt. The purpose of the parade was to humiliate eighty-five of the Native Cavalry, who had refused to use the cartridges, even after being told that they were not of the offensive kind. While the entire parade watched, the eighty-five were stripped of their uniforms and fastened with leg-irons, the task taking several hours. They were then marched off to serve ten years' imprisonment.

The following day, Sunday, while most of the British officers were preparing for evening service, along with their families, the outraged regiments mutinied and released the condemned men. They killed as many British as they could find and set fire to a number of buildings, then marched off on the road to Delhi.

Everyone was shocked at the news. The Duffs' older son Alexander Groves was at this time serving as an army surgeon at Meerut, and it was almost certain that he would have been among those massacred. It was only later that they found out that he had been sick in bed and had escaped the attention of the mutineers, and by chance, his bungalow was one that had escaped the torch. For Alexander and his colleagues, this was a disaster extending far beyond the present massacre and that to follow. It was the complete breakdown of all that they had been doing to help the native people of India. None better than they knew the importance of a man's faith and dignity,

[1] See James Hewitt (ed.), *Eye-Witnesses to the Indian Mutiny* (Reading: Osprey Publishing, 1972); J. A. B. Palmer, *The Mutiny Outbreak at Meerut in 1857* (Cambridge: Cambridge University Press, 1966).

and had they not fully realized that in their teaching method? The change from one faith to another was a personal issue, and had to be a voluntary undertaking, and this had been the whole policy laid down by Alexander from the start of his work. All that he could do now was to await the outcome of the present emergency, and use such influence as he had to persuade those in power to change their policy.

General Hewitt had one thousand five hundred British troops under his command at Meerut and could quite easily have stopped the mutineers on their way to Delhi but, disastrously, he did nothing. In spite of John Lawrence's protests, General Anson, the commander-in-chief who had hurried down from Simla, refused to take possession of Delhi while it was still possible to do so. The mutineers reached Delhi and the gates were opened by their sympathisers, and a widespread massacre of Europeans began. All Europeans at the palace were slaughtered, officers at the encampment were cut down, and the position could have been much worse had not five British soldiers risked their lives to blow up the magazine before they escaped. They were all awarded the Victoria Cross. The mutiny spread death and destruction all over India until the execution of a rebel leader, Tatya Tope, in 1859. The mutineers failed to overthrow the British because they were unorganised and could not match their military strategy and decisive leadership.

In Calcutta, the Europeans were issued rifles to defend themselves. The mission house was absolutely unprotected, in the heart of the native city and far away from other European quarters, yet the missionaries had no thought of leaving it. A plan had been made to seize Fort William. The night chosen for the desperate act was that on which the Maharaja of Gwalior had invited the European community to an exhibition of fireworks, across the river, at the Botanic Gardens. On that evening, as if by a gracious intervention of providence, there was a heavy storm of thunder and rain, so that the entertainment was postponed. The British troops, therefore, had not left the fort, the holding regiment being the 78th Highlanders (later Seaforth Highlanders). All sepoys were immediately disarmed in Calcutta and a strict discipline enforced. Thus Calcutta was spared the carnage of the other cities. In a report made by Alexander on 20 July, he describes a tragic incident:

Heavier and heavier tidings of woe! About a week ago it

was known that Sir Henry Lawrence – whose defence of Lucknow with a mere handful, amid the rage of hostile myriads, has been the admiration of all India – had gone out to attack a vast body of armed rebels; that his *native* force, with characteristic treachery, had turned round upon him at the commencement of the fight – and that, with his two hundred Europeans, he had to cut his way back, with Spartan daring, to the Residency. It was also known that, on that occasion, the brave leader was severely wounded; and two days ago intelligence reached us, which, alas! has since been confirmed, that on the 4th instant he sunk under the effects of his wounds. What shall I say? It is impossible for me to express the grief of heart which I feel in thus recording the death of Sir Henry Lawrence . . .

Peace was at last restored and the Free Church Presbytery fixed Sunday, 25 October, as the day of special service, which they appointed Dr Duff to conduct. Members of the government were present in the crowd of worshippers. The government had gagged the press during the uprising, but speech was still free.

Lady Charlotte Canning had been keeping her Queen informed of events by her writings and illustrations. This kept Her Majesty up to date in a way which no other source could supply. She continued this correspondence, including photography at a later stage, until she died in November 1861, and there is no doubt that her efforts had a great bearing on the Queen's attitude to India and its people. The beautiful and gifted Countess Canning was buried at one of her favourite spots overlooking the Hooghly River. In March 1862, Lord Elgin became Viceroy. Lord Canning returned to England, in ill health and heart-broken over the loss of his wife. He died on 17 June and was buried in Westminster Abbey.

How had the months of mutiny and massacre affected the Church of India? For by 1857 there was a native church, pastors and flocks, in the great cities and scattered among the villages. Few, save the missionaries who had been blessed to bring it to birth, and officials of the Lawrence stamp who fostered its growth, knew of what stuff its members were made. Native Christian were simply identified by the rebels with the governing class, but were generally offered their lives at the price of denying their Lord. At the end of 1857 the native church was 150,000 strong.

In the eight years ending in 1863, which formed the third and last period of his service in India, Alexander enjoyed a foretaste, at least, of that which is generally denied to the pioneers of philanthropy. 'One soweth and another reapeth', is the law of the divine kingdom. He rejoiced in reinforcements of young missionaries from Scotland, and all around he saw the indirect results of his whole work since 1830.

Dr Duff's Bengal Mission went on growing. It had never been so prosperous, spiritually and educationally, as in the Mutiny year. Then it moved into the new college buildings in Neemtolla Street, for which he had raised £15,000 in Scotland, England, and the USA. The year 1859–60 was a time of trial for the mission staff. 'Know ye not that there is a prince and a great man fallen this day in Israel?' were the words from which Alexander, on 24 July, 1859, preached a discourse on the life and death of the great-hearted Swiss missionary Lacroix. Death did not stop there. In a few months, and in one afternoon, cholera carried off Dr Ewart, a pillar of the mission and Alexander's student friend. This was followed by the death of the Rev Gopeenath Nundi, killed at Futtehpore.

Alexander became president of several societies and was commisioned to be one of those who drew up the constitution for the University of Calcutta. In the early years of the university, Alexander led the senate, and of his leadership one of his colleagues, Dr Banerjea, wrote, 'To his gigantic mind the successive Vice-Chancellors paid due deference, and he was the virtual governor of the university'. Dr Duff was the first person who insisted on education in the physical sciences, and strongly urged the establishment of a professorship of physical science for the university. The Viceroy was, by his office, Chancellor of the University, and he appointed the Vice-Chancellor for a term of two years. Lord Elgin naturally turned to Sir Charles Trevelyan, who had been sent out as his financial colleague in council. But although the honour had been well won, that official would not consider it so long as it had not been offered to one whom he thus declared worthier:

Calcutta, 22 March, 1863

My Dear Dr Duff, – I have written to Sir R. Napier requesting that he will submit to the Governor-General my strong recommendation that you should be appointed

Vice-Chancellor of the University, and entirely disclaiming the honour on my part if there should have been any idea of appointing me. It is yours by right, because you have borne without rest or refreshment the burden and heat of the long day, which I hope is not yet near its close; and, what concerns us all more, if given to you it will be an unmistakable public acknowledgment of the paramount claims of national education, and will be a great encouragement to every effort that may be made for that object.

Very sincerely yours,

Ch. Trevelyan.

Alas! by that time 'the long day' was already overshadowed, so far as residence in India was concerned. In July, 1863, his old enemy, dysentry, laid him low. To save his life, the doctors hurried him off on a sea voyage to China. He had dreamed that the coolness of such a Himalayan station as Darjeeling would complete the cure. But he was no longer the youth who tried to fight the disease in 1834, and had been beaten home in the struggle. He had worked like no other man in East and West, for a third of a century. He took the trip and returned by Bombay and Madras to Calcutta, and there he quietly set himself to prepare for his departure for Scotland.

The varied communities of Bengal were roused, not to halt the homeward movement, the pain of which to him, as well as the loss to India, they knew to be overborne by a divinely marked necessity, but to honour the venerable missionary as not even governors had ever been honoured. It was resolved to unite men of all creeds in one memorial of him. A committee, of which Bishop Cotton, Sir Charles Trevelyan, and the leading Indians and representatives of the other cities of India were members, resolved to reproduce, in the centre of the educational buildings of Calcutta, the Maison Carrée of Nismes. The marble hall, the duplicate of that exquisite gem of Greek architecture in an imperial province, was to be used for and to symbolise the catholic pursuit of truth. But, as there were Indian admirers of the man who thought this too Christian, so there were many of his own countrymen who desired to mark more vividly his particular genius as a missionary.

The first result accordingly was the endowment in the university of the Duff Scholarships, to be held, one by a student of his own college, one by a student of the Eurasian institutions for which he had done so much, and two by the best students of all the affiliated arts colleges, soon to number fifty-seven. The Bethune Society and the Doveton College procured oil portraits of their benefactor by the best artists. His own students, Christian and non-Christian, placed his marble bust in the hall where so many generations of youths had sat at his feet.

A few of the Scottish merchants of India, Singapore and China offered him £11,000. The capital he destined for the invalided missionaries of his own Church. On the interest of this sum he thenceforth lived, refusing all the emoluments of the offices he held. The Free Church of Scotland wanted the missionary to continue the work in the West. He knew that his health would prevent further service in the East, so Alexander and Anne said farewell to India for the last time. A beautiful house awaited them at 22 Lauder Road in the Grange district of Edinbugh, gifted to them by Sir William Mackinnon and other kind friends and admirers.

Alexander and Anne parted when they left India. His doctors insisted that he should have some months' enforced rest and suggested he take the Cape route home. In the spacious cabins and amid the quiet surroundings of an East Indiaman, the journey would be much preferred to the scorching heat of the Red Sea route. As he knew that this would be his last visit to the East, he would like to visit South Africa, and possibly meet some of many friends. He calculated that, in his new work back home, it would be an advantage to have a clearer picture of the situation in the field and meet some of the missionaries with whom he would be in contact. He gladly accepted the advice to go by the Cape route!

At first it may appear curious that Anne should not accompany her husband, who at that time was far from well, and that her tender care and attention would not be of considerable help to him, but there was a sad and very valid reason for her action. Completely unknown to Alexander, the stress of actual work at the Institution, the caring for her husband, and the climate of Bengal, not to mention some of the terrifying adventures of shipwrecks and mutiny, had taken toll of her strength, and she was now more than aware that she might not have much time left to be with her husband. Should her beloved Alexander have to carry on alone in life, she wanted to return to Edinburgh and prepare his home at Lauder Road, and have a little while with her remaining children. It is certain that Alexander knew nothing of this position, as such letters as are available, sent to her on his South African tour, make no reference to her health or indeed his concern. As far as he knew, she was going ahead to prepare their new home.

The wearied, wasted missionary went on board the last, and the best of the East Indiamen, the *Hotspur*, on Saturday, 20 December, 1863. In command was Captain Toynbee, the foremost sailor of the day. During the voyage, as they left Natal for the Cape, another famous Scotsman was boldly crossing the Indian Ocean for Bombay. David Livingstone, having just completed his great Zambezi expedition, made the trip in the little *Lady Nyassa* steam launch, manned by seven natives who had never before seen the sea, far less sailed upon it.

They had invalid soldiers on board and Alexander visited them all daily. He also interested himself in a school amongst the soldiers' children, and in the illness of a Mrs Ellis, the wife of a missionary going home for her health. The contrast between his patience and the impatience of others on board who were not as ill as he was, was noticed even by the servants. A young cavalry officer on board remarked, 'If all missionaries were like Dr Duff, India would be a different place'. The captain was struck by Alexander's memory when he reproduced the tale of the 1830 shipwreck so accurately that not a point jarred on the captain's nautical ear.

In mid-January Mrs Ellis, having taken a turn for the worse, died peacefully. Alexander solemnly consigned her body to the deep next morning, but the presence of her two children, too young to know their loss, touched the hearts of all. Some ten days later, on 29 January, they were opposite Cape Agulhas and the following morning they turned the Cape and at dawn they were a little to the south of Table Mountain. The ship anchored at Cape Town, exactly six weeks after leaving Calcutta. No sooner was Alexander ashore than he was met by the Rev Mr Morgan, minister of the Established Church, who took him to his manse. He then resolved to proceed to Kaffraria by the ordinary land route. It was a distance of some seven hundred miles, which made it necessary for him to obtain a wagon and eight mules. While collecting the equipment, he saw many of the Cape Town notabilities. The Bishop and Dean, the Hon. Mr Rawson, the Colonial Secretary, who took him to his beautifully situated house at Wynberg and persuaded him to stay overnight. On Saturday he went by train to Stellensbosch and stayed with Mr Murray, one of the professors of the Theological Seminary of the Dutch

Reformed Church. On the following Monday he went by rail to Wellington, on Tuesday he took a covered cart to Worcester. On his journey he would sleep in his wagon if the weather was fine and dry. He found out that normal custom of travelling was to stop every two or three hours, unyoke the animals, let them roll in the sand for about an hour, let them drink, then yoke them all together again and drive on! He visited all the missions from Cape Town to Port Elizabeth; from Grahamstown to King Williamstown, then north through the Orange Free State, then east to Natal. The time was three years before the first diamond was found.

He visited the principal African mission station at Lovedale on the 17 March, 1864. He pursued the long and difficult track through Basutoland with its French mission stations. At Queenstown, in April, he saw hoar-frost for the first time for many years. After visiting Maritzburg, he returned from Port Natal to Cape Town. It is obvious that his doctors did not plan his itinerary! He reached Edinburgh on the 10 August 1864, just in time to address the Commission of the General Assembly.

17

Professor, and Moderator Again

Of domestic joy and social life, Alexander knew less than most public men, less even than most Britons who lived and worked in India. Even now, with his perpetual self-imposed life's work-load, he could only give to family and friends the time which the exhausted body forced him to steal from his incessant activity. What to most men forms the sum of life, was with him an accident of living. It was as well that his fine physique had been the willing slave of his tempestuous spirit, and it was as well that he had, in his wife Anne, a totally devoted partner, who, even more than him, sacrificed herself beyond all normal human limits. He was her great earthly love, the manifestation of her divine love.

Their earthly home, wherever it might be, was the manifestation of the house of their Lord, and now, at Lauder Road in Edinburgh, only Anne knew that this would be their penultimate house which they could share together. She knew that she had but a short time to live, but could, at least, share the remainder of her time with him in the house on earth in which she knew her husband would spend the rest of his days. For Anne, this would not be the end; she would be leaving her husband for a while, but she would soon be joining her little girl Annie, and her elder son, Alexander, who had also been taken away by the dreaded dysentery, and they would all unite in time in the final family of their Lord. Their remaining son and daughter were now both married and had children, and Anne was able to see much of them in her last days.

After reporting to the committee in August, 1864, Alexander speedily took himself north to Perth, in order to take part in the ordination of the Rev W. Stevenson as a missionary to Madras. The following week he again took part in the ordination of yet another missionary to Madras, and addressed a vast meeting. The local press reported: 'Notwithstanding his enfeebled health his voice was distinctly heard over the large audience, and his eloquent and seasonable address was listened to with close attention and evident delight.'

His strength would not allow him to be present at the General Assembly of 1865, but Dr Murray Mitchell, who represented him, announced a home income for foreign missions in the previous year of £27,000, besides £3,000 from the English Presbyterian Church. He heard at this time from India, that the Viceroy, Sir John Lawrence, had visited in state and presided at the first examination at the 'Duff College' in Calcutta.

Now that Alexander was permanently settled in Scotland, he felt that the time had come to lay broad foundations of the missionary enterprise to which he regarded all his previous home campaigns as preparatory. Here, as in India, he must leave behind him a system based on and worked by living principles, which would grow and expand and bless the people long after he was forgotten. To this end he determined to set up a professorship of evangelistic theology, a practical missionary institute, and a missionary quarterly review. He was to prepare lectures for the Chair, and lecture in the three colleges of Edinburgh, Glasgow and Aberdeen. He refused all income from his work, including his salary as a professor, but donated the total sum to the Missionary Institute. Not only as professor of evangelistic theology, but as superintendent or, so far as presbyterian parity allowed, director of foreign missions of his Church, Alexander had the care of all the churches till the day of his death. He was also the adviser, referee, and fellow-helper of the other missionary agencies of Great Britain and America.

On 22 February, 1865, after being tenderly nursed by her daughter and the widow of Dr Mackay, Anne Scott Duff died. To the remaining son, William, now in Calcutta, the widowed father two days later wrote a letter epistle of heart-breaking yet triumphant words, from which we quote the following:

> I at once write the fulness of my own sorrow and yours, when I say that I am now writing as a wifeless husband to a motherless son; and at the same time the fulness of my joy and yours, when I say that, through faith in the atoning blood and righteousness of the Lamb of God for sinners slain, the most loving, lovable, and beloved of wives and mothers is now one of the bright spirits that shine in white array in the realms above . . . Praised be God then, there is no incompatibility between the fulness of natural sorrow and the fulness of gracious joy. God, the tender and compassionate God, has not forbidden us to sorrow over

departed friends – and least of all over the departure of one who has been the desire and the light of my eyes and a vitalizing element of my life . . . the most faithful and devoted partner of my life-long joys and sorrows in many climes and amid many eventful scenes. And true it is, that though endeavouring to restrain and control my feelings to the utmost before others, I have again and again found relief in a burst of tears, while in my solitary musings – ah! how solitary and lonely now! – my eyes have become sore with weeping. And what I have yielded to myself, though I trust in God within the limits of undue excess, I cannot ask my darling not to yield to in due and allowable measure. For such yielding in due measure to the outbursting of natural sorrow is consecrated by a higher, nobler, grander example than even that of the father of the faithful, even the example of the eternal Son of God Himself . . . Yes! the most touching, the most affecting verse in the whole Bible, as an embodiment of the fulness and overflow of natural feeling, is the short solitary one, 'Jesus wept', wept at the tomb of His beloved friend, where others were weeping too, mingling His tears in sympathy with theirs – and that too at the very moment when He knew as no other one did or could that a marvellous resurrection work was to be by Himself achieved.

Heaven ought now to have new attractions for you and for us all; . . . among the secondary ones must be the meeting and the greeting of loved ones on earth in their glorified forms. In this sense it is that I have ventured to say that heaven itself has new attractions for you and me and the other members of our now desolated family. My own father and mother, saintly as they were on earth, were there before. Your little brother, who had 'not sinned after the similitude of Adam's transgression', was there; your sister, dear little sweet gentle Annie, through grace, I trust was there. And now my faithful loving spouse – my other half, who sustained and cheered and comforted me, and was herself not merely the light of my dwelling, but my very home itself; and your precious mother, who so fondly nursed and cherished you, ever ready to deny and sacrifice herself if she could only minister to your comfort and joy and happiness – she too is gone. She is not, for God hath taken her, taken her to the temple above, to serve Him and enjoy Him for ever there.

It tended to soothe us exceedingly to find that during the last twelve hours, at least, she had no pain whatever, and that life went gradually, gradually ebbing away, till she literally fell asleep in Jesus. As there was no pain you cannot imagine the singularly sweet, placid and tranquil expression of her countenance even in the paleness of death. To us it was a heart-rending spectacle. But our prayer was that the Lord might give us the spirit of simple, absolute resignation to His holy will. And our prayer has been wonderfully answered. What my own feelings are, I dare not venture to attempt to describe; nor would I if I could. They are known to the Searcher of hearts, and can only find relief in prayer. The union cemented by upwards of thirty-eight years of a strangely eventful life in many climes and amid many perils and trials and joys, so suddenly, so abruptly brought to a final close in this world – oh! it is agony to look at it in *itself*. But when I turn to the Saviour and the saintly one now in glory, I do see the dark cloud so lustred with the rainbow of hope and promise, that I cannot but mingle joy with my sorrow, and we can all unite in praising the Lord for His goodness, His marvellous loving-kindnesses towards us in our hour of sore trial . . .

Those who, outside her own home, knew Anne best, were the Bengali Christians of Cornwallis Square in Calcutta. When the news of her death reached them their sorrow found expression through their minister, the Rev Lal Behari Day, from the pulpit of the mission church. In the course of his address he said that in his twenty-two years' experience since his baptism, he had not seen 'a more high-minded and pure-souled woman, of loftier character of greater kindliness'.

Her distinguished husband was engaged in a mighty work, and she rightly judged that, instead of striking out a path for herself of missionary usefulness, she would be doing her duty best by upholding and strengthening him in his great undertaking. Mrs Duff rightly judged that her proper province was to become a ministering angel to her husband who was labouring in the high places of the field, who had to sustain greater conflicts than most missionaries in the world, and who, therefore, required more than most men the countenance, the attentions, the sympathy, and the consolations of a loving companion.

From now on Alexander was emphatically alone, though ever cared for with filial devotion and friendly affection. His spiritual experience became still deeper, his power to comfort sufferers like himself more remarkable and more sought after. In all his correspondence to the close of his life, and in his personal intercourse with those he loved, there was now a touch of tenderness, ever before felt but now more freely expressed. He had no partner to express his feelings for him. As the tall figure began to stoop more visibly, and the expressive mouth came to be concealed under a still more eloquent beard of venerable whiteness, and the once great and powerful voice soon became wearied into an almost unearthly whispering, new love went forth to one whose chivalrous simplicity was daily more marked. The flash of the eye and the rapid remark told that there was no abatement of the intellectual force or the spiritual fire; while the pen was never more ready for action in any good cause and for every old friend, especially in the cause he had made his own all through life. As grandchildren climbed on his knees, and grew up around him, at school and college, he renewed his youth. All children he delighted in; with all he was a favourite.

To the General Assembly of 1867, in an oration full of his old fire, but of diminished volume, he illustrated the principle on which he had acted all his life and sought to support his whole missionary work. In his lengthy address there was a new warmth, as can be seen from the following extract:

> On one occasion, when in Calcutta, I received a letter from an officer who had served in the Sindh campaign. He had received between three thousand and four thousand rupees as his share of the prize money. I had seen him only once, when he happened to be passing through Calcutta. Having taken him to visit our Institution, he was greatly struck with it. In the letter, he sent what he called a tithe of his prize money, amounting to upwards of three hundred rupees, as a thank-offering to God. I thanked him warmly for his liberality; and in doing so happened to refer to the 29th chapter of Chronicles, and 14th verse, stating that it was a blessed thing to have the means of giving, but that it was still more blessed when God was graciously pleased to give us the disposition to part with these means. Some two or three weeks afterwards, I received a second letter from

the same officer, containing the whole of the rupees which
he had received for his prize money, accompanied with the
remark, 'I had often read that chapter and that passage, but
it had never struck me in that light before; and I thank
God for putting it into my heart to do as I have done.'
He then desired me to acknowledge the receipt of the
sum in a particular newspaper, but stated that I was not to
mention his name, but to say that it was from 1 Chronicles
xxix: 14. That was not all. When the time arrived that he
was able to retire upon a pension, instead of coming home
. . . he . . . became a practical missionary in India . . .

The university session of each year after his appointment as
Professor of Evangelistic Theology was a period of unusual toil
and even hardship to Alexander. Besides the often harassing
and always anxious cares arising from his management of
the foreign office of his Church, and the multitudinous calls
of committees, societies, and other organizations, he had to
discharge his college duties in the three cities of Edinburgh,
Glasgow, and Aberdeen successively. He had much travelling in Scotland in winter, and after so much time in Bengal the contrast was not favourable to comfort or health.
Hardly had April set him free from lecturing, when May
brought on the fatigues of the General Assembly. After that
he would flee, not for rest but for solitude in his work,
to the friendly shades of Auchendennan on the shores of
Loch Lomond, or to Patterdale in the Lake District. Or he
would gratify the expatriate crave for travel by a tour on
the continent, out of the beaten track and alone, till the
'commission' of the Assembly called him back in the middle of August. The greater part of his writing, preparing
lectures and correspondence was done at these two retreats.

By nothing so much as by tours on the continent of Europe
did Alexander at once keep up the catholicity developed by
his Indian experience, and the elasticity of spirit which was
essential for the work he continued to the last year of his life.
Almost every alternate year he so planned his time as to give
him the two months from the middle of June to the middle
of August to this highest form of recreation. Now he was in
Holland, now on the northern shores of the Mediterranean.
Again duty drove him as far east as the Lebanon; another
year found him exploring Russia; and another found him in
Norway. He met many interesting associates, gave speeches

when invited, wrote of his travels, and extended his evangelical mission. In a letter to Lady Aberdeen, in 1871, we find him writing:

The tour in Holland was most seasonable. I twice visited that country, and I did so with much interest. There is much in its past history of a stirring and ennobling character, on high Christian grounds; though, alas, in these latter days, there has in this respect been much lamentable degeneracy. My second visit was by invitation from a union of evangelical societies, who were to hold a meeting in a wood near Utrecht. Some fifteen or sixteen thousand of the still remaining good people of Holland assembled on the occasion. In several parts of the wood some half-dozen rustic pulpits were erected. The avowed object was to give an account of the different Missions throughout the world; but in so doing full liberty was given to the speakers to shape their remarks so as to bear directly on the rationalism and other errors now unhappily prevalent in Holland, . . . I seldom enjoyed any gathering so much.

He visited Nijni Novgorod, St Petersburg, Moscow, and Troitsa (the Oxford of Russia). At seeing the heartless irreverence of the Russo-Greek priests and the superstition of the people, he declared that he had not, even in the idolatries of the East, seen anything more degraded. He visited Stockholm and Hamburg and many other places. Alexander was continually on the move, both in body and mind. He only rested when asleep, and sometimes this was of short duration, for health reasons or keeping to schedule. Could it be that he missed his wife and did not wish to be alone with the thoughts of her? There was his family including his grandchildren, he did not have the best of health, and never knew when his old trouble would flare up and lay him low, yet he kept going, relentlessly.

In January, 1871, while he was having breakfast with his daughter (who was pregant, and shortly thereafter gave birth to a baby girl whom she named Anne, having already a son named Alexander Duff), she received a letter from her husband Dr Watson in Glasgow, in the middle of which was the remark, 'How shocked your father will be to hear of the death of Sir Henry Durand'. Alexander was not only stunned, he could not help bursting into tears. Not only had he lost one of the truest and best of friends, but India had lost the greatest, wisest, ablest and most upright of her public men, as he wrote a letter of sympathy to Lady Durand. Until his own death, he remained on affectionate counsellor to her and her children.

In April, 1871, Lord Shaftesbury wrote to Alexander: 'Will you allow your honoured and illustrious name to be placed on the lists of the Vice-presidents of the Bible Society?' Alexander was glad and indeed highly honoured to accept and he gave an address in Exeter Hall shortly thereafter.

The time of Alexander's final return to Scotland seemed favourable for church union. Freed from the evil legacies of history, the United States had set the world an example of ecclesiastical equality and spiritual freedom. The Scottish Disruption of 1843, following secessions from the Kirk in the previous century, had supplied another national argument and model of the same kind. In 1863, the Assembly unanimously took the first step towards incorporation with the United Presbyterian Church, itself the result of previous unions. In 1867 Dr Duff was appointed to a seat in the committee of the leading men of both Churches and all parties in these Churches, who invited him to join them.

Alexander's accession to the ranks of the union divines was considered important for another reason. It was clear as early as 1867 that the prospects of union with the United Presbyterian Church, at least, began to be clouded. Retaining his unique position aloof from parties Alexander yet felt constrained, publicly and privately, to use all the influence of his character and his power of moral persuasion in favour of union. To have done otherwise, between two Churches of the same origin, confession, ritual, race, and history, differing only in their views on church government, would have been to prove false to his Master and to his whole life. But he always used this influence in a way which did not alienate the anti-unionists, and which so far prevailed with them as to result in a compromise, and in the effort after a still wider union proceeding on more national lines.

By 1870 the division between the union majority and the separatist minority had become so wide that the Assembly committed the subject for discussion to each of the seventy presbyteries. In that of Edinburgh, towards midnight in November, Alexander proposed a peaceful solution. It shared the immediate fate of all attempts at peace-making during the white heat of controversy, but bore fruit when the hour of reflection came. The Reformed Presbyterian Church, oldest of the non-established churches in Scotland, had meanwhile joined the negotations and was ultimately incorporated with the Free Church. This one passage from Alexander's address may serve as an illustration of the spirit which animated the first missionary of the Church of Scotland in his impassioned advocacy of union:

What is the design of the present negotiations? Is it not to bring into closer corporate alliance the three largest of the non-established Presbyterian Churches of Scotland, between whom there seem to exist no real differences on grand, vital, essential, doctrinal points, and, by so doing, to repair at least some of the widest breaches in our once happily united Scottish Zion; and that, too, not as an end in itself, however blessed, but as a means to a more glorious end – even that of the more effective evangelization of the sunken masses at home, and of the hundreds of millions of heathens abroad? Such being the central object, and the grand ultimate end in view, who would envy the sorry vocation of any one that laboured to throw obstacles in the way, instead of helping to remove such as may now exist; or strove to widen instead of lessening the breaches which all deplore; or to magnify any differences which may be discovered, instead of attempting, without any unworthy compromise, to reduce them, in their intrinsic and relative proportions, to the very uttermost? But the work of reconstruction and reconsolidation would not be completed until, in some practicable way, by which any 'wood, hay, or stubble', in our respective edifices, or any 'untempered mortar' in their walls, being wisely disposed of, the present established and non-established churches might be all reunited on a common platform, in one Reformed National Church – national, at least, in the sense of embracing within its fold the great bulk of our Scottish population.

When the General Assembly of 1873 was approaching, the controversy had become so embittered that the separatist minority plainly hinted they would secede if the majority exercised its constitutional right by legislatively carrying out union. Now was the time for the peacemaker. The whole Church turned to Dr Duff as the one man who could avert the crisis. In the end, a 'middle measure' was carried, as a compromise, so that ministers of the United

Presbyterian Church were made eligible, and could be called as ministers of the Free Church, and *vice versa*. The system worked well, but it was neither union nor incorporation. Since that time the cause of union made rapid strides, but along another road – in the Act of Parliament of 1874, and the declaration of the Moderator of the Established Church, acknowledging the wrong done in 1843, and in the union in 1876 of the Free and Reformed Presbyterian Churches. The United Presbyterian Church was to join with the Free Church in 1900, and most members of the resulting United Free Church rejoined the established Church of Scotland in 1929.

Alexander was again the Moderator of the General Assembly in 1873, and he delivered in part, and published in full, his opening addresses, under the title of *The World-Wide Crisis*. As partially reported at the time they had caused much discussion in the daily newspapers. Surveying the world as it is, and the history of the race in the light of God's truth ever and again arresting the degeneracy of men left to themselves, he said in effect to his own distracted Church and to all the divided Churches of Christendom: 'Cease your petty strifes; unite and fight against your one enemy'. Far removed from the shallow sensationalism of the prophecy-expounders whose only use is to destroy each others' theories, he yet spoke as a seer who felt the world growing evil because the Church had become cold. With an imperial insight he swooped down the ages upon the conscience, he traced the increasing purpose of God in Christ which runs through them all, he marshalled in Miltonic array the forces of darkness, and he closed his opening address by setting against each man's 'neglect of duty, its terrible doom', a consummation of glory in the heavens. The *Spectator* pronounced the address a 'plea for the true conception of Church work by comparison with the trifle which engrossed his auditors. It struck the right key-note and it did not go without its reward.'

The closing address was as practical as the previous one was elevated. The Education Act he pronounced an 'equitable compromise', such that 'it will now be the fault of the local boards and of the electors of the boards if everywhere we shall not have a religious education with the free use of the Bible and Shorter Catechism'.

The death of Dr Candlish in 1873 once more left vacant the office of Principal of New College, Edinburgh. Now that Dr Duff was home and was a professor in the college, it seemed natural as well as becoming that one so venerable and of such reputation in all the Churches as well as his own, should preside in the senatus. Alexander had no thought of filling such an office. As the duty of a peacemaker had induced him to become Moderator at a crisis which he had successfully warded off, he had no intention, at this time, of giving up his other active work for a more honorary kind.

Dr Rainy, whom Dr Candlish's death had made the leader of the old union majority, was proposed to fill the post as principal and Alexander would have been delighted to see the son of an old personal friend in the seat. But, when he learned that the appointment of Dr Rainy would arouse the old anti-union bitterness into violent opposition, he became willing again to throw himself into the breach. In the interests of peace he had seemed to bring about as Moderator, he was willing to be appointed principal. However, he underestimated the strength of ecclesiastical partisanship, even when, for the unity of Christ's Church, it was directed to the purest ends. He considered the position very carefully, and after controversy in the newspapers and the General Assembly of 1874, resigned his two offices. He only withdrew the resignation after a deputation of leading members on both sides had conveyed to him the essential need for him to remain at his posts.

The conclusion of the affair formed an occasion for the display of simple Christian magnanimity on Duff's part. Principal Rainy happened to be absent from the first meeting of the senatus after his appointment. Alexander at once consented to preside. Again, when the session 1875 had opened, Alexander took occasion to allude, before all the students, to the introductory address, in terms which we find Dr Rainy thus reciprocating in a private letter to him, dated 25 November: 'My absence was accidental. but I can hardly regret it, having heard of the very kind way in which you took occasion to speak of my address. I set it down entirely to your own generosity of feeling, but I do not value it the less on that account.' Alexander's long friendship with the writer's father, Dr Harry Rainy, became still closer. After, as before, the controversy, it was plainly seen that the principalship was nothing to the man whose whole life had been a self-sacrifice, except as the means to the end of the unity of his Church and the consequent enlargement of its missionary zeal and enterprise.

Many sought Duff's advice on Indian affairs. In 1874, Miss Florence Nightingale consulted him, as, 'the first authority living on the state of the population in Bengal', submitting to him a proof of one of her many earnest papers on the sanitary and economic condition of India. His reply called forth from her this acknowledgment:

35, South Street, Park Lane, W., 19 August, 1874

My Dear Sir, – I cannot thank you enough for your long, most wise and kind letter: full of hints invaluable to me. I am the more obliged, because I feel that you can ill afford the time and strength to write it. I could have wished that it had been otherwise, and that I might have reaped a little more of your unique experience about our poor Ryots. But whatever you do must be of incalculable importance in God's world and God's work, that I can only pray for God's blessing on whatever work you are doing, and not wish it otherwise. This is merely a word of grateful acknowledgement. I hope that, more than uncertain as my life is, it may not be the last time that I may enjoy some communication with one whom I have ever considered as one of the most favoured of God's servants, and in His name I ask for your prayers and blessing. I am, ever yours faithfully and gratefully,

Florence Nightingale.

On 25 April, 1876, Alexander completed the seventieth year of his busy life. The college session was at an end; the universities had crowned their winter course with the usual ceremonial of graduation; the ecclesiastical and philanthropic societies, of which he was an active member, were preparing for May meetings. Never of late had Alexander felt so well, though always wearied by the attempt to master the details of his varied and excessive duties, as when, spiritually braced by the exercises of a Scottish communion season, he addressed himself to the task of, yet again, rousing the General Assembly to its duty to the foreign missions. But the first stage of what was to prove his fatal illness was at hand. In a letter to Lady Durand, acknowledging receipt of a large donation for his college in Calcutta, he alluded to an accident and an illness which his doctor considered far more serious than he did:

. . . towards the end of May, I met with an accident, having fallen from a considerable height, heavily on my back in my study, my head knocking against a desk and getting sadly gashed. This confined me to my bedroom for weeks. When getting well and able to move about towards the end of July, I was suddenly seized with a violent attack of illness which disabled me for about two months. Since October, however, by God's great goodness, I have enjoyed ordinary health.

The double warning was unheeded, and the old man of seventy-one persisted in discharging his office and professorial duties all through the session of 1876–77, travelling much between Edinburgh, Glasgow and Aberdeen in the rigour of a Scottish winter, and for the first three months of 1877 longing for the familiar surroundings of his home, his home which had been prepared for him by his loving and now departed wife, Anne.

Intellectually he seemed to grow in keenness of observation and energy. The great public events which marked the close of Mr Gladstone's administration, the transfer of power to his rivals, and the consistent attitude of the Scottish people throughout, were viewed by him from a higher level than that of his party. Like most British people who have lived abroad, he looked at affairs as they affected not only domestic politics, but the welfare of the the great peoples of East and West. Liberty, the free development of the nations under Christian institutions or influences, was what he sought, whether in his own country and its colonies or in America, similarly for India and Russia and Turkey. The longer he lived out of India, above all, the more did he concern himself with its progress. of which he had sown many of the seeds.

He took great interest in the proposed visit by the Prince of Wales to India. How would the Prince act in a rapid tour through the feudatory states as well as the ordinary provinces, when all the chivalry of India, Hindu and Muslim, would be at the feet of the Queen's eldest son, when multitudes of the people and all the Christian officials would crowd around his Royal Highness? The Churches and communities which sent forth their future sovereign that he might thus prepare himself for the responsibilities of empire, did well to be in earnest about it.

Alexander's mind went back to the time when the great Prince of Evangelists, Charles Simeon, visited his own parish in Moulin by reason of the fact that the local people would not allow him to travel further on the Sabbath. The Prince of Wales, following the order by the Marquis Wellesley, eighty years before, had made the order in India that observance of the Sabbath was essential for the Europeans. The Prince of Wales ordered that his officials take steps to ensure that there would be no travel or public functions held on Sundays. Her Majesty expressed a similar wish. Alexander felt that the tour proved to be the most remarkable 'found in the annals of all time', and some thought that such a titular and political proclamation of the Empire should have been made at the time, on 1 November, 1858, when Queen Victoria assumed direct sovereignty, as Empress of India, from the East India Company.

On no day of all his later years was Alexander happier than of that of the one patron saint tolerated but forgotten by Scotsmen, till they go abroad. Their Churches had agreed with those of England and Ireland to observe St Andrew's Day, 30 November, annually as a time of intercession with God for an increase in the number of missionaries. In the hall of the Free Church General Assembly a congregation attended a service which was led by a representative of each of the three branches of the old historic Kirk. It was at this time that Dean Stanley opened the nave of Westminster Abbey to some great preacher, lay or clerical, of one of the Reformed Churches. It happened, unfortunately, that Alexander was committed to preside at the Scottish intercessory service of 1876, and could not accept the honour of being asked by Dean Stanley to preach in Westminster Abbey.

As was inevitable, his age and his state of health, had for some time, played a significant part in the role which he attached the greatest importance of all: that of encouraging the young students to go out into the world as missionaries. He knew that with his experiences in the field and the position he now held in the Church and at the university, no one was better qualified to perform this all-important task, but he had already lost the powerful and expressive voice with which he was able to communicate his passionate beliefs, and his mind was taken back to his early student days at St Andrews, when he had to listen to the aged yet learned professors, before the dynamic Dr Chalmers came to spread fire and enthusiasm throughout the establishment. As he lectured the young students, in a voice that at times was reduced to almost a whisper, and at times would require him to leave the lecture hall to regain his strength, it hurt him deeply to know that the youths before him did not have the encouragement that he himself had been given. No longer was there feedback and participation from the students. Yes, they were interested in all that the great man had done, but they did not need to attend lectures to learn of this. He would see them sit uneasily and, often as not, the lectures were not fully attended. Alexander knew the reason better than they, but what could he do? Circumstances beyond earthly control would change all this in the near future. Alexander had murmurings, as he later admitted, that his Lord may have another place for him, but until then, he would do that which had been divinely commanded.

Alexander had sought health in his beloved solitude of Patterdale in the Lake District of England; but the long walks to which the convalescence tempted him brought on persistent jaundice. The disease continued to gain on him in spite of a residence for six weeks at the German bath of Neuenahr, of the skill of his son-in-law, Dr P. H. Watson, and of the loving attention of his devoted daughter and grandson. He was with difficulty brought back by slow stages to Edinburgh. There he wrote letters, resigning all the offices he held in the Church and in many societies, religious and benevolent. Not that he expected to die shortly. He resolved to devote his whole nature to a renewed advocacy throughout Scotland of the duty of more faithfully carrying out Christ's last commission. He did not, at this time, resign either the offices of professorship and convenership.

To escape the northern winter he went to the sheltered Devonshire retreat of Sidmouth, where two years previously he had found rest. At his last meeting with George Smith before he left Edinburgh, he heard of the relief of the famine-stricken millions in Southern India, and his half audible voice seemed to gain momentary strength as he blessed God for the liberality of the Christian people who had saved them. He was succeeded in his office of president of the Anglo-Indian Evangelization Society by Lord Polwarth, and was placed in the honorary position of its patron along with the great statesman who was to die soon after him, Lord Lawrence.

Summoned from Calcutta by telegraph, his only remaining son, William, who was now also serving Christ in India, reached his side just a month before he passed away. When the first joy of seeing his son was over, Alexander said, 'I am in God's hands, to go or stay. If he has need of me he will raise me up; if otherwise it is far better.' That was on 12 January,

1878. Alexander then pleaded with William to go to Scotland to visit his children, who had been left there, like his own in former days. William did not want to leave his father without permission from the doctors and this was given on the 16th. After a rapid journey, he returned to Sidmouth on the 20th. As strength permitted, Alexander dictated, and William jotted down in a notebook almost his exact words.[1] As the days of weakness passed on, the poison in the blood gaining on the body but the brain holding untouched the citadel of the soul, he said on 24 January:

> I had intended, if spared, to resign next May abso-lutely both offices [the professorship and convenership]. It seemed the natural course of procedure when entering on my jubilee year – the fiftieth year of being a missionary of the Established Church of Scotland. If God spared me my intention then was, after being thus liberated from neces-sary official duties, to give myself wholly to the completion of the work which was only begun by the establishment of the missionary professorship; that is, to try and rouse the people of Scotland to a sense of the paramount duty of devoting themselves to the cause of Missions, and secure the means of establishing an endowment of a Home and Foreign Missionary Institute, based upon the most unsectarian and comprehensive principles of the glorious and blessed gospel of Christ. If I saw this accomplished, or a solid prospect of its being soon accomplished, I should feel, as far as my humble judgment could discern, that my work on earth to promote the glory and honour of my blessed Saviour was completed, and would be ready to exclaim with old Simeon, 'Now lettest Thou thy servant depart in peace'. But if all this were to be unexpectably unhinged, and a totally different course in Providence opened up, I was prepared – thanks, eternal thanks, to the Great Jehovah, I was equally ready and willing – to submit to any change which He in His infinite wisdom, goodness and love might be pleased to indicate.

Then, exhausted, he whispered, 'I am very low and cannot say much, but I am living daily, habitually in Him.'
On the same day he dictated the names of some fifty friends

[1] The notes were incorporated in W. Pirie Duff, *Memorials of Alexander Duff, D.D.* (London: Nisbet, 1890).

to whom he desired a memorial of his affection to be sent from his library, specifying in one case the volumes to be given, which were the works of De Quincey.

On 27 January Alexander seemed to rally so far as to dictate replies to many messages of prayerful sympathy from such old friends as Sir Charles Trevelyan, Mr Hawkins, General Colin Mackenzie, and others. February found him still dying, but ever brightening in spirit and living much in the past. On 2 February he alluded to the prospect of soon being laid beside the dust of his wife. Of the good and great men like Chalmers and Guthrie, whose remains lay in the Grange cemetery, he said with earnestness, 'There's a perfect forest of them.' The following day the hand of death became more evidently visible. Still he could ask for his grandchildren, and was ever careful to thank his loving ones for their ministrations. When, in the evening, his daughter repeated to him the twenty-third psalm as he lay apparently unconscious, he responded at the end of each verse.

Even on Saturday, the 9th, the departing saint could recognise the voices he loved, but his only response then was a grasp of the hand. Without acute suffering, and in perfect peace, he lingered on until Tuesday morning, 12 February, 1878. 'He was just like one passing away into sleep; I never saw so peaceful an end,' was the remark of a friend.

Next morning telegrams and long and intensely appreciative sketches of the missionary in *The Times* and *Daily News*, and in all the Scottish newspapers, carried the sad but not unexpected news wherever the English language was read. In India, Africa, America and Canada alike, where he had been personally known and where his great works followed him, the journals and ecclesiastical bodies gave voice to the public sorrow. In Edinburgh, to which his remains were at once conveyed from Sidmouth, the burial of Alexander Duff was to prove to be a lesson in Christian unity not less impressive than his own eloquent words and whole career.

18

Last Journey

The funeral of Alexander Duff, D.D., LL.D., took place on 18 February, 1878. A private service was held for the family in a house in Brunstfield Place, opposite the Bruntsfield Links and within one hundred yards of Barclay Church, where the public service was to take place. Christians of all denominations met around his bier, as he had often taught them to do in the field of Foreign Missions. The Lord Provost Boyd, the magistrates and council, in formal procession, represented civic Scotland. Professors and students of the four universities and the Royal High School marched in vast company past Bruntsfield Links, which were covered by the citizens and by crowds from the country, while the deep-toned bell of Barclay Church slowly clanged forth the general grief. For the first time in Scottish ecclesiastical history the three Kirks and their Moderators, the representatives of the English, American and Indian Churches through their missionary societies and officials, trod the one funeral march. The scene was described by Lord Polwarth, in a letter to Lady Aberdeen:

> I have today stood at the grave of our dear old Dr Duff, and was asked to act as one of the pall-bearers, as being a personal friend and as representing you. I felt it a very great honour, and one of which I am very unworthy, but I believe few there loved him more truly than I did. Somehow I felt strongly attached to him from our first meeting. He was a truly great man, and all Edinburgh and far beyond seemed to feel that today. It was a solemn sacred sight. Such crowds of people lining the streets and all along the meadows; such a long, long line of carriages, such an assemblage of men belonging to all the Churches! The great missionary societies were all represented, the city, the universities. As we walked into the cemetery, we walked through a long row of students! I stood at the foot of the open grave and watched the coffin lowered down. Mary's words were, 'His coffin should be covered with

palm branches.' I felt not sorrowful in one sense, for he was weary, weary in the work. I climbed up the long, long stairs to his room in the Free Church offices today, but he will climb up no more in weariness. Then I felt it was the grave of a Christian hero and conqueror, and came away with the desire that I, even I, and many others may be enabled to unite and bear the standard he bore so nobly.

I noticed close behind me a black lad gazing with his big rolling eyes into the grave. How many there would have been from India had it been possible. One thing was forced on one's mind – how utterly all the petty divisions which now separate Christians sink out of sight when one comes near the great realities.

Many tributes were published. The Prime Minister, Gladstone, praised Alexander as: '. . . one who not only stood in the first rank for intelligence, energy, devotion and advancement in the inward and spiritual life' among missionaries like Carey and Marshman:

. . . but who likewise so intensely laboured in the cause that he shortened the career which Providence would in all likelihood have otherwise committed to him, and he has reaped his reward in the world beyond the grave at an earlier date than those whose earthly career is lengthened into a long old age . . .

One of Duff's former pupils, Harish Chandra Mittra, although remaining unconvinced of the truth of Christianity, testified from the Indian side:

. . . I would mention at the very outset that I am an unworthy pupil of the great and good man about whom I intend to speak to you this evening. Although Dr Duff, my most revered teacher, has gone down to the grave at the venerable age of seventy-two, yet I cannot but deeply lament his death. In the death of Dr Duff, Scotland has lost one of the noblest sons, the Protestant Church of Great Britain one of its brightest ornaments, and India, poor, benighted, hapless India and the civilized world one of its greatest orators, and a truly great and good man . . .

. . . One could not be in the company of Dr Duff, even for a few minutes, without feeling that he was a

messenger from above. There was a felt moral sweetness
in his presence and contact which tended to instil a calm
of pure and perennial happiness in the troubled soul
. . . In a word, he was a visible impersonation of the
omnipotence of Christian love; and it was this deep
Christian love for his fellow-men that, in spite of the
noblest sentiment of patriotism which burned in his
heart, led him to spend the manhood of his strength
among the people of India, with a view to elevate them
to a higher platform of moral and intellectual greatness
and glory . . .

A memorial church was built at Kirkmichael, the neighbouring parish to that in which he was born, which at the
time of writing this biography is being used as a furniture
store; and in 1889, Sir William Muir, when Principal of the
University of Edinburgh, with Dr George Smith and friends
of evangelical missions, united and erected a celtic cross as a
national monument to Alexander Duff at Pitlochry Church in
Perthshire, Scotland. Kind and thoughtful as these memorials
are, we may ask why he was not honoured in Edinburgh, the
capital city of Scotland, by sharing a place of honour with
Knox, Chalmers, Guthrie, Ramsay, Walter Scott, Robert Burns
and other great Scotsmen? A reason could be that, unlike the
others mentioned, Alexander Duff led two lives. The first life
ended when his wife died and his second life began thereafter.
It is more than likely if Alexander had retired on returning to
Scotland from India for the last time, he would have shared an
honoured place in his capital city. The great man's work was
known to all, and the results were there to prove it, both at
home and in India, but it would seem that he was judged and
regrettably almost forgotten during his less dramatic second
life as a widower, and it is mainly this aspect which requires
further investigation today.

People are judged by how they behave and by what they
achieve. In Alexander's case, during later life his behaviour
did little to influence the young radicals who sat at his feet
in the lecture halls. He was aware of this fact. Had he not
once been one of them sitting at the feet of Chalmers? The
students had read all about the Disruption and indeed were
daily living with the results of it, and however he was judged
and admired by his contemporaries, the young students linked
this elderly stooping figure with the whispering voice, with the

disunity and sectarianism between the Churches in which they had chosen to serve.

It was true that they were fully aware of his past record and what he had achieved, but all they saw now was the animated manifestation of the troubles past and present, and was it not their ambition to free the Church from this sectarian strife and unite in the prime objective of spreading the gospel? The result of his great work was in India, not before the eyes of the students. It was true that photography was now able to convey physical images of the country in which he served, and of his Institution, colleges, schools and missions spread throughout Bengal, but the eye is the least reliable of our senses, and we must be aware that at that time, society had not yet had time to adapt to acceptance of this new dimension and by nature, relied on the age-old interpretation by reading and the spoken word. Alexander was now unable to give this three-dimensional mental picture as he once was able to do with his passionate oratory. Through no fault of his own, health now limited his powers, and there was another all-important reason which we shall consider shortly. The young theological students had not yet mastered their chosen craft and developed the compassion that would understand his situation.

Alexander was fully aware of the position, had he not been there before? He watched as they sat uneasily in class. There was little or any participation between teacher and students as in his own younger days under Chalmers. There was no fun, or indeed laughter, as there had been with Chalmers. It would remind Alexander of the dry-as-dust days at St Andrews when the lecturers read from yellowed sheets, in monotonous tones, before the arrival of Chalmers. Notes were now taken by the students, something which Alexander and his contemporaries never had to do. At times classes were poorly attended.

The other reason for the dramatic change in Alexander during the second part of his life which lasted thirteen years was, without doubt, the loss of his wife. When Anne died he lost the great stimulus essential to his being. He lost her loving care, her encouragement and her presence at his side. He felt the full impact of this when he was alone in their house at Lauder Road. As he gazed out from the window and saw the beautiful rolling hills, her favourite view, his eyes filled with tears as he was now alone looking at something she had seen for him, and wondering how much more in their lives she had seen and done for him in the past. The tears which he shed were for himself as he realized that from now on her eyes would no longer share his view of life, those eyes which he now knew were part of his sight life. For the first time he turned his thoughts to his children, those dead and those still living, and to his grandchildren, to all of whom she had passed his own love. He now knew the domestic love which had been forever overshadowed by divine love and this was borne out, when on his death-bed, he pleaded with his son William to to go and visit his children in Scotland before attending to his father.

Alexander and Anne had the greatest love of all as their individual love of God was ever present and manifested itself in their love for each other, even to the denial and sacrifice of their children's presence and reciprocating love. All this was now revealed to Alexander. He carried on the good work in his last thirteen years and accomplished a great deal in the continuance of his missionary and other undertakings, but the main, and most important aspect of directly attracting the young to the all-important work in the missionary field, did suffer. There was this vital loss of continuity which resulted, quite simply, in people, even those in the Churches forgetting Alexander.

Not so for the people in India. Even today, the people of the world remember the Mutiny, with the loss of some 1,500 Europeans killed, but not the Indian people. Their memory of that era is of Dr Alexander Duff, the great Scotsman who saved the lives of hundreds of thousands by his efforts and where the evidence is there to see in his schools, colleges, missions, in the University of Calcutta and, most important of all, in the fact that he was directly responsible in preparing them to govern their own country.

Every year, professors and students from India pay homage to Dr Duff by visiting the little cottage at Achnahyle Farm in Moulin, Perthshire. Sadly, there are few other visitors who show interest in his works, with the positive exception of the biographer, a fellow clansman, whose own mother, Georgina Laird Duff, was born in this parish and to whose memory this biography is now dedicated.